ISO 9001:2000
for Small Businesses

Ray Tricker

BUTTERWORTH
HEINEMANN

OXFORD   AUCKLAND   BOSTON   JOHANNESBURG   MELBOURNE   NEW DELHI

Butterworth-Heinemann
Linacre House, Jordan Hill, Oxford OX2 8DP
225 Wildwood Avenue, Woburn, MA 01801-2041
A division of Reed Educational and Professional Publishing Ltd

℞ A member of the Reed Elsevier plc group

First published 1997
Reprinted 1997, 1998, 1999, 2001
Second edition 2001

British Library Cataloguing in Publication Data
A catalogue record for this book is available from the British Library

Library of Congress Cataloguing in Publication Data
A catalogue record for this book is available from the Library of Congress

ISBN 0 7506 4882 1

Composition by Genesis Typesetting, Laser Quay, Rochester, Kent
Printed and bound in Great Britain by Clays Ltd, St Ives plc

Contents

Foreword

During the past few years there has been a growing demand for an assurance of quality before a contract is let. This is not an entirely new concept, for quality has always played an important role in securing new markets as well as retaining those markets that already exist, but without doubt, in these days of competitive world markets, quality assurance has become even more relevant.

To meet this requirement, manufacturers and suppliers have had to recognise the importance of quality and the fact that it can only be achieved through efficient company organisation and a determination by management to meet the increased quality requirements of their potential customers.

This concept is not just related to the larger manufacturing companies and suppliers. It also affects the smaller companies, even those employing only two or three people. In fact, no matter how large or small the company, there has to be an increasing reliance on quality and the recommendations of ISO 9000 in order to meet customers' requirements.

In fact, for anyone wanting to sell their product in a multi-national European or American market, the ISO 9000 publications are essential reading. Together they provide a comprehensive set of rules and regulations, specifications and recommendations that enable a manufacturer (or supplier), large or small, to set up workable quality assurance procedures and operate within their constraints.

Many books have already been written on the topic, but most of these appear to automatically assume that the reader belongs to a large manufacturing or supply company. Indeed most of these larger companies will probably already have an established, fully certified, Quality Management System in place. Small to medium size manufacturing companies and/or service industries now need to set up similar systems, but on a smaller scale, and show that they too can work in conformance with ISO 9001:2000.

This book, with its series of examples and audit procedures, shows how the smaller company can benefit from the requirements of ISO 9001:2000 and in so doing, gain entry into these more lucrative markets.

The aim of this book is to enable readers, at very little expense, to set up an ISO 9001:2000 compliant Quality Management System for themselves. But *ISO 9001:2000 for Small Businesses* is not **just** a book – it also includes a complete Quality Management System on disk capable of being reproduced by any company without having to employ a specialist to do it for them and provide a detailed self-assessment plan.

The main parts of the book are as follows:

- Background to ISO 9000;
- Structure of ISO 9001:2000;
- The importance of Quality Control and Quality Assurance;
- Quality Management System;
- Quality organisational structure;
- Example Quality Manual;
- Self-assessment.

For convenience (and in order to reduce the number of equivalent or similar terms) the following, unless otherwise stated, are considered interchangeable terms within this book.

- product – hardware, software, service or processed material;
- organisation – manufacturer and/or supplier.

Preface

With the increased demand for quality in everything that we do or make nowadays has come the need to have some formalised set of rules to work to. Up until a few years ago, however, there were no formalised standards for assuring a manufacturer's (or supplier's) quality. Quality procedures and guarantees were therefore required and the Military – as so often happens in these cases – came to the rescue.

NASA (in their capacity as controlling body for the US Space Program and with their requirement for the highest level of equipment reliability) were the first to produce a set of procedures, specifications and requirements. These become known as Military Specifications (Mil Specs) and manufacturers and suppliers, regardless of their size, were required to conform to these requirements if they wanted to provide equipment for this lucrative military market.

The North Atlantic Treaty Organisation (NATO), under the American influence, then produced a series of quality assurance procedures which were known as the NATO Allied Quality Assurance Publications (AQAPs). These were republished by the British Ministry of Defence (MOD) as the Defence Standard (DEF STAN) 05 series of procedures.

Civilian firms and contractors quickly realised the necessity of ensuring that manufacturers and suppliers should abide to a set of quality standards and the British Standards Institution (BSI) formally adapted the DEF STAN 05 series into a virtually identical set of documents known as the BS 5750 series. This standard was then copied by other nations and a common series of recommendations known as the ISO 9000:1994 series of 'Standards for Quality Assurance' were produced.

Under existing international agreement, all international standards have to be re-inspected five years after publication. In accordance with this agreement, the 1994 versions of ISO 9000 series have now been revised with more emphasis being placed on the need for customer satisfaction and the use of a more modular, process approach to quality management. The main change caused by this new review process, however, is the amalgamation of the previous (similar) requirements contained in the ISO 9001:1994, ISO 9002:1994 and ISO 9003:1994 standards into a single ISO 9001:2000 requirements standard.

ISO 9001:2000 now identifies the basic disciplines of a Quality Management System and can be used by manufacturers, suppliers, service industries and end users – large or small – with equal effect. This standard specifies the national, regional and international accepted procedures and criteria that are required to ensure that products and services meet the customers' requirements.

These disciplines, processes, procedures and criteria can be applied to any firm, no matter its size – whether they employ just a few people or many thousands. It can also be used by companies to set up their own Quality Management System and can form the basis for assessing a manufacturer's Quality Management System (i.e. to ensure that a supplier or service industry has the ability to provide satisfactory goods and/or services).

Part One
The Background to ISO 9000

In Part One, the necessity and the interoperability of quality standards is discussed, the historical background of ISO 9000 is presented and the basic requirements of ISO 9001:2000 are explained. The UK Government's support of Quality Management Systems is also briefly examined.

1
ISO 9000

1.1 ISO 9000

Wherever you go nowadays, it seems that you are always hearing the word 'quality' especially in relation to the requirements of 'ISO 9000', but even though these have become everyday words, they are often misused, misquoted and misunderstood. But why is this? Well, normally you will find that when most people talk about the quality of an object, they are talking about its excellence, perfection and/or value. In reality, of course, they should be talking about how much it meets its designed purpose and comes up to the manufacturer's or supplier's original specifications. Referring to the quality of a single article is, of course, fairly simple. Problems occur, however, when one has to talk about complex systems. Then it can become very difficult indeed to assess a level of quality.

Quality

"The degree to which a set of inherent characteristics fulfils requirements".

Figure 1.1 The accepted definition of quality

So what exactly is **meant** by the word quality? There are many definitions but the most commonly accepted definition of quality is 'the degree to which a set of inherent characteristics fulfills requirements'. (ISO DIS 9000:2000).

But customers are not just interested in the level of quality 'intended' by the manufacturer or supplier, they are far more interested in the maintenance of quality level and want an assurance that the product (i.e. hardware, software, service or processed material) that they are buying truly meets the quality standard that they were initially offered and/or recommended.

This customer requirement has, quite naturally, had a sort of knock-on effect which has meant that manufacturers and suppliers (especially in the larger companies) have now had to pay far more attention to the quality of their product than was previously necessary. Organisations have had to set up proper Quality Management Systems in order to control and monitor all stages of the production process **and** they have had to provide proof to the potential customer that their product has the guaranteed – and in some cases

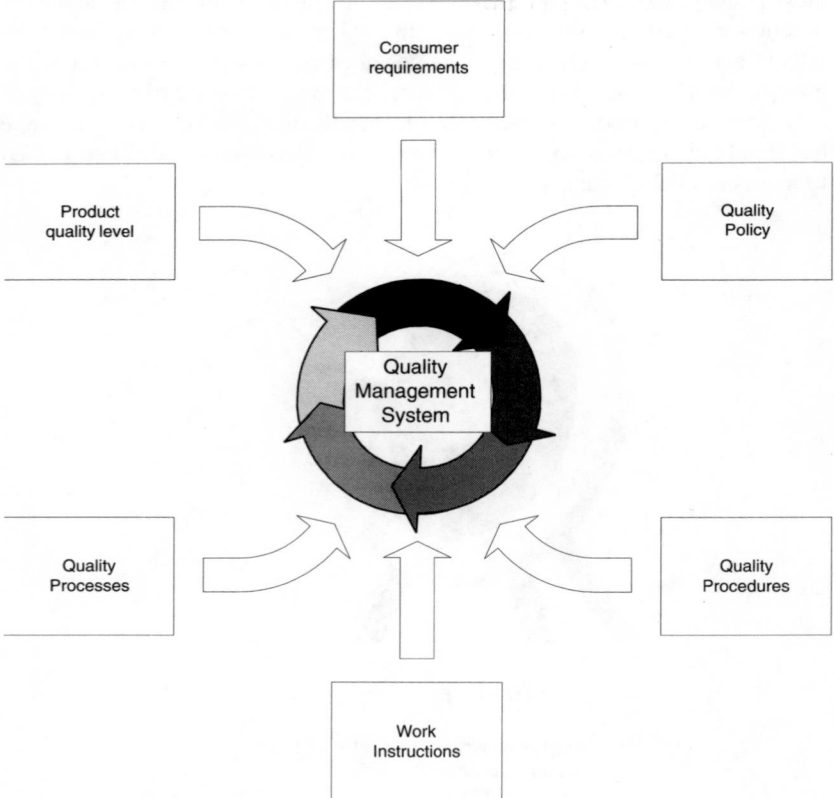

Figure 1.2 Meeting the customer's requirement for quality

certified – quality required by the customer. In other words, the manufacturer or supplier has had to work within a Quality Management System (QMS) in order to provide some degree of quality assurance for their product.

Unfortunately, with the current trend towards microminiaturisation, most modern day products have become extremely complex assemblies of components compared to those which were available a few years ago. This has meant that many more people are now involved in the manufacture or supply of a relatively simple object and this has increased the likelihood of a production fault occurring.

In the same way, the responsibility for the quality of a product has also been spread over an increasing amount of people which has meant that the manufacturer's and/or supplier's guarantee of quality has, unfortunately, become less precise.

Within the European Union (EU), there is a potential marketplace of some 350–400 million people. In America the potential is similar and selling to these markets is an extremely competitive business which has meant an increased reliance on internationally agreed quality procedures and recommendations in order to gain a foothold in these markets. This is where ISO 9001:2000 really proves its worth.

Figure 1.3 Main producers of national standards within Europe

1.2 Interoperability of standards

As the British Standards Institution (BSI) Secretary, Mr Geoff Strawbridge, said in an article entitled 'Setting the scene for European standards, testing and certification post 1992' – standards are as international as the markets they serve.

Currently, the main producers of national standards in Western Europe are:

- United Kingdom – British Standards Institution (BSI);
- Germany – Deutsch Institut fur Normung e.v. (DIN);
- France – Association Français de Normalisation (AFNOR).

Outside Europe the most widely used standards come from:

- America – American National Standards Institute (ANSI);
- Canada – Canadian Standards Association (CSA).

Figure 1.4 Main producers of national standards outside Europe

There are, of course, others (e.g. Japan and Saudi Arabia). Europe and North America, however, are the main two and although these countries publish what are probably the most important series of standards, virtually every country with an industrial base has its own organisation producing its own set of standards. This can obviously lead to a lot of confusion, especially with regard to international trade and tenders. For example, if America were to invite tenders for a project quoting American (ANSI) national standards as the minimum criteria, other countries might find it difficult to submit a proposal, either because they didn't have a copy of the relevant standard, or

they wouldn't find it cost effective to retool their entire works in order to conform to the requirements of that particular national standard.

The situation in Europe has been made even more difficult when the European Union (EU) – in an attempt to stop national standards forming trade barriers to community trade – produced even more regulations!

On the defence electronics side of the fence there is little change. The United Kingdom Ministry of Defence (MOD-UK) use Defence Standards (DEF STANS), the American Division of Defence (DOD) use Military Standards (Mil-Std) and the North Atlantic Treaty Organisation (NATO) use NATO Allied Quality Assurance Publications (AQAPs) and most other nations have their own particular variations.

From a more civilian point of view the International Telecommunications Union (ITU) Committees (i.e. The International Telegraph and Telephony Consultative Committee (CCITT) and the International Radio Consultative Committee (CCIR)) also publish recommendations.

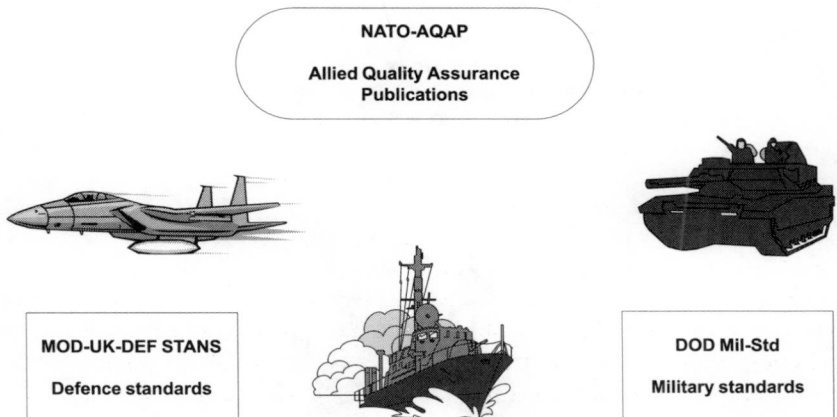

Figure 1.5 Military standards

For this reason there has been a steady growth in international standardisation and ISO, (International Standards Organisation) and the IEC (International Electrotechnical Commission), are now the standards bodies that most countries are affiliated to – via, that is, their own particular National Standards Organisation (NSO).

Like ITU documents, these ISO and IEC standards (ISO is mainly concerned with industrial standards whilst IEC refers to electrical equipment) were initially published as 'recommendations', but they are now accepted as international standards – in their own right.

The standards themselves are drawn up by International Technical Committees which have been approved by ISO or IEC member countries and there are now many hundreds of different ISO and IEC standards available.

But national bodies and national standards cannot dictate customer choice. A product that may legally be marketed need not be of universal appeal.

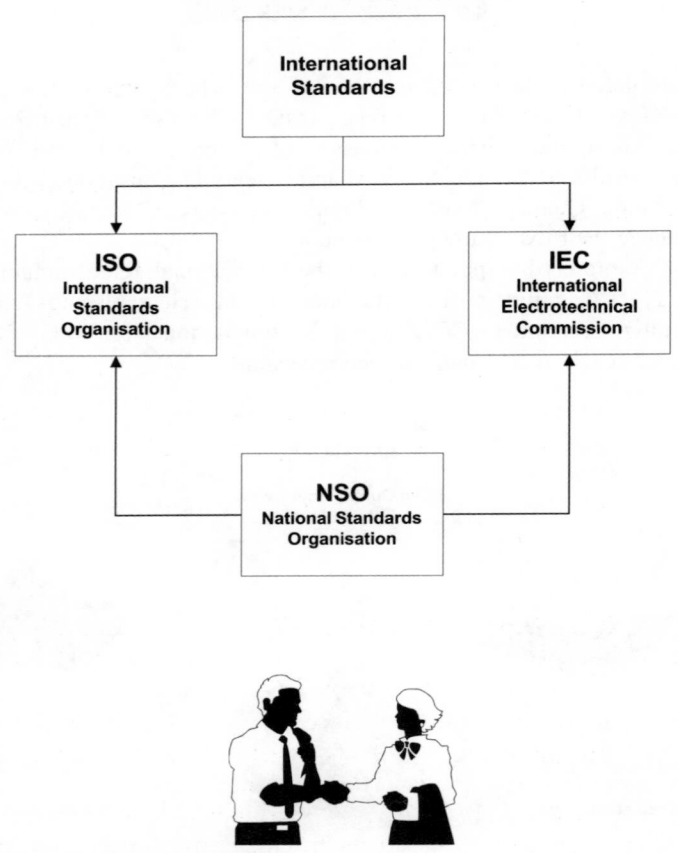

Figure 1.6 International standards

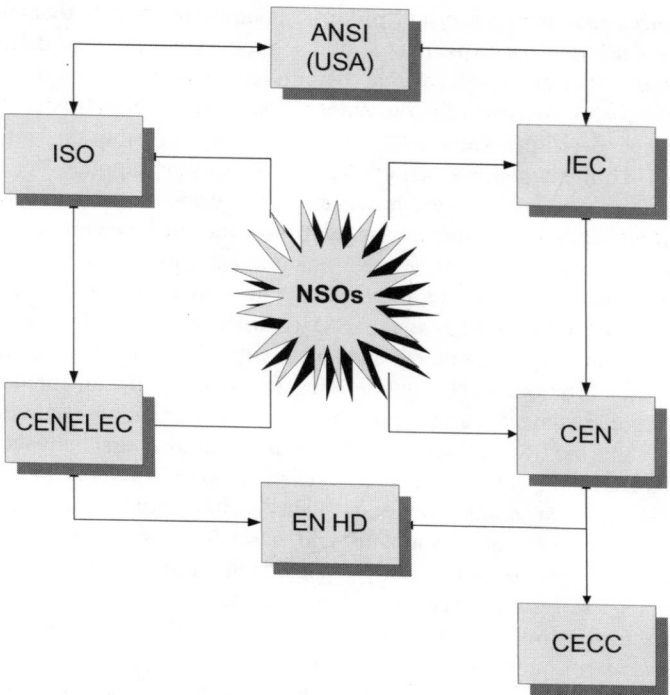

Figure 1.7 Inter-relationship of the standards bodies and committees

Indeed, where different national standards persist they will do so as a reflection of different market preferences. For industry to survive in this new, 'liberalised' market, therefore, it must have a sound technological base supported by a comprehensive set of internationally approved standards.

Quality has thus become the key word in today's competitive markets and there are now more than 80 countries with similar organisations – most of which are members of ISO and IEC. Figure 1.7 shows the inter-relationship of these standards and committees.

1.3 The demand for standardisation of Quality Management Systems

The growing demand for assurance of quality **before** a contract is awarded has reinforced the already accepted adage that quality products play an important role in securing new markets as well as retaining those markets that already exist. Without doubt, in these days of competitive world markets, quality assurance has never been more relevant. No longer can suppliers rely on their reputation alone.

The drive towards quality-led production now means that today's major purchasers are not just **expecting** a quality product but are also **demanding** proof that a company is capable of producing quality products and/or providing quality services. The provision of this proof is normally in the form of an independent third-party certification and this is possibly the single most important requirement for a manufacturer, company or supplier.

Up until a few years ago, however, there were no viable third-party certification schemes available. But with an increased demand for quality assurance during all stages of the manufacturing processes, came the requirement for manufacturers to work to a recognised set of standards.

Within the United Kingdom the BSI (British Standards Institution) had already published a number of guides to quality assurance (for example BS 4891:1972), and quickly set about providing an acceptable document that would cover all requirements for a two-party manufacturing or supply contract.

This became the BS 5750 series of standards which were first published in the United Kingdom during 1979. These standards supplied guidelines for internal quality management as well as external quality assurance and they were quickly accepted by manufacturers, suppliers and purchasers as being a reasonable minimum level of quality assurance that they could be expected to work to. The BS 5750:1979 series thus became the 'cornerstone' for national quality.

But in the meantime America had been working on their ANSI 90 series and other European countries were also busily developing their own sets of standards. Quite naturally, however, as the BSI had already produced and published an acceptable standard, most of these national standards were broadly based on BS 5750.

In 1981, the Department of Trade and Industry (DTI) formed a committee called FOCUS to examine areas where standardisation could benefit the competitiveness of British manufacturers and users of high technology – for instance Local Area Network (LAN) standardisation. Owing to the wider international interest concerning quality assurance, ISO then set up a Study Group during 1983 to produce an international set of standards that all countries could use.

This initiative, the Open Systems Interconnection (OSI), ensured that products from different manufacturers and different countries could exchange data and interwork in certain defined areas. In the United States, the Corporation of Open Systems (COS) was formed in 1986 to pursue similar objectives.

1.4 The background to the ISO 9000 set of quality standards

ISO was established as a United Nations Agency in 1947 and is made up of representatives from more than 90 countries including BSI for the United Kingdom and ANSI for the United States. The work of ISO has increased

ORGANISATION
INTERNATIONALE DE
NORMALISATION

INTERNATIONAL
ORGANIZATION FOR
STANDARDIZATION

considerably since it first got under way and a great number of standards are now available and have already been adopted.

From the consumer's point of view, the importance of international (i.e. ISO) standards is that all major agencies are now committed to recognising their requirements. Equipment, modules and components can now be designed and built so that they will be acceptable to all member countries. In this way interoperability is assured.

Similar to quality standards from other countries, ISO's first attempt at producing an international standard for quality management (i.e. the ISO 9000:1987 set of standards) were very heavily based on BS 5750 Parts 1, 2 and 3. They followed the same sectional layout except that an additional section (ISO 9000:1987 Part 0 Section 0.1) was introduced to provide further guidance about the principal concepts and applications contained in the ISO 9000 series.

ISO 9001:2000

ISO 9001:1994
ISO 9002:1994
ISO 9003:1994

BS 5750:1987
ISO 9000:1987
EN 29000:1987

OSI
COS
FOCUS

BS 5750:1979

BS 4891:1972

AQAP

Figure 1.8 The background to ISO 9001:2000

When ISO 9000 was first published in 1987 it was immediately ratified by the UK (under the direction of the Quality Management and Statistics Standards Committee) and republished by the BSI (without deviation), as the new BS 5750:1987 standard for QMSs.

Similarly, on 10 December 1987 the Technical Board of the European Committee for Standardisation (Commission European de Normalisation Electrotechnique – CEN) approved and accepted the text of ISO 9000:1987 as **the** European Standard – without modification – and republished it as EN 29000:1987.

Table 1.1 Comparison chart of equivalent standards to ISO 9000 (1–4), 9001, 9002, 9003 and 9004 (1–4)

Standard no.	Equivalent standard								
	AS	ASQC	BS	CSA	DIN	EN	IEC	JIS	NFX
ISO 9000	AS 3900	ASQC Q90		CSA Q9000	DIN ISO 9000	EN 29000		JIS-Z9900	NFX 50-121
ISO 9000/1		ASQC Q9000-1	BS EN ISO 9000-1		DIN EN ISO 9000 PT1	EN ISO 9000/1			NFX 50-121
ISO 9000/2	AS 3900.2	ASQC Q9000-2							
ISO 9000/3		ASQC Q9000-3	BS 5750 PT13 (1991)	CSA Q9000.3	DIN ISO 9000 PT3	EN 29000 PT3			NFX 50-121/3
ISO 9000/4	AS 3900.4		BS 5750 PT14 (1993)		DIN ISO 9000 PT4	EN 60300 PT1	IEC 300 PT1		
ISO 9001	AS 3901	ASQC Q9001	BS EN ISO 9001	CSA Q9001	DIN EN ISO 9001 DIN ISO 9001	EN ISO 9001		JIS-Z9901	NFX 50-131
ISO 9002	AS 3902	ASQC Q9002	BS EN ISO 9002	CSA Q9002	DIN EN ISO 9002 DIN ISO 9002	EN ISO 9002		JIS-Z9902	NFX 50-132
ISO 9003	AS 3903	ASQC Q9003	BS EN ISO 9003	CSA Q9003	DIN EN ISO 9003 DIN ISO 9003	EN ISO 9003		JIS-Z9903	NFX 50-133
ISO 9004	AS 3904	ASQC Q9004-1		CSA Q9004	DIN ISO 9004	EN 29004		JIS-Z9904	
ISO 9004/1		ASQC Q9004-1	BS EN ISO 9004-1		DIN EN ISO 9004 PT1	EN ISO 9004/1			
ISO 9004/2	AS 3904.2	ASQC Q9004-2	BS 5750 PT8 (1991)	CSA Q9004.2	DIN ISO 9004 PT2	EN 29004 PT2			NFX 50-122-2
ISO 9004/3	AS 3904.3	ASQC Q9004-3							
ISO 9004/4	AS 3904.4	ASQC Q9004-4	BS 7850 PT2 (1994)						

At that time official versions of EN 29000:1987 existed in English, French and German. CEN members were allowed, however, to translate any of these versions into their own language and they then had the same status as the original official versions.

Note: Up-to-date lists and bibliographical references concerning these and other European standards may be obtained on application to the CEN Central Secretariat (Rue Brederode 2, Boite 5, B–1000, Brussels, Belgium) or from any CEN member.

BS 5750:1987 was, therefore, identical to ISO 9000:1987 and EN 29000:1987 except that BS 5750 had three additional guidance sections. Consequently, BS 5750 was not just the British Standard for Quality Management Systems it was also the European **and** the international standard.

But, if all of these titles referred to the same quality standard, why not call the standard by the same name?!

Well that is exactly what happened. ISO, realising the problems of calling the same document by a variety of different names was confusing (even a bit ridiculous!), reproduced (in March 1994) the ISO 9000:1994 series of documents. By the year 2000 more than 60 countries had ratified ISO 9000 as their accepted quality standard. Table 1.1 shows national standards equivalent to the ISO 9000:1994 series.

Although the most notable change between the 1987 and the 1994 versions of the ISO 9000 standard was the streamlining of the numbering system, there were also around 250 other changes, the main ones being that:

- it became an explicit requirement that all members of an organisation (down to supervisory level at least) had job profiles (descriptions) to define their authority and responsibility;
- design reviews were now compulsory throughout the Work Package lifetime;
- documentation control was extended to ensure that all data was kept up to date.

Most of the 250 changes were intended to clarify the standard, making it easier to read. They did not significantly alter the way in which most companies were running their businesses; they simply sought to improve it.

1.5 ISO 9001:2000

1.5.1 Background to the ISO 9001:2000 standard

When ISO 9000 was first released in 1987, it was recognised as being largely incomplete and required the auditors to fill in lots of the gaps. The first revision of ISO 9000 in 1994 got rid of many of these problems. However, an organisation could still conform to the standard but at the same time produce

Figure 1.9 The background to ISO 9001:2000

substandard products that were of a consistent poor quality! There was clearly a major loophole that enabled organisations to comply with the requirements of ISO 9000:1994 but without having to **improve** their quality!

Some managers also found it extremely difficult to see the real benefit of having to commit more and more manpower and finance in maintaining their ISO 9000 certification. Whilst most organisations accept that the initial certification process is worthwhile and can result in some very real benefits, these are mainly one-offs. Once ISO 9000 had been fully adopted within an organisation, it was often felt that these savings could not be repeated. The ISO 9000 certificate has been hanging on the wall in the reception office for many years but third party surveillance visits don't tell them much more than they already knew from their own internal audits. Quite a few organisations also felt that they had gone well beyond ISO 9000 and apart from associating the organisation with a quality standard, there was little or no actual benefit to be gained from having to continually pay out for re-certification and surveillance fees.

On the other hand, however, BSI frequently come across organisations who initially sought ISO 9000 registration (because it was a requirement to continue business with a client), but having seen the benefits they, in turn, have pushed it on down their supply chain, thus increasing the requirement for ISO 9000 certification.

So as the 1990s progressed, more and more organisations started reaping benefits from the existing ISO 9000:1994 requirements but as the standard became more popular the inadequacies of ISO 9000:1994 became more apparent. For example:

- some organisations did not need to carry out all the 20 elements making up ISO 9000:1994 in order to be a quality organisation;

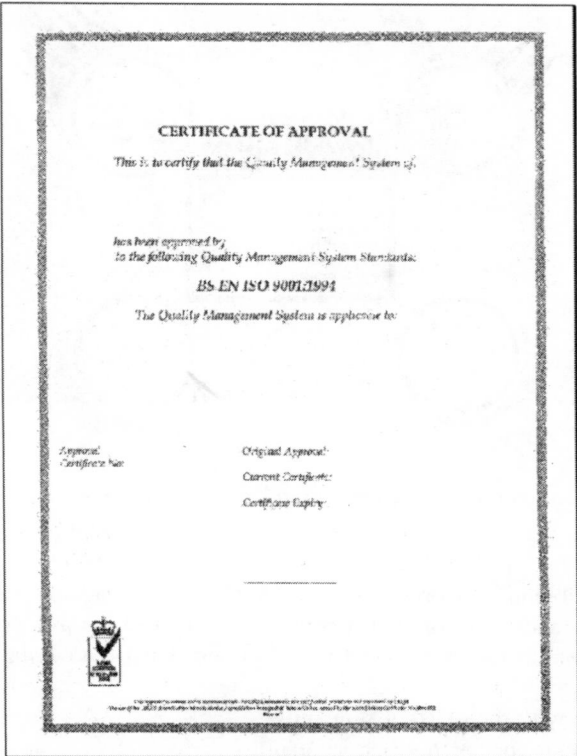

Figure 1.10 A typical ISO 9001:1994 certificate

- the standard was too biased towards manufacturing industries thus making it difficult for service industries to use;
- the requirements were repeated in other management systems, resulting in duplication of effort (e.g. ISO 14001 environmental management and BS 8800 management of health and safety);
- many organisations wanted to progress beyond the confines of ISO 9000 towards Total Quality Management (TQM);
- the language used was not clear and could be interpreted in many different ways;
- the standard was very inflexible and could not be tailored to specific industries, etc;
- the standard did not cater for continual improvement.

The reasons went on and on and there was clearly a need for revision.

Fortunately, help was on its way for under existing international agreement, **all** International standards have to be re-inspected, five years after publication, for their continued applicability. In accordance with this agreement, ISO/

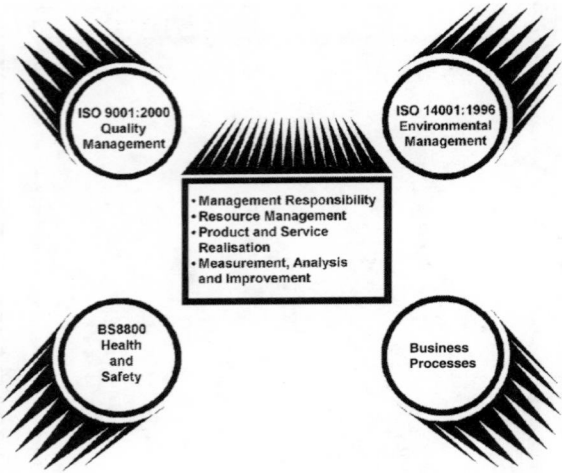

Figure 1.11 The common elements from ISO 9000, BS 8800 and ISO 14001

TC176 (ISO Technical Committee No 176 'Quality Management and Quality Assurance') conducted a global survey of over 1000 users and organisations for their views on ISO 9000:1994 using a questionnaire covering:

- problems with the existing standards;
- requirements for new/revised standards;
- possible harmonisation and interoperability between quality management, environmental management and health & safety standards.

The primary objective of this exercise was to make ISO 9001:2000:

- more compatible with the other management systems;
- more closely associated to business processes;
- more easily understood;
- capable of being used by all organisations, no matter their size;
- capable of being used by all types of industries and professions (i.e. manufacturers **and** service providers);
- a means of continually improving quality;
- future proof.

1.5.2 The revision process

The revision process was the responsibility of ISO TC–176. Initial specifications and goals were established following extensive user surveys and these were followed by a user verification and validation process, to ensure that the standards produced would actually meet the requirements of the user.

ISO

FDIS

DIS

CD2

CD1

WD3

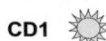

WD2

WD1

Figure 1.12 The revision process

The program of work was as follows:

4th quarter 1997	1st Working Draft (WD1) for use by TC–176
1st quarter 1998	2nd Working Draft (WD2) for use by TC–176
2nd quarter 1998	3rd Working Draft (WD3) for use by TC–176
July 1998	Committee Draft (CD1) issued for ballot
November 1999	Committee Draft (CD2) issued for ballot
November 1999	Draft International Standard (DIS) for comment and vote by Member Countries*
September 2000	Publication of Final Draft International Standard (FDIS)
December 2000	Publication of International Standard (ISO)

---

* Once Draft International Standards have been adopted by the technical committees they are then circulated to member bodies for voting. Publication as an International Standard then requires a two-thirds majority of the votes.

1.5.2.1 Factors considered during the revisions of the standards

Some of the factors considered during the development of the draft standards included:

- the problems with ISO 9001:1994's 20-element model and its current bias towards manufacturing organisations;
- the increased use of the ISO 9000 standards by regulated industries and their subsequent need for change;
- the proliferation of guideline standards in the ISO 9000:1994 family (most of which were not fully used!);
- changed user requirements with more emphasis on meeting customer needs;
- the difficulties that small businesses were having in trying to meet the requirements of the standards;
- the need to be more compatible with other management system standards (e.g. ISO 14001 for environmental management);
- incorporation of the ISO 9000 standards into specific sector requirements standards or documents;
- the adoption of process-oriented management and the need to assist organisations in improving their business performance.

The interest shown by users in improving ISO 9000:1994 was obvious by their response to the questionnaires which resulted in over 6000 comments on each of the first and second sets of committee drafts. The results of the survey clearly showed the need for a revised ISO 9000 standard, which would:

- be split, so that one standard (i.e. ISO 9001:2000) would address requirements, whilst another (ISO 9004:2000) would address the gradual improvement of an organisation's overall quality performance;
- be simple to use, easy to understand and only use clear language and terminology (a definite plus for most readers of current international standards!);
- have a common structure based on a 'process model';
- be capable of being 'tailored' to fit all product and service sectors and all sizes of organisations (and not just the manufacturing industry);
- be capable of demonstrating continuous improvement and prevention of nonconformity;
- provide a natural stepping stone towards performance improvement;
- be more orientated toward continual improvement and customer satisfaction;
- have an increased compatibility with other management system standards;
- provide a basis for addressing the primary needs and interests of organisations in specific sectors such as aerospace, automotive, medical devices, telecommunications, and others.

The survey also indicated that organisations were finding it increasingly difficult to do business in the world marketplace without ISO 9000. Organisations, therefore, needed this recognition, but gaining ISO 9000 certification shouldn't be that difficult provided that they followed the basic requirements of this standard. The growing confusion about having three quality standards available for certification (i.e. ISO 9001:1994, 9002:1994 and 9003:1994) was another problem and so it was recommended that the requirements of all three standards be combined into one overall standard (i.e. ISO 9001:2000).

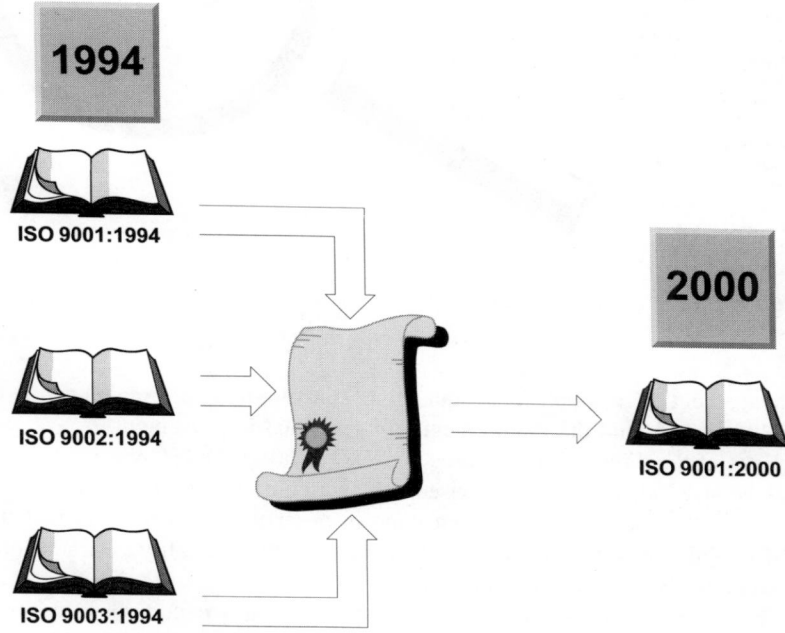

Figure 1.13 Simplified certification with only one standard

ISO emphasise, however, that the year 2000 revision of the ISO 9000 standards **does not** require the rewriting of an organisation's current QMS documentation! They point out that the major change has been from a 'system based' to a more 'process based' management approach, which can be easily addressed by organisations who have a fully documented QMS that already complies with the 1994 standard.

1.5.2.2 Key changes in the standards

In ISO 9001:2000, the 20 elements contained in section four of ISO 9001:1994 have been replaced by four major sections covering the

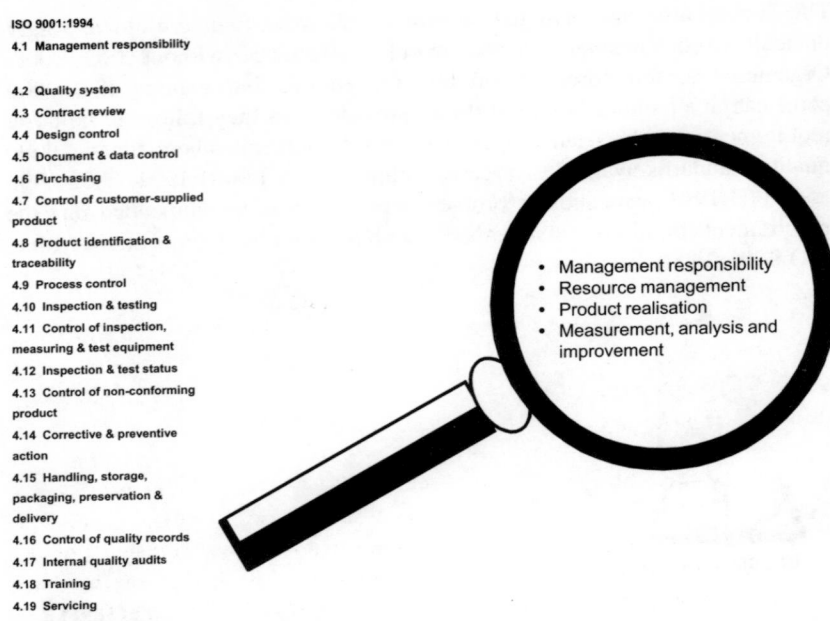

ISO 9001:1994

4.1 Management responsibility

4.2 Quality system
4.3 Contract review
4.4 Design control
4.5 Document & data control
4.6 Purchasing
4.7 Control of customer-supplied product
4.8 Product identification & traceability
4.9 Process control
4.10 Inspection & testing
4.11 Control of inspection, measuring & test equipment
4.12 Inspection & test status
4.13 Control of non-conforming product
4.14 Corrective & preventive action
4.15 Handling, storage, packaging, preservation & delivery
4.16 Control of quality records
4.17 Internal quality audits
4.18 Training
4.19 Servicing

- Management responsibility
- Resource management
- Product realisation
- Measurement, analysis and improvement

Figure 1.14 How 20 went into 4!

management of resources, the quality of the product, the maintenance of quality records and the requirements for continual improvement.

Each of the three main standards (i.e. ISO 9000:2000, ISO 9001:2000 and ISO 9004:2000) now have a revised title, which no longer includes the term 'quality assurance'. This has been done in order to reflect the fact that the QMS requirements specified in these standards address quality assurance of a product as well as customer satisfaction.

They have been designed so that ISO 9000:2000 now includes a description of the basic approach to quality management as well as including a revised vocabulary to reflect the usage of new and revised terms and associated definitions contained in ISO 9001:2000 and ISO 9004:2000.

ISO 9001:2000 is focused towards 'providing confidence, as a result of demonstration, in product conformance to established requirements' and includes a clause entitled 'permissible exclusions'. This clause allows organisations to formally 'exclude' certain non-applicable requirements of the standard, yet still claim conformance to it. However, only those organisations that can **prove** that the nature of their products, customers and/or the applicable regulatory requirements do not need to meet the full requirements of ISO 9001:2000, are allowed these exclusions. For example, organisations whose products require no design activities (and who would have previously sought ISO 9002:1994 certification) can claim to be in compliance with ISO 9001:2000 by excluding the requirements for design and/or development.

ISO 9004:2000 is focused towards providing 'benefits for all interested parties through sustained customer satisfaction'. ISO 9004:2000 also includes the requirements of ISO 9001:2000 in text boxes inserted in appropriate places (which means, I suppose that organisations only need to purchase 9004 and not both of the standards – funny old world!). In addition, ISO 9004:2000 includes an annex giving guidance on 'self-assessment' to enable an organisation to check the status of their own QMS. I feel that this will prove very useful for organisations who are considering applying for ISO 9001:2000 certification, but are unsure what additional quality documentation will be required.

It should be noted, however, that ISO 9001:2000 and ISO 9004:2000 have been developed as a 'consistent pair' of QMS standards, based on eight quality management principles with a common process-oriented structure and harmonised terminology. They are designed to be used together, or may be used as stand-alone documents.

One specific change to ISO 9001:2000 and ISO 9004:2000 that was brought about late in the day concerned the usage of the term 'product'. During the Committee Draft stages, it became apparent that there was a need to have a single word that described an organisation's output as well as the service that it provided. Consequently in the new standards, 'product' has been defined as 'a process, which uses resources to transform inputs into outputs' and there are four agreed generic product categories, namely:

- hardware (e.g. engine, mechanical part);
- software (e.g. computer program);
- services (e.g. transport);
- processed materials (e.g. lubricant).

In practice, most products will be combinations of these four generic product categories. Whether the combined product is then called hardware, processed material, software or service will depend on the dominant element.

Although upgrading an organisation's QMS to ISO 9001:2000 will be fairly simple if that organisation is already certified to ISO 9001:1994, the impact on organisations who are currently only registered to ISO 9002:1994 and 9003:1994 (i.e. organisations not involved in the design and manufacture of a product) will probably be more difficult. Greater documentation will now be required by these organisations in order to demonstrate why service and design functions do not apply to their organisations and more detailed records will be needed.

1.5.2.3 Accreditation and certification/registration

Following consultation between ISO/TC 176, the International Accreditation Forum (IAF) and the ISO Committee on Conformity Testing (ISO/CASCO), a joint communiqué was issued which included the following statements:

- 'Accredited certificates to the new ISO 9001 shall not be granted until the publication of ISO 9001:2000 as an International Standard'.
- 'ISO 9001:2000 will require auditors and other relevant certification/registration body personnel to demonstrate new competencies'.
- 'Certification/registration bodies will need to take particular care in defining the scope of certificates issued to ISO 9001:2000, and the 'permissible exclusions' to the requirements of that standard'.
- 'Certificates issued to ISO 9001:1994, ISO 9002:1994 or ISO 9003:1994 shall have a maximum validity of 3 years from the date of publication of ISO 9001:2000'.

However, although organisations already registered to the 1994 standard will have up to three years following publication of the ISO 9001:2000 in which to re-certify, I would strongly recommend that these organisations make a start on the transition to the new standard as soon as possible. By agreement, those organisations which have previously used ISO 9002:1994 and ISO 9003:1994 will be permitted to work to this new international standard by reducing the scope of their conformance. For example, when a customer needs a particular type of product and/or service that does not necessarily require all the QMS requirements, then they can be excluded. This exclusion can be made, **provided** that the organisation does not reduce the scope of its QMS or exclude any QMS requirements that affect the organisation's ability to provide a conforming product and/or service. All exclusions need to be defined in the organisation's Quality Manual and naturally, reducing the scope of conformance will not absolve the organisation from providing a product and/or service which meets customer requirements.

As previously mentioned, the 2000 revision is also an attempt to harmonise the common quality management elements of ISO 9000 with those contained in the ISO 14001 environmental management system standard and, to some degree, the health and safety requirements of standards such as BS 8800. The overall intention is to enable an organisation to run one management system that addresses quality, the environment **and** health and safety.

It has to be said, however, that much of the old standard has been preserved and the revisions that have been made have been aimed mainly at closing the gap between ISO 9000, QS 9000 for the automotive industry and TR 9000 for the telecommunications industry etc.

1.5.3 The 'consistent pair'

ISO 9001:2000 and ISO 9004:2000 have been developed together – with the same sequence and structure – in order to form a 'consistent pair' of quality management standards. Their primary aim is to give ISO 9000 a more global applicability, to relate modern quality management to the actual processes and activities of an organisation and to promote continual improvement and achievement of customer satisfaction.

These two international standards are designed to be used together, but can also be used independently. ISO 9001:2000 specifies the **requirements** for a QMS (that can be used for internal application by organisations, certification, or contractual purposes), ISO 9004:2000 gives **guidance** on a wider range of objectives aimed at improving an organisation's overall performance. ISO 9004:2000 is not, however, meant as a guideline for implementing ISO 9001:2000 neither is it intended for certification or contractual use.

Both standards are based on eight quality management principles, which reflect best management practices. These eight principles are:

- customer focused organisation;
- leadership;
- involvement of people;
- process approach;
- system approach to management;
- continual improvement;
- factual approach to decision making;
- mutually beneficial supplier relationship.

In summary, the aim of ISO 9001:2000 is that it:

- is flexible enough to fit any sort of organisation (the manufacturing emphasis is gone);
- no longer consists of 20 isolated elements;
- has a new quality process management model;
- defines responsibilities and authorities within the process areas;
- has a new emphasis on the identification of stakeholders and how the organisation plans to meet their needs;
- includes quality planning (similar to the automotive industries advanced quality planning shown in QS 9000:1995 'Quality system requirements');
- sets a requirement for the regular review of quality objectives;
- provides a flexible approach to quality documentation;
- provides useful rules for presenting the Quality Manual;
- enables an organisation to assure that its infrastructure is sufficient to meet its quality objectives;
- provides a method for continually reviewing the work environment and its effect on quality;
- emphasises the identification and review of customer needs and expectations;
- needs a formal review of an organisation's ability to meet customer needs;
- emphasises close communications with customers;
- includes process capability studies;
- includes design control based on project management;
- includes expanded validation of design requirements;

- requires configuration management;
- gives a better definition of the function of purchasing and procurement;
- verifies purchased products;
- validates the output of processes within an organisation;
- replaces service requirements with delivery and post delivery service requirements;
- closely integrates with ISO 10012 'Quality Assurance Requirements for Measuring Equipment' concerning the use of measurement and inspection equipment;
- needs process measurements and process audits;
- documents how a product is measured and evaluated using a Quality (Control) Plan;
- includes the requirement for regular revalidation of products or services to ensure that they continue to meet customer expectations;
- requires a formal system of measuring customer satisfaction;
- gives a more aggressive definition of corrective and preventive action;
- requires a formal policy on continuous improvement;
- is in line with other management systems.

Thus all organisations, whether private or public, large or small, involved in the production of manufactured goods, services, or software, now have tools available to organise their activities and which will achieve internal and external benefits.

1.5.4 Compatibility with ISO 14001:1996

ISO 9001:2000 is intended to be compatible with other management system standards, in particular, those relating to environmental management, occupational health & safety and financial management, etc. In producing ISO 9001:2000, TC/176 have made sure that the requirements of ISO 14001:1996 'Environmental management systems – Specifications with guidance for use' have been carefully considered and a very good degree of compatibility now exists between these two standards. Work is already underway to produce a revised edition of ISO 14001 (scheduled for the year 2002) with the aim of achieving even more compatibility between these management standards.

ISO 14001 is ISO's equivalent to the UK's BS 7750 – the world's first Environmental Management System (EMS). It specifies the requirements for an EMS against which a third party may certify an organisation for environmental purposes.

ISO 14001 is voluntary and is not affected by any mandatory requirements for a company to register. It was adopted by the CEN in September 1996 and now supersedes all other European national standards, including BS 7750. ISO 14001 is sufficiently flexible to take account of an organisation's size and nature. It recognises that the level of complexity of certification should be appropriate to individual requirements.

1.5.4.1 ISO 14001 versus ISO 9001:2000

Although there is some overlap between these two standards, the all important difference is that quality management (ISO 9001) is applied to the process stream of a business (i.e. production) while the environmental standard (ISO 14001) is applied to all aspects of an organisation's activities. So, although they share comment elements, there are vital differences in scope and approach. ISO 9001 is primarily aimed at achieving customer satisfaction by producing the product or service at the most competitive price. An EMS, by contrast, aims to improve an organisation's environmental performance by evaluating the environmental impact of its products and services and taking steps to reduce or control them.

1.5.4.2 Possible integration

Whilst ISO 9001:2000 does not, however, include any requirements that are specific to ISO 14001 (or, indeed, any of the other management systems), it does, nevertheless, allow an organisation to align and integrate its own QMS with other (related) management system requirements. In some cases, it may even be possible for an organisation to adapt its existing management system(s) in order to establish a QMS that complies with the requirements of ISO 9001:2000.

1.5.5 The ISO 9000:2000 family of standards

ISO 9000:2000 Quality Management Systems – fundamentals and vocabulary (superseding ISO 8402:1994 'Quality Management and Quality Assurance – Vocabulary' and ISO 9000–1:1994 'Quality Management and Quality Assurance Standards – Guidelines for selection and use' and ISO 9000–3: 1997).

Describes fundamentals of QMSs and specifies the terminology for QMSs.

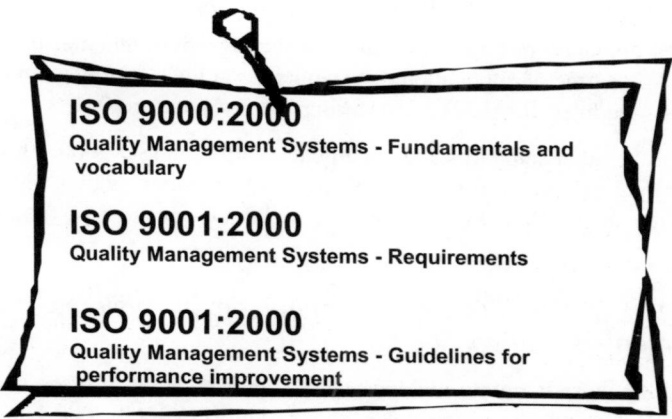

ISO 9000:2000
Quality Management Systems - Fundamentals and vocabulary

ISO 9001:2000
Quality Management Systems - Requirements

ISO 9001:2000
Quality Management Systems - Guidelines for performance improvement

Figure 1.15 The ISO 9000:2000 family

ISO 9001:2000 Quality Management Systems – requirements (superseding ISO 9001:1994 ' Quality Systems – Model for quality assurance in design, development, production, installation and servicing', ISO 9002:1994 'Quality Systems – Model for quality assurance in production, installation and servicing' and ISO 9003:1994 'Quality Systems – Model for quality assurance in final inspection and test').

Specifies the requirements for QMSs for use where an organisation's capability to provide products that meet customer and applicable regulatory requirements needs to be demonstrated.

ISO 9004:2000 Quality Management Systems – guidelines for performance improvement (superseding ISO 9004–1:1994 'Quality Management and Quality System Elements – Guidelines).

Provides guidance on QMSs, including the processes for continual improvement that will contribute to the satisfaction of an organisation's customers and other interested parties.

For completeness, a new standard will be introduced to assist auditing systems against ISO 9001:2000, this will be:

ISO 19011 Guidelines on auditing quality and environmental management systems (to supersede ISO 10011–1:1990 ' Guidelines for Auditing Quality Systems – Auditing', ISO 1011–2:1991 'Guidelines for Auditing Quality Systems – Qualification criteria for quality system auditors', ISO 1011–3:1991 'Guidelines for Auditing Quality Systems – Management of audit programmes', as well as ISO 14010:1996 'Guidelines for Environmental Auditing – General principles', ISO 14011:1996 'Guidelines for Environmental Auditing – Audit procedures – Auditing of environmental management systems' and ISO 14012:1996 'Guidelines for Environmental Auditing – Qualification criteria for environmental auditors').

Provides guidance on managing and conducting environmental and quality audits. At the time of publication this standard is at the Committee Draft stage, but it is scheduled for publication during the 3rd quarter 2001.

As all of the other standards and documents within the ISO 9000:1994 family were submitted for formal review by ISO member bodies during the committee stages, they will probably be withdrawn in the near future.

1.5.5.1 ISO 9000:2000 quality management systems – fundamentals and vocabulary

To ensure a more harmonised approach to standardisation (and the hopeful(!) achievement of coherent terminology within the ISO 9000:2000 family), the development of ISO 9000:2000 was completed in parallel with ISO

Figure 1.16 The way to ISO 9000:2000

9001:2000, ISO 9004:2000, the future ISO 14001 standard for environmental management and all other existing and planned management standards.

ISO 9000:2000 now includes a revision of the current ISO 8402:1995 'Quality Management and Quality Assurance – Vocabulary' standard, provides a more formal approach to the definition of terms, specifies terminology for QMSs and will assist:

- those concerned with enhancing mutual understanding of the terminology used in quality management (e.g. suppliers, customers, regulators);
- those internal or external to the organisation who assess the QMS or audit it for conformance to the requirements of ISO 9001:2000 (e.g. auditors, regulators, certification/registration bodies);
- those internal or external to the organisation who give advice on QMSs appropriate to that organisation;
- developers of related standards.

ISO 9000:2000 also provides an introduction to the fundamentals of QMSs and following publication of this standard, ISO 8402:1995 has been withdrawn.

1.5.5.2 ISO 9001:2000 Quality management systems – requirements

The current ISO 9001:1994, ISO 9002:1994 and ISO 9003:1994 family of standards have now been consolidated into a single revised ISO 9001:2000 standard. Organisations that have previously used ISO 9002:1994 and ISO 9003:1994 will be allowed to be certified to ISO 9001:2000 through 'permissible exclusions' of that standard's requirement by omitting those requirements that do not apply to their particular organisation.

Figure 1.17 The way to ISO 9001:2000

With the publication of ISO 9001:2000, there is now, therefore, a single quality management **'requirements'** standard that is applicable to all organisations, products and services. It is the only standard that can be used for the certification of a QMS and its generic requirements can be used by **any** organisation to:

- address customer satisfaction;
- meet customer and applicable regulatory requirements;
- enable internal and external parties (including certification bodies) to assess the organisation's ability to meet these customer and regulatory requirements.

For certification purposes, an organisation will have to possess a documented management system which takes the inputs and transforms them into targeted outputs. Something that effectively:

- says what they are going to do;
- does what they have said they are going to do;
- keep records of everything that they do – especially when things go wrong.

The basic process to achieve these targeted outputs will encompass:

- the client's requirements;
- the inputs from management and staff;
- documented controls for any activities that are needed to produce the finished article;
- and, of course, delivering a product or service, which satisfies the customer's original requirements.

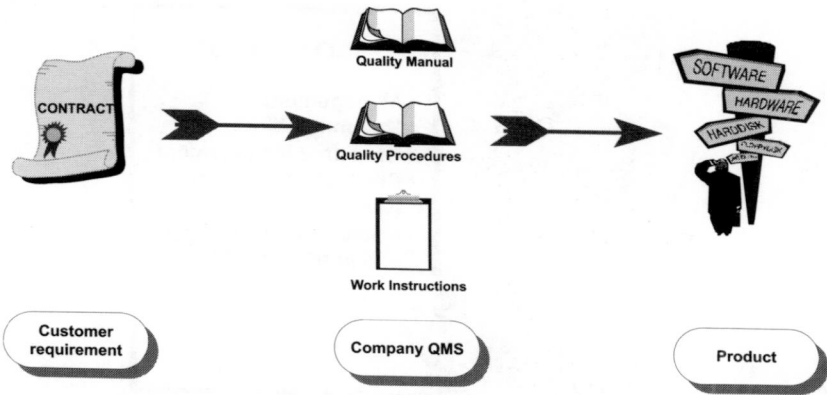

Figure 1.18 The basic process

The adoption of a QMS has to be a strategic decision for any organisation and the design and implementation of their QMS will be influenced by its varying needs, objectives, products provided, processes employed and the size and structure of that organisation. As ISO are quick to point out, however, it is not the intention of ISO 9001:2000 to insist on a uniform structure to a QMS or uniformity of documentation. The QMS requirements specified in this standard should always be viewed as complementary to the product technical requirements.

This latest revision process has made ISO 9001:2000 into a far more generic standard than the previous 20-element ISO 9001:1994 structure. It adopts the process management approach widely used in business today and more clearly addresses the QMS requirements for an organisation in order to demonstrate its capability of meeting customer requirements. It is now also more compatible (indeed linked with) the ISO 14001:1996 standard for environmental management and includes the relevant managerial requirements found in national/international health and safety management standards.

The ISO 9001:2000 standard is the only standard within the 2000 edition to which an organisation can be certified. It includes all the key points from the previous 20 elements of ISO 9001:1994, but integrates them into four major generic business processes, namely:

- management responsibility (policy, objectives, planning, system, review);
- resource management (human resources, information, facilities);
- product realisation (customer, design, purchasing, production, calibration);
- measurement, analysis and improvement (audit, process/product control, improvement).

The new structure of ISO 9001:2000 is shown in Tables 1.2–1.6.

ISO 9001:2000

- Management Responsibility
- Resource Management
- Product and Service Realisation
- Measurement, Analysis and Improvement

Figure 1.19 The four major generic business processes of ISO 9001:2000

Table 1.2 The structure of ISO 9001:2000 – Sections 1–4

Section	Sub section	Sub-sub section	Title
1			**Scope**
	1.1		General
	1.2		Application
2			Normative reference
3			Terms and definitions
4			Quality Management System
	4.1		General requirements
	4.2		Documentation requirements
		4.2.1	General
		4.2.2	Quality Manual
		4.2.3	Control of documents
		4.2.4	Control of quality records

Table 1.3 The structure of ISO 9001:2000 – Section 5

Section	Sub section	Sub-sub section	Title
5			Management responsibility
	5.1		Management commitment
	5.2		Customer focus
	5.3		Quality policy
	5.4		Planning
		5.4.1	Quality objectives
		5.4.2	Quality management system planning
	5.5		Responsibility, authority, communication
		5.5.1	Responsibility and authority
		5.5.2	Management representative
		5.5.3	Internal communication
	5.6		Management review
		5.6.1	General
		5.6.2	Review input
		5.6.3	Review output

Table 1.4 The structure of ISO 9001:2000 – Section 6

Section	Sub section	Sub-sub section	Title
6			Resource management
	6.1		Provision of resources
	6.2		Human resources
		6.2.1	General
		6.2.2	Competence, awareness, training
	6.3		Infrastructure
	6.4		Work environment

Table 1.5 The structure of ISO 9001:2000 – Section 7

Section	Sub section	Sub-sub section	Title
7			Product realisation
	7.1		Planning of product realization
	7.2		Customer-related processes
		7.2.1	Determination of requirements related to the product
		7.2.2	Review of requirements related to the product
		7.2.3	Customer communication
	7.3		Design and development
		7.3.1	Design and development planning
		7.3.2	Design and development input
		7.3.3	Design and development outputs
		7.3.4	Design and development review
		7.3.5	Design and development verification
		7.3.6	Design and development validation
		7.3.7	Control of design and development changes
	7.4		Purchasing
		7.4.1	Purchasing process
		7.4.2	Purchasing information
		7.4.3	Verification of purchased product
	7.5		Production and service provision
		7.5.1	Control of production and service provision
		7.5.2	Validation of processes for production and service provision
		7.5.3	Identification and traceability
		7.5.4	Customer property
		7.5.5	Preservation of product

Table 1.6 The structure of ISO 9001:2000 – Section 8

Section	Sub section	Sub-sub section	Title
	8		Measurement, analysis and improvement
		8.1	General
		8.2	Monitoring and measurement
		8.2.1	Customer satisfaction
		8.2.2	Internal audit
		8.2.3	Monitoring and measurement of processes
		8.2.4	Monitoring and measurement of product
	8.3		Control of non-conforming product
	8.4		Analysis of data
	8.5		Improvement
		8.5.1	Continual improvement
		8.5.2	Corrective action
		8.5.3	Preventive action

1.5.5.3 Process approach

Any activity that receives inputs and converts them to outputs can be considered as a process. Often, the output from one process will directly form the input into the next process.

For organisations to function effectively, they will have to identify and manage numerous interlinked processes. This systematic identification and management of the processes employed within an organisation (and particularly the interactions between such processes) is referred to as the 'process approach'.

Throughout ISO 9001:2000, the requirement for continuous improvement is frequently (and heavily) emphasised. The following process model clearly shows how the four major sections of ISO 9001:2000 (i.e. management responsibility, resource management, product realisation and measurement, analysis and improvement) inter-relate and how the improvement processes continuously revolve around all other aspects of quality management.

Each of these four sections is then sub-divided into a series of elements or sub-sections but, the most important requirement is the first which **demands**

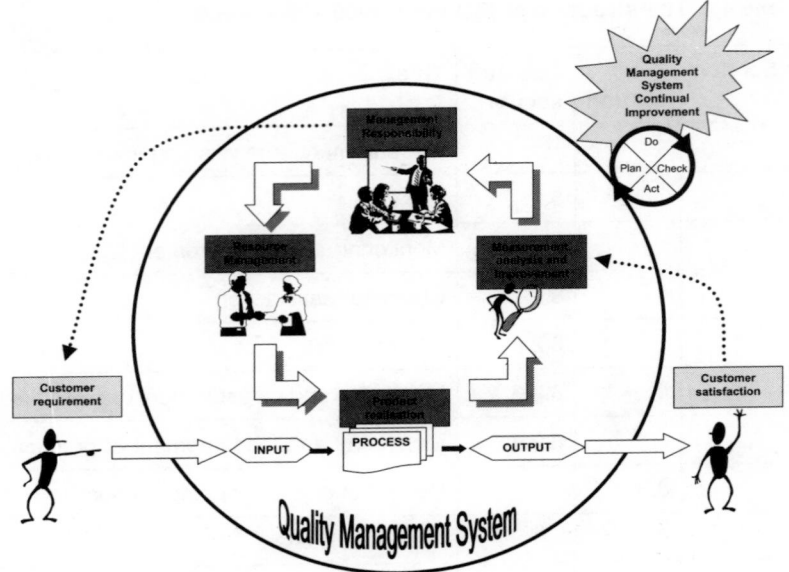

Figure 1.20 The ISO 9000:2000 process model

Herne European Consultancy Ltd

Quality Policy

Within Herne European Consultancy Ltd we are committed to provide products and services which meet the customers' specified contractual and project requirements. We are totally committed to setting and achieving quality standards that are capable of meeting, in **all** respects, the specified requirements and reasonable expectations of our customers.

Herne European Consultancy Ltd shall develop and maintain a Quality Management System that conforms to the requirements of ISO 9001:2000 so that we can provide and maintain a consistently high quality in all work we undertake. Our Quality Management System shall ensure that proper communication, work control and accountable records are generated for all work undertaken

All members of Herne European Consultancy Ltd staff are charged with promoting these aims and are required to familiarise themselves with the contents of this Quality Manual which defines the Quality Management System that has been established and adopted as the means for achieving these declared objectives. Everyone connected with Herne European Consultancy Ltd shall be supported according to their individual needs for personal development, training and facilities.

The Quality Manager based at the Herne European Consultancy Ltd main office is my appointed management representative responsible for monitoring and ensuring the correct and effective implementation of Herne European Consultancy Ltd Quality Management System as a whole.

Total Quality Management **shall** be applied to every aspect of our activity and quality **shall** be the responsibility of everyone, in every activity, throughout Herne European Consultancy Ltd.

Managing Director
Herne European Consultancy Ltd

Figure 1.21 A commitment to quality

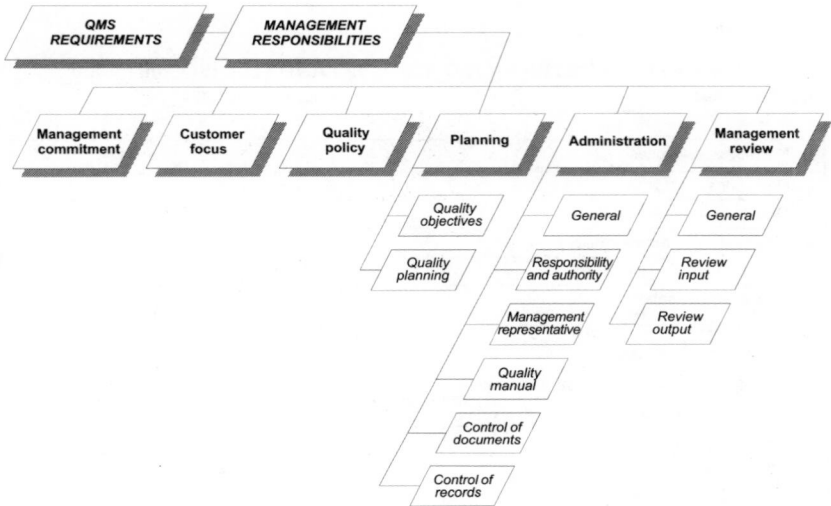

Figure 1.22 Quality Management System requirements and management responsibilities

that everyone shall be involved in quality in order for it to succeed and that it must be management-led and that there must be a commitment to quality – at the highest level.

For clarity, the QMS requirements and management responsibilities can be combined as shown in Figure 1.22.

Organisations seeking to change over their existing ISO 9000:1994 QMS to the 2000 edition are referred to Figure 1.23 that shows the correlation between the existing key elements from ISO 9001:1994 and the clauses of ISO 9001:2000.

1.5.6 Major changes caused by ISO 9001:2000

1.5.6.1 The process model

ISO 9001:2000 uses eight quality management principles which reflect best practice and which are designed to enable a continual improvement of the business, its overall efficiency and be capable of responding to customer needs and expectations.

The eight principles contained in ISO 9001:2000 are of primary concern to an organisation, as they will affect an organisation's overall approach to quality. They are:

1. Customer focused organisation
Organisations depend on their customers and therefore should understand current and future customer needs, should meet customer requirements and should strive to exceed customer expectations.

COMPARISON BETWEEN ISO 9001:1994 AND FDIS ISO 9001:2000	
ISO 9001:1994	**FDIS ISO 9001:2000**
1. Scope	1
2. Normative reference	2
3. Definitions	3
4. Quality system requirements	
4.1 Management responsibility	
4.1.1 Quality policy	5.1, 5.3, 5.4.1
4.1.2 Organisation	
4.1.2.1 Responsibility & authority	5.5.1
4.1.2.2 Resources	5.1, 6.1, 6.2.1, 6.3
4.1.2.3 Management representative	5.5.2
4.1.3 Management review	5.6.1, 5.6.2, 5.6.3, 8.5.1
4.2 Quality system	
4.2.1 General	4.1, 4.2.1, 4.2.2, 5.1, 5.4.1
4.2.2 Quality system procedures	4.2.1
4.2.3 Quality planning	5.4.2, 6.2.1, 7.1
4.3 Contract review	5.2, 7.2.1, 7.2.2, 7.2.3
4.4 Design control	7.2.1, 7.3.1, 7.3.2, 7.3.3, 7.3.4, 7.3.5, 7.3.6, 7.3.7
4.5 Document & data control	4.2.1, 4.2.3
4.6 Purchasing	7.4.1, 7.4.2, 7.4.3, 7.4.4
4.7 Control of customer-supplied product	7.5.4
4.8 Product identification & traceability	7.5.3
4.9 Process control	6.3, 6.4, 7.1, 7.5.1, 7.5.2, 8.2.3
4.10 Inspection & testing	7.1, 7.4.3, 7.5.1, 7.5.3, 8.1, 8.2.4
4.11 Control of inspection, measuring and test equipment	7.6
4.12 Inspection & test status	7.5.3
4.13 Control of non-conforming product	8.3
4.14 Corrective & preventive action	8.4, 8.5.2, 8.5.3
4.15 Handling, storage, packaging, preservation & delivery	7.5.1, 7.5.5
4.16 Control of quality records	4.2.4
4.17 Internal quality audits	8.2.2, 8.2.3
4.18 Training	6.2.1, 6.2.2
4.19 Servicing	7.1, 7.5.1
4.20 Statistical techniques	8.1, 8.2.3, 8.2.4, 8.4

Notes
1. Reference numbers are given in numerical order, not in order of significance.
2. The clause numbers in ISO 9001:2000 are as follows:
    5.x.x - Management Responsibility
    6.x.x - Resource Management
    7.x.x - Product Realisation
    8.x.x - Measurement, Analysis and Improvement

Figure 1.23 Correlation between the clauses of ISO 9001:1994 and ISO 9001:2000

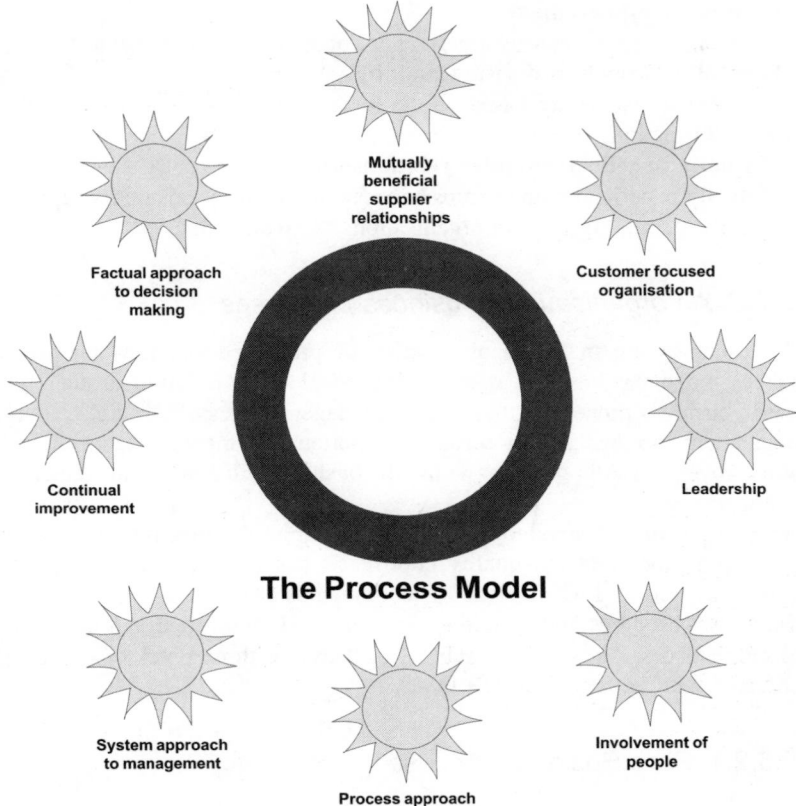

Figure 1.24 The process model

2. Leadership
Leaders establish unity of purpose, direction, and the internal environment of their organisation. They create the environment in which people can become fully involved in achieving the organisation's objectives.

3. Involvement of people
People at all levels are the essence of an organisation and their full involvement enables their abilities to be used for the organisation's benefit.

4. Process approach
A desired result is achieved more efficiently when related resources and activities are managed as a process.

5. System approach to management
Identifying, understanding and managing a system of inter-related processes for a given objective contributes to the effectiveness and efficiency of the organisation.

6. Continual improvement

Continual improvement is a permanent objective of any organisation.

7. Factual approach to decision making

Effective decisions are based on the logical and intuitive analysis of data and information.

8. Mutually beneficial supplier relationships

Mutually beneficial relationships between an organisation and its suppliers enhance the ability of both organisations to create value.

1.5.6.2 An organisation's business processes

All businesses are made up of a series of processes which when placed together make the business operate. ISO 9001:2000 is based around four generic business processes, these being management responsibility, resource management, product and/or service realisation and measurement, analysis and improvement. All processes within the business will contain an element of all four processes.

Processes are the keys to providing a clear understanding of what an organisation does and the quality controls it has in place to control their business activities. ISO 9001:2000 recommends the use of 'processes' to define how resources and activities are combined, controlled and converted into deliverables. As shown in Table 1.7, there are three types of processes associated with an organisation's QMS.

1.5.6.2.1 Core Business Process

A company's organisational processes making up their QMS normally comprise a Core Business Process supplemented by a number of supporting

Table 1.7 Core Business and supporting processes

Core Business Process	Describing the end-to-end activities involved in an organisation manufacturing or supplying a deliverable.
Primary supporting processes	The basic set of activities which, when combined into a logical sequence, takes you from receipt of an order (or marketing opportunity) through to the realisation of the finished product or service.
Secondary supporting processes	Those activities that are vital to attaining the desired levels of quality but which are seen as supporting the primary supporting processes.

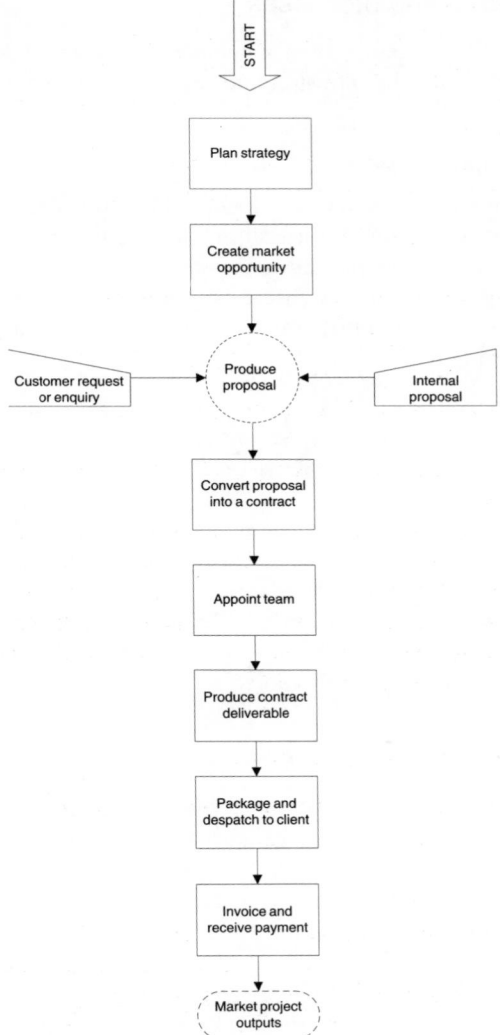

Figure 1.25 The Core Business Process

processes which describe the infrastructure required to produce the contact deliverable (or market opportunity) on time.

The Core Business Process describes the end-to-end activities involved in producing a contract deliverable or marketing opportunity. It commences with the definition of corporate policy and ends when the product is manufactured and/or marketed.

A process owner with full responsibility and authority for managing the process and achieving process objectives should always be nominated.

1.5.6.2.2 Supporting processes

The Core Business Process is then supplemented by a number of supporting processes that describe the infrastructure required to manufacture (or supply) the product on time.

Primary supporting processes

All businesses revolve around taking inputs and putting them through a series of activities that turn them into useful outputs, be that a product or service. These activities are the supporting processes.

Of course the only way to ensure repeat orders is to control quality. Consequently, it is essential that you define your quality policy and objectives for each supporting process.

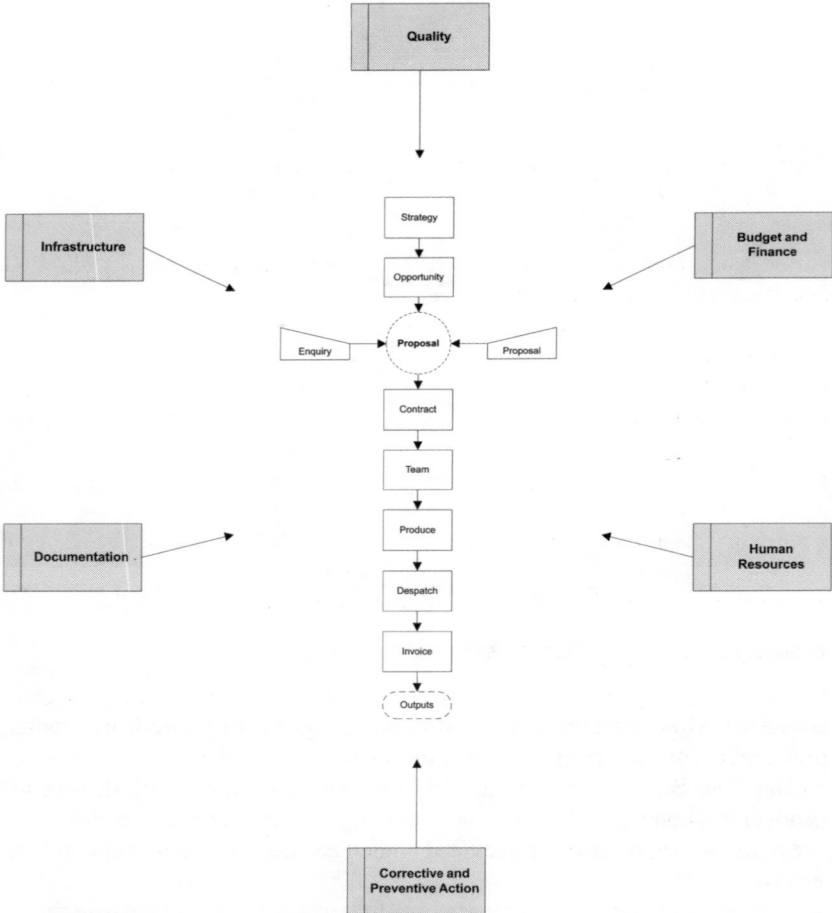

Figure 1.26 Supporting processes

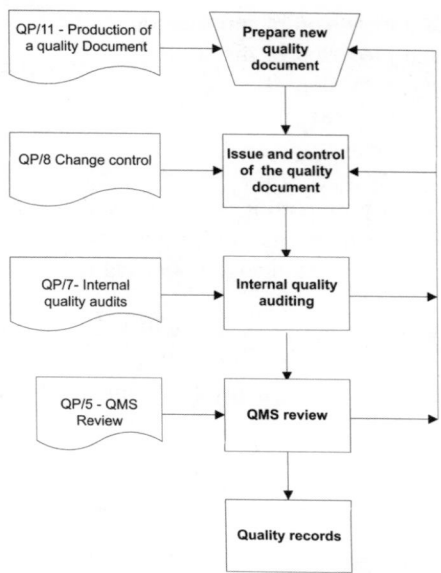

Figure 1.27 Flowchart showing typical primary supporting process

For each process within the flowchart there will be an organisation documentation detailing:

- **objective** – what the process aims to achieve;
- **scope** – what the process covers;
- **responsible owner** – who is ultimately responsible for implementing the process;
- **policy** – what the organisation intends doing to ensure quality is controlled;
- **key performance indicators** – those items of objective evidence that can be used as a way of monitoring performance of the process;
- reference to **supporting system documentation** (QPs and WIs).

Secondary supporting processes

In addition to primary supporting processes there will also be a number of **secondary supporting processes** that run in parallel with and support the primary supporting processes. These secondary supporting processes are equally important as they control all other activities that may influence the quality of the product.

Secondary supporting processes may include such things as:

- identification and provision of suitable staff;
- management and support of staff;

- identification and provision of information;
- identification and provision of materials;
- identification and provision of equipment and facilities;
- management of the QMS;
- continual improvement.

The purpose of secondary supporting processes is to document those activities that are essential for supporting and achieving the primary supporting processes. An example of a secondary supporting process is shown in Figure 1.28.

These secondary-supporting processes will have an identical structure to the primary supporting processes, and will also have their own associated supporting documentation (e.g. Quality Procedures (QPs) and Work Instructions (WIs)).

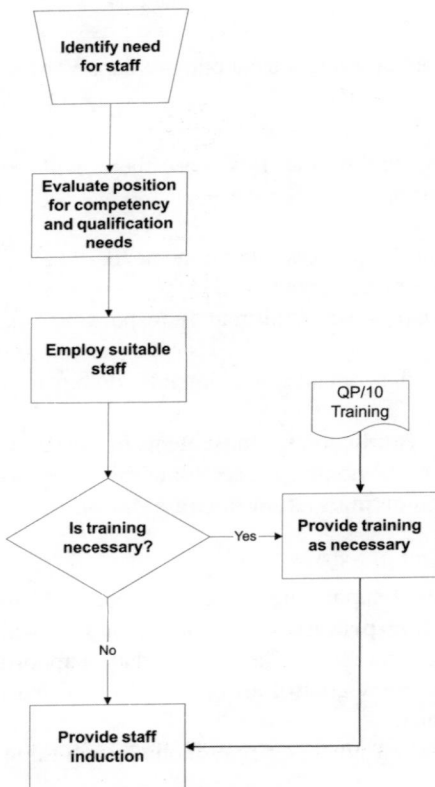

Figure 1.28 An example of a secondary supporting process flowchart for the identification, provision, management and support of staff

1.5.6.2.3 Inter-relationship of process documentation

All processes are documented to give a complete picture of how to perform the activity to a consistent level of quality. The level of detail varies depending whether it is a:

- **Process** – an outline of its objective, scope and key performance indicators;
- **Quality Procedure** – an enlargement of the process explaining how it is controlled;
- **Work Instruction** – the 'fine print' required to perform a specific activity.

All these documents are explained in more detail elsewhere in this book.

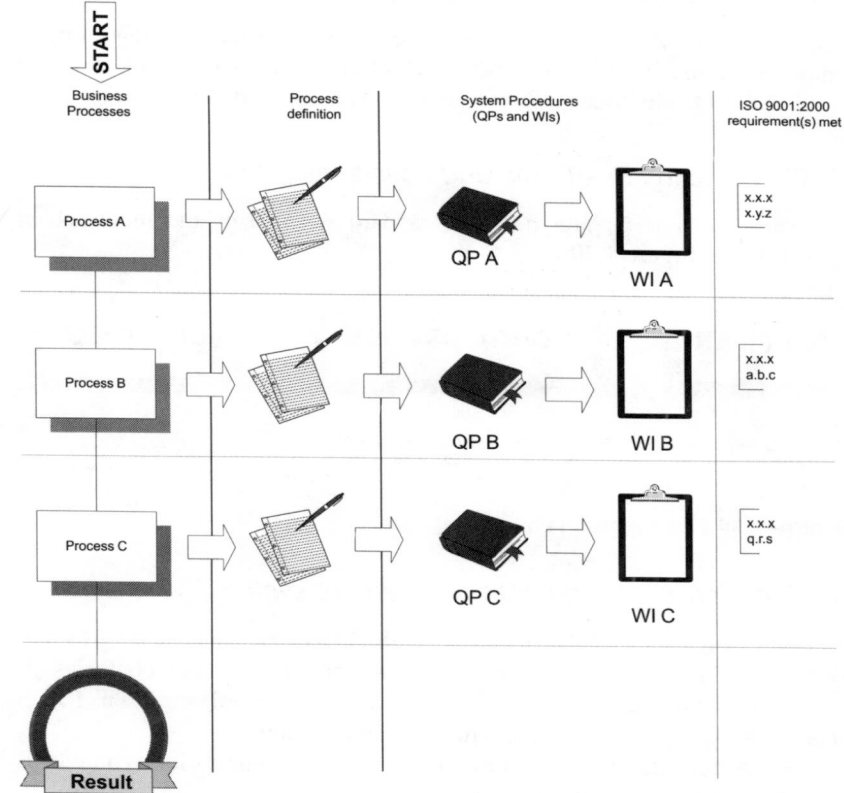

Figure 1.29 The inter-relationship of documented processes within QPs/WIs

Note: By using a matrix such as this, it is possible to identify the parts of ISO 9001:2000 which are met by each process.

1.5.7 Brief summary of ISO 9001:2000 requirements

ISO 9001:2000 is made up of eight sections which are summarised below.

1.5.7.1 Section 1 – Scope

This short section explains what the standard covers and emphasises its primary objective of achieving customer satisfaction by meeting customer requirements. In this context, customer satisfaction is achieved through the:

- effective application of a QMS;
- process for continual improvement of that system;
- prevention of non-conformity.

1.5.7.2 Section 2 – Normative reference

Another short section directs the reader to other standards that form a **mandatory** input to ISO 9001:2000. In this instance the only reference is 'ISO 9000:2000, Quality Management Systems – Fundamentals and vocabulary'.

1.5.7.3 Section 3 – Terms and definitions

This third section explains how the standard is based on the supply chain shown in the Figure 1.30.

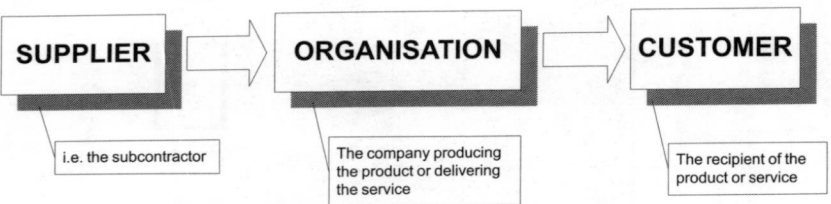

Figure 1.30 The supply chain

1.5.7.4 Section 4 – quality management system

This basically states that an organisation **shall** have a documented QMS that defines the processes necessary to ensure that the product conforms to customer requirements. This QMS must be implemented, maintained and, most importantly, continually improved by the organisation.

This section also clearly states the types of documentation required to comply with the standard, as follows:

- **Quality Manual** – establishing and maintaining an organisational 'Rule Book';
- **Control of documents** – establishing and maintaining a documented procedure for the control of QMS documents;

- **Quality records** – controlling and maintaining quality records;
- **system level procedures** – used to detail the activities needed to implement the QMS;
- **procedures** that clearly describe the sequence of processes necessary to ensure the conformity of a product or service;
- **instructions** that describe the physical operating practices and controls within each process.

It should always be remembered, however, that the extent of the QMS documentation (which may be in any form or type of medium) is dependent on the:

- size and type of the organisation;
- complexity and interaction of the processes;
- competency of personnel.

1.5.7.5 Section 5 – Management responsibility

This section consists of the majority of the old ISO 9001:1994 management responsibility and quality requirements all rolled together. It is broken down into the following sub-sections that cover the requirements for:

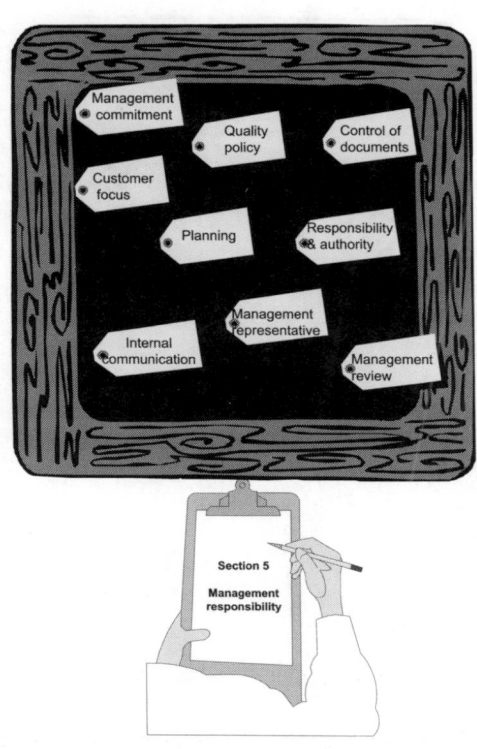

Figure 1.31 Section 5 – Management responsibility

- **Management commitment** – top (i.e. senior) management committing, fully, to the development and improvement of the QMS. (Without their commitment the system will fall at the first hurdle);
- **Customer focus** – determining, fully understanding and documenting customer requirements; ensuring compliance with identified statutory legislation (e.g. EC Directives, other national and international standards etc.);
- **Quality policy** – ensuring that it is appropriate for the purpose, understood by everyone and reviewed for continued suitability;
- **Planning** – clearly stating management's quality objectives and policy on quality in an established, fully documented, QMS;
- **Administration** – identifying and planning the activities and resources required to achieve quality objectives;
- **Management representative** – appointing someone (or some people) to be responsible for the implementation and improvement of the organisation's QMS;
- **Management review** – carrying out regular reviews of the QMS to ensure it continues to function correctly (and to identify areas for improvement).

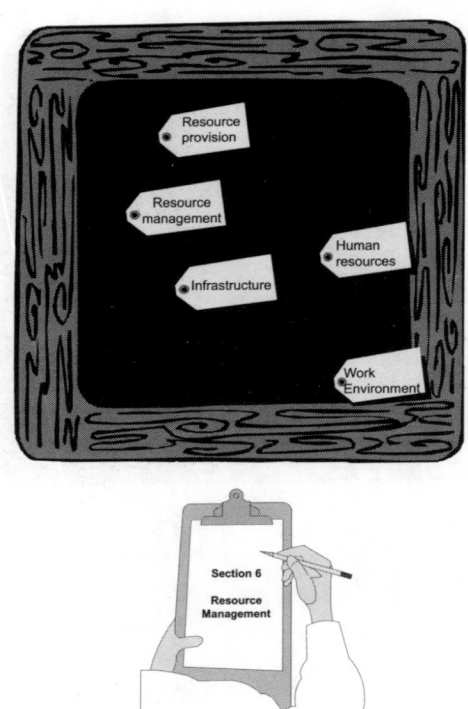

Figure 1.32 Section 6 – Resource management

1.5.7.6 Section 6 – resource management

This section covers resources with regard to training, induction, responsibilities, working environment, equipment requirements, maintenance etc. It is broken down into the following sub-sections:

- **Provision of resources** – identifying the resources required to implement and improve the processes that make up the QMS;
- **Human resources** – assigning personnel with regard to competency, education, training, skill and/or experience;
- **Infrastructure** – identifying, providing and maintaining the workspace, facilities, equipment (hardware and software) and supporting services to achieve conformity of product;
- **Work environment** – identifying and managing the work environment (e.g. health and safety, ambient conditions etc.).

1.5.7.7 Section 7 – product realisation

Section 7 absorbs most of the 20 elements of the old ISO 9000:1994 standard, including process control, purchasing, handling and storage, and measuring

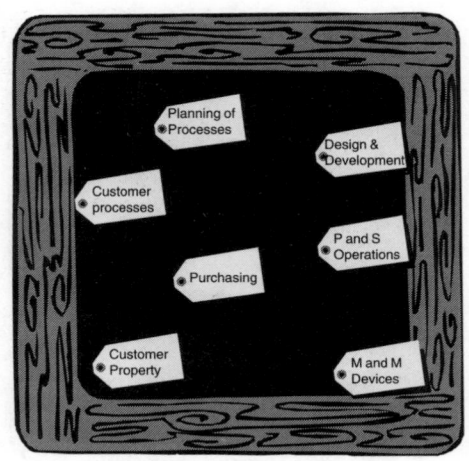

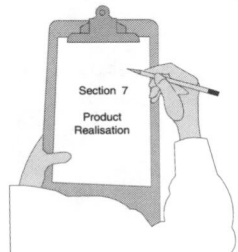

Figure 1.33 Section 7 – Product realisation

devices. This section is broken down into a number of sub-sections that cover the requirements for:

- **Planning of realisation processes** – clearly defining and documenting the processes used to ensure reliable and consistent products (e.g. verification and validation activities, criteria for acceptability and quality records etc.);
- **Customer-related processes** – identifying customer, product, legal and design requirements;
- **Design and development planning** – controlling the design process (e.g. design inputs, outputs, review, verification, validation and change control);
- **Purchasing** – having documented processes for the selection and control of suppliers and the control of purchases that affect the quality of the finished product or service;
- **Production and service operations** – having documented instructions that control the manufacture of a product or delivery of a service;
- **Customer property** – identifying, verifying, protecting and maintaining customer property provided for use or incorporation with the product;
- **Control of measuring and monitoring devices** – their control, calibration and protection.

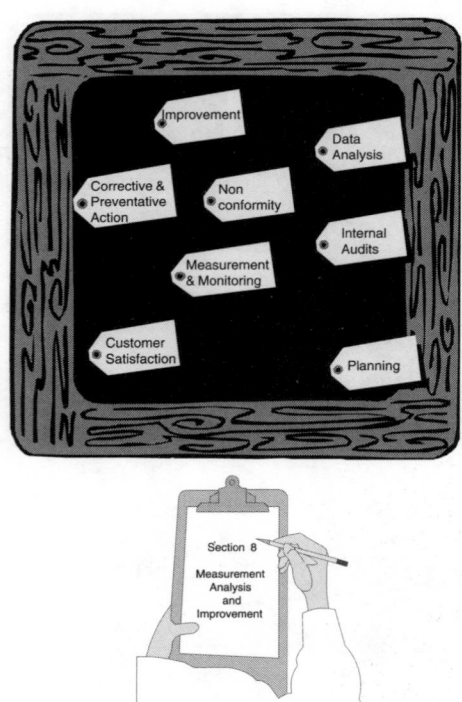

Figure 1.34 Section 8 – Measurement, analysis and improvement

1.5.7.8 Section 8 – Measurement, analysis and improvement

This section absorbs the former inspection and measurement control sections of ISO 9001:1994 and includes requirements for:

- **Planning** – defining the requirements for measurement analysis and improvement (including statistical analysis);
- **Customer satisfaction** – monitoring customer satisfaction/dissatisfaction as a measurement and improvement of the QMS;
- **Internal audits** – conducting periodic internal audits to confirm continued conformity with ISO 9001:2000;
- **Measurement and monitoring of processes and product** – defining processes to monitor the performance of the QMS and the products and services delivered by the organisation;
- **Non-conformity** – controlling non-conformity and its rectification;
- **Data analysis** – collecting and analysing statistical data obtained from the organisation's measuring and monitoring activities to find areas of improvement;
- **improvement** – planning for continual improvement of the QMS;
- **Corrective and preventive action** – having available procedures to address corrective and preventive action.

1.5.8 ISO 9004:2000 Quality Management Systems – guidelines for performance improvement

ISO 9004:2000 provides guidance on all aspects of a QMS, including the processes for continual improvement, that contribute to the satisfaction of an organisation's customers and other interested parties. The guidance provided in this standard is generic and is applicable to all organisations, regardless of

ISO 9004:2000

Figure 1.35 The reason for ISO 9004:2000

the type, size and the product provided. It is based on sound quality management principles that provide an understanding of quality requirements and their application to improve the performance of an organisation.

ISO 9004:2000, therefore, is aimed at improving an organisation's overall quality performance and provides a stepping stone to Total Quality Management (TQM). In the words of the standard, 'ISO 9004:2000 is, therefore, designed to go beyond quality management requirements and provide organisations with guidelines for performance improvement through sustained customer satisfaction'. In doing so it:

- provides guidance to management on the application and use of a QMS to improve an organisation's overall performance;
- is recommended as a guide for organisations whose management wishes to move beyond the minimum requirements of ISO 9001:2000 in pursuit of increased performance improvement;
- defines the minimum QMS requirements needed to achieve customer satisfaction by meeting specified product requirements;
- can also be used by an organisation to demonstrate its capability to meet customer requirements.

Note: ISO 9004:2000 is **not** a guideline for **implementing** ISO 9001 and is **not** intended for certification, regulatory or contractual use.

1.6 Certification

1.6.1 Who can certify an organisation?

There are a number of companies available to carry out ISO 9001:2000 certification (e.g. TÜV, BSI, SGS Yarsley, etc.) and it really depends on where the organisation's main market is going to be as to whom is eventually chosen.

BSI is the recognised world leader in setting quality and safety standards for industry. BSI's main offices are in London which, in addition to conference rooms which host ISO committees, has a huge administration block for the update and dissemination of standards. They also have a large library containing copies of all the BS, EN, IEC, ISO and ANSI standards together with the majority of all the other industrial and management standards. BSI Inc is a separate company under US law with 11 regional offices and a corporate office in Reston, VA. They recently acquired CEEM (Center for Energy and Environmental Management) which was founded in Fairfax, VA, in 1979 and is now located in their Reston offices. As well as providing the usual certification services, BSI Inc (through CEEM) provide training in all ISO 9000/14000 topics including BSI's well-established Quality Managers and Lead Auditors courses.

1.6.2 What is required for certification?

A fully documented, auditable QMS that is totally supported by senior management and one that is implemented throughout the organisation.

The QMS shall consist of:

- a **Quality Manual** – describing how an organisation meets the requirements of ISO 9001:2000 (objectives, goals, roles, organisation and responsibilities, etc.);
- **Processes** – describing the end-to-end activities involved in project management;
- **Quality Processors** – describing the method by which the processes are managed;
- **Work Instructions** – describing how individual tasks and activities are carried out.

1.6.3 Who will be responsible for quality within an organisation?

ISO 9001:2000 requirement:

'5.5.2 Management representative
Top management shall appoint a member of management who, irrespective of other responsibilities, shall have responsibility and authority that includes:

- *ensuring that processes needed for the quality management system are established, implemented and maintained;*
- *reporting to top management on the performance of the quality management system, and any need for improvement;*
- *ensuring the promotion of awareness of customer requirements throughout the organisation;*
- *liaison with external parties on matters relating the quality management system'.*

An organisation, therefore, needs a Quality Manager who has the full support of senior management. They need to appoint someone who is fully versed in the requirements of ISO 9001:2000 and who is capable of acting as a catalyst and management coach. This post will initially have to be full-time whilst the organisation is setting up their QMS, but could probably reduce to part-time following certification.

The Quality Manager's prime qualities should include:

- approachability;
- an ability to establish two-way communication with all levels of the company personnel.

The Quality Manager shall report to the Managing Director and must be independent of all responsibilities that may adversely affect quality performance.

1.7 Assistance (in the UK) for obtaining a Quality Management System

1.7.1 Government assistance

Following publication of the 1982 White Paper entitled 'Standards, Quality and International Competitiveness' and via its National Quality Campaign, the UK Government are also promoting the wider use of quality control, quality assurance and QMSs within industry.

As part of this National Quality Campaign, the UK Government – in this case the Department of Trade and Industry (DTI) – offers assistance to small and medium-sized companies in order to 'bring awareness of quality through the application of modern quality management techniques'.

1.7.1.1 DTI Business Links

Currently, over 100 Business Links (see *Yellow Pages*) are now open to help small and medium companies to cut costs, to grow, increase sales and export. They are also there to help companies operate at the leading edge of design, quality and delivery and to face the challenge of international competition. The President of the Board of Trade has stated that the object of Business Links is to pool the important support services in an area to improve the effectiveness and quality of support to customers. They are places where services are tailored to fit individual customers' needs and where trust is built through a long-term relationship with a personal business adviser.

Business Link services include personal business advisers who work with a company over time and put together a package of support; access to specialist counsellors in design, exports and innovation and technology; information and advice on grants; finance and taxation; consultancy; health checks/diagnostics services; export services; and training courses.

1.7.1.2 National Quality Information Centre

The National Quality Information Centre (NQIC) was set up in 1984, in consultation with the DTI, to provide an information source on standards, training courses and quality generally and to assist the DTI's National Quality Campaign. It is run by the Institute of Quality Assurance (IQA) with the aim of assisting industry and commerce in obtaining information about how to improve quality in their activities and the products and services they provide.

The Centre's main commercial services, in addition to enquiries, are its bibliography or abstracts service, quality journals from the American Society for Quality Control and European Organisation for Quality, and a wide range of books for sale. The Centre plans to open a library in the near future for the benefit of those wishing to carry out serious study.

For further details contact:

The National Quality Information Centre
Tel: 020 7245 6722
Fax: 020 7245 6755
www.iqa.org/info/information.html

Institute of Quality Assurance

1.7.2 Assistance for the smaller company

Most small firms are either unable or unwilling to undertake the complicated procedures required to achieve certification and registration to ISO 9000. With this in mind, BSI launched (in 1994) a low-cost, no-fuss BSI/QA Small Business Service. A customer service helpline is also available to provide assistance.

Further details of this facility are available from:

BSI Customer Services and Information
Tel: 020 8996 7000
Fax: 020 8996 7001
www.bsi.org.uk

1.7.3 Assistance in setting up a Quality Management System in America

Assistance in setting up a QMS in America may be obtained from two standards bodies. The American Society for Quality (ASQ) are responsible for quality management systems and standards whilst the American Society Testing & Materials (ASTM) responsibilities lie in the provision of quality statistics for the implementation of Total Quality Management (TQM).

1.7.3.1 American Society for Quality

The American Society for Quality (ASQ) provides:

- guidelines for the selection and use of the appropriate internal quality management and external quality assurance standards. This includes clarification of the relationships and differences between the principal quality concepts;
- guidelines and recommendations for the implementation and development of quality management and quality systems;
- assistance on the particular vocabulary used within the quality management and quality assurance fields (i.e. supplying specific terms applicable to the preparation and use of quality management and quality assurance standards);
- details of all elements that should be considered in quality systems within a laboratory.

Further details are available from:

American Society for Quality (ASQ)
Tel: 001 414 272 8575
www.asq.org

1.7.3.2 American Society Testing & Materials

The American Society Testing & Materials (ASTM) provide individual case studies to illustrate examples of how to establish and maintain Total Quality Control (TQC). In addition, ASTM are able to provide statistics for the application of Total Quality Management (TQM) and the latest information on standardisation, particularly with emphasis on documentation planning and control. Further details are available from:

American Society Testing & Materials (ASTM)
Tel: 001 610 832 9585
www.astm.org

Part One has explained the background to the ISO 9000 recommendations. It has described how ISO 9001:2000 can be used to the best advantage and it has shown how much importance is being placed on companies (large and small) in having ISO 9001:2000 certification or proving that they have an effective QMS that ensures that they work in conformance with that standard.

In Part Two the structure of the ISO 9000:2000 series is explained and the various clauses and elements making up ISO 9001:2000 are reviewed.

Part Two

The Structure of ISO 9001:2000

In Part One the background to the ISO 9000 recommendations and requirements have been explained.

In Part Two the structure of ISO 9001:2000 is explained and details provided of the various clauses and elements contained in the ISO 9001:2000 sections are reviewed.

2

The structure of
ISO 9001:2000

Although the formal procedures contained in ISO 9001 are mainly used by larger companies, there is absolutely no reason why smaller companies cannot adapt these procedures to suit their own purposes.

For example, ISO 9001:2000 Section 7.3 states that 'an organization shall plan and control the design and development of a product'. Perhaps your company does not have a design office and this activity is achieved by an individual. Although all of the requirements of Section 7.3 are probably inappropriate, the procedures are still the same – so why not use them!

A detailed description of the main sections making up ISO 9001:2000 now follows.

2.1 Section 1 – Scope

2.1.1 Section 1.1 General

Section 1.1 General requirements	The organisation shall demonstrate its ability to: • consistently provide a product that meets customer and regulatory requirements; • enhance customer satisfaction through the application of their QMS.

This short section contains an explanation of the contents of the standard and states the basic requirements for achieving customer satisfaction through the effective application of a Quality Management System (QMS).

2.1.2 Section 1.2 Application

Section 1.2 Permissible exclusions	If there are clauses that an organisation does not need to meet in order to fulfil the requirements of this standard, these clauses may be excluded. They may be due to: • the nature of the product; • customer requirements; • applicable regulatory requirements.

Section 1.2 emphasises that all the requirements of this International Standard are generic and are applicable to all organisations regardless of type, size and product provided.

If any of the requirements contained in Section 7 cannot be applied owing to the nature of the organisation, then provided that the exclusion(s) do not affect the organisation's ability, or responsibility to provide a product that fulfils customer and/or applicable regulatory requirements, then it can be considered an exclusion.

If, for instance, the organisation manufactures a product that does not have any design and/or development input (e.g. previous and/or similar designs) then Clause 7.3.2 could be excluded.

Note: The **only** clauses that may be excluded are those from Section 7.

2.2 Section 2 – Normative reference

Section 2 Normative reference	This section lists standards that form a **mandatory** input to ISO 9001:2000.

This section requires an organisation to take into consideration ISO 9000:2000:Quality Management Systems – Fundamentals and vocabulary, when applying ISO 9001:2000.

2.3 Section 3 – Terms and definitions

Section 3 Terms and definitions	In addition to those terms defined within ISO 9000:2000, an organisation shall make a note of the specific terms used to describe the supply chain.

This section covers the specific use of terminology to describe the supply chain.

The word 'product' is defined so as to cover all manufacturing and service outputs and so, whenever the term 'product' occurs, it can also mean 'service'.

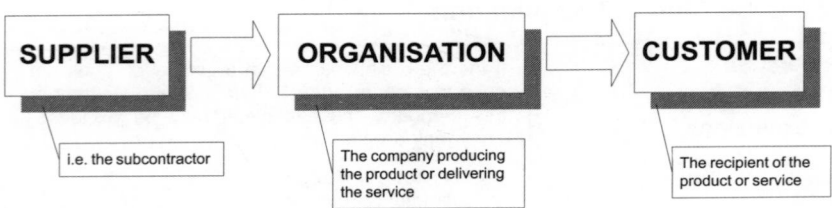

Figure 2.1 The supply chain

Note: In this ISO standard the definition of a product is 'the result of a process'. A product may be defined as:

- hardware;
- software;
- services;
- processed materials.

The definition of a supply chain is shown in Figure 2.1.

2.4 Section 4 – Quality Management System

Section 4 of ISO 9001:2000 covers the requirements for all organisations to establish, document, implement, maintain and continually improve a QMS in accordance with the requirements of this standard.

2.4.1 Section 4.1 General requirements

Section 4.1 General requirements	The organisation shall establish, document, implement, maintain and continually improve a QMS. that ensures and covers: • identification of processes; • their operation and control; • the availability of resources and information; • measurement, monitoring, analyse and support; • achievement of planned results; • continual improvement; • management (in accordance with the requirements of ISO 9001:2000).

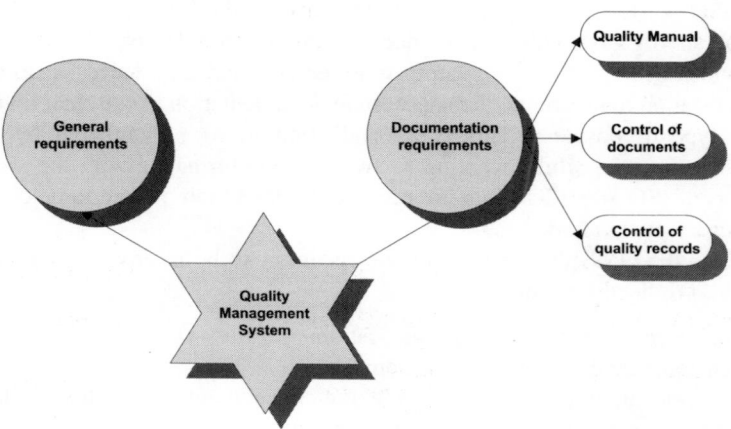

Figure 2.2 Quality Management System

The management of any organisation will rely on a number of different management disciplines, the most important of which, is quality management. As this is the core of all organisational structures, the activities and processes that affect performance improvement will need to be described and defined by management. They will also need to ensure that they are clearly understood by the whole workforce, monitored (i.e. to evaluate improvement on a continuing basis) and managed. Self-assessment can be a very useful tool to evaluate improvement and ISO 9004:2000 helps organisations by providing an annex containing 'Guidelines for self-assessment'. For the assistance of small businesses, I have also included a section (see Part Seven) on 'self-assessment' which includes check sheets against the requirements of ISO 9001:2000 and examples of Stage Audit checklists.

An organisation's self-assessment should be completed on a regular basis. Indeed, the use of self-assessment methodology can provide an overall view of the performance of the organisation and the degree of maturity of its QMS. It can also help to identify areas that need improving and determine priorities.

2.4.2 Section 4.2 Documentation requirements

2.4.2.1 Section 4.2.1 General

Section 4.2 General documentation requirements	The QMS documentation shall include: • a Quality Manual; • specific statements regarding quality policy and quality objectives; • documented procedures that clearly describe the sequence of processes necessary to ensure the conformity of the product; • documented instructions to ensure the effective operation and control of the processes; • quality records

As ISO 9001:2000 is a generic requirements standard it doesn't state exactly what an organisation's quality documentation should look like. It merely provides details of the mandatory requirements and then leaves it up to the organisation to determine the appropriate documentation to suit their own size and type of business. This is a good point to be remembered by small businesses who, whilst wanting to 'work in conformance with the requirements of ISO 9001:2000' do not necessarily **need** their system to be certified against that standard.

Thus the QMS documentation and records can be in any form or in any media provided that they meet:

• the needs of that particular organisation:
• customer and contractual requirements;
• the relevant international, national, regional and industry sector standards;
• the relevant statutory and regulatory requirements.

2.4.2.2 Section 4.2.2 Quality Manual

Section 4.2.2 Quality Manual	The organisation shall: • establish and maintain a Quality Manual; • include details of any ISO 9001:2000 exclusions; • include details of associated documented procedures; • indicate the sequence and interaction of processes.

One of the requirements of ISO 9001:2000 (see Section 4.2.1) is to define the documentation required to support an organisation's QMS. The primary purpose of this quality documentation is to express the quality policy and describe the QMS. This documentation serves as the basis for implementing and maintaining the system and should be capable of controlling the effective operation of the QMS.

Details of the quality documentation are usually found in an organisation's Quality Manual, which will provide information about all of the quality policies, processes, and their associated Quality Procedures (QPs) and Work Instructions (WIs). Depending on the size of the organisation, the Quality Manual will also, probably, include standard formats for data collection, data reporting and quality records. It will also have to show (and justify) if certain requirements from ISO 9001:2000 have been omitted.

There are no set rules about what should or should not be included in a Quality Manual. It all rather depends on the structure and business of the organisation concerned. As a Quality Consultant, I always recommend that organisations address **each** requirement contained in ISO 9001:2000 separately, and in turn, to ensure that none of the essential (i.e. mandatory requirements) are left out. As previously described, organisations are allowed to leave out the non-relevant sections of ISO 9001:2000 provided, that is, that details are included in the organisation's Quality Manual. At Part Six I have provided a complete example of a Quality Manual together with a number of example QPs and WIs which can be used as a template for your own Quality Manual.

For your assistance, a soft copy of this 'generic QMS' is available by email from the author at stingray@herne.demon.co.uk. If you wish to customise this publication to suit your own purposes, the easiest method is to instruct your computer (using the 'find and replace all' facility) to replace 'Herne European Consultancy Ltd' with your own company's name. Each section of the Quality Manual and **all** of the QPs and WIs should then be read and carefully modified to reflect your own company's business.

If you require further assistance please feel free to contact me at 'stringray@herne.demon.co.uk'.

2.4.2.3 Section 4.2.3 Control of documents

Section 4.2.3 **Control of documents**	The organisation shall instigate a documented procedure for the quality control of documents. This procedure shall include processes for: • controlled distribution of documents; • approval of documents prior to issue; • review, updating and re-approval of documents; • identifying the current revision status of documents; • ensuring that only relevant versions of applicable documents are available at points of use; • ensuring that documents remain legible, readily identifiable and retrievable; • identifying, distributing and controlling documents from an external source; • controlling obsolete documents.

ISO 9001:2000 requires an organisation to establish and maintain procedures for the control of all their documents and data such as hard copy and/or electronic media, especially those relating to quality assurance and quality control. Indeed, where the term 'documented procedure' appears within ISO 9001:2000, this requires the procedure to be established, documented, implemented and maintained.

All documentation used by the organisation in support of its QMS and/or the execution of a contract (e.g. specifications, customer orders, plans, drawings, manuals, operating procedures, national and international standards and codes of practice etc.) must be controlled to ensure that:

• they are issued to the appropriate personnel;
• they are revised and reissued as necessary;
• all obsolete versions are removed from the point of use.

Value of documentation

Documentation enables communication of intent and consistency of action. It is therefore a necessary element within a QMS. Its use contributes to:

• achievement of product quality and quality improvement;
• provision of appropriate training;
• ensured repeatability and traceability;
• provision of objective evidence;
• evaluation of the effectiveness of the system.

The production of documentation should not be an end in itself but should be a value-adding activity.

Quality Manual

Normally the Quality Manual and it associated processes, procedures, plans and instructions are maintained by the Quality Manager who ensures that the appropriate items, at the correct revision levels, are issued to all who need them within the organisation.

Support documentation

National and international standards, codes of practice and so on should be maintained by the General Manager and/or the Engineers who are responsible for ensuring that the appropriate documents are available within the organisation and are issued at the correct revision levels. External suppliers of documentation should be contacted on a regular basis to ascertain that the documents held remain current.

Document distribution

The distribution of standard documents should be controlled and recorded on distribution lists, which also show the current issue status. A master list of all documents should be maintained which clearly shows the current status of each document. This list needs to be available at all locations where operations effective to the functioning of the QMS are performed and this distribution list needs to be reviewed and updated as changes occur and all invalid and/or obsolete documents/data must be immediately removed.

Document changes

All changes (e.g. modified wording, new procedures to be adopted etc.) that need to be made to a previously issued document or data should, ideally, be approved by the same person who performed the original review and approval. Where appropriate, the nature of the change should be indicated on the document and master copies of the revised documents retained as records of the changes.

Contract documents

Each contract should have a separate file which contains all the relevant information applicable to that contract.

2.4.2.4 Section 4.2.4 Control of quality records

Section 4.2.4 Control of quality records	The organisation shall establish a documented procedure for the: • control; • maintenance; • identification; • storage; • retrieval; • protection; • retention time; • disposition; of all quality records.

The question is often asked, why bother to keep records?

Nothing is worse than ordering a product or service, finding a firm to meet the delivery time, but then not being able to use it because the relevant documentation (e.g. working instructions), has still to arrive. It is, therefore, vitally important for the supplier to ensure that the documentation for the assembly, installation, commissioning and operation are provided to the purchaser well before delivery and that these are both comprehensive and clear.

The progress of a product throughout its life cycle, its many maintenance cycles, during storage and operational use etc. will doubtless produce a considerable amount of records. Product improvement relies heavily on the availability of records such as the results of previous audit reports, customer feedback and failure reports gathered in the design office and from the shop floor. From a contract point of view, the maintenance of a complete historical record of all the alterations made to a contract, concessions allowed, variations permitted by the purchaser and specifications changed need to be recorded. Indeed it is usually a contract requirement for organisations to have available, at all times, sufficient records to be able to demonstrate that their products continue to comply with the relevant contract requirements and specifications. Quality records that can be analysed to provide inputs for corrective and preventive action, process improvements etc. are also very important to the quality of the product.

The above are only a few of the examples which show why records should be maintained and ISO 9001:2000 makes it a mandatory requirement that all records that are required for the QMS **shall** be controlled.

2.5 Section 5 – Management responsibility

2.5.1 Section 5.1 Management commitment

Section 5.1 Management commitment	Management shall demonstrate their commitment to developing and improving their QMS by: • conducting regular management reviews; • establishing organisational objectives and quality policies; • ensuring the availability of necessary resources; • ensuring everyone is aware of the importance of meeting customer, regulatory and legal requirements.

Top management should always try to create an environment where people are fully involved and in which their QMS can operate effectively. They should use the principles of quality management as a basis for:

• establishing the organisation's quality policies and quality objectives;
• ensuring that customer requirements are recognised;

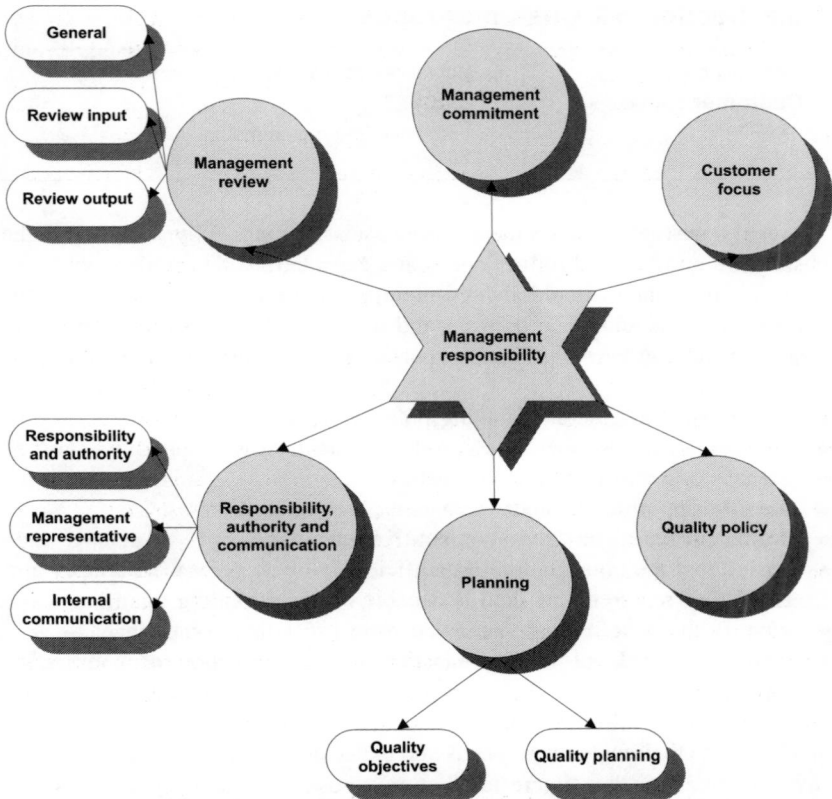

Figure 2.3 Management responsibility

- ensuring that processes are available (and implemented) that enable customer requirements to be fulfilled and quality objectives to be achieved;
- ensuring that an effective QMS is established, implemented and maintained to achieve these objectives;
- ensuring the availability of necessary resources;
- comparing the achieved results against the quality objectives that were set by top management;
- evaluating the ongoing effectiveness of their organisation's quality policies and quality objectives;
- deciding on actions for improvement;
- defining responsibilities and authorities – e.g. who is responsible for managing, performing and verifying that the end product meets the organisation's quality requirements;
- nominating a management representative (or representatives – depends on the size of the organisation) for quality matters.

2.5.2 Section 5.2 Customer focus

Section 5.2 Customer focus	Customer needs and expectations shall be: • determined; • converted into requirements; • fulfilled.

To satisfy customer requirements, organisations must fully understand the customer's current (and future) needs and expectations. In an ideal world, of course, management should always attempt to exceed their customers' needs and expectations and in so doing, stand to gain follow-on orders. To define customer and end-user needs and expectations, an organisation should:

• identify its customers (including potential customers);
• determine the customer's key product characteristics;
• identify and assess market competition;
• identify opportunities and weaknesses;
• define financial and future competitive advantages;
• ensure that the organisation has sufficient knowledge of the statutory and regulatory requirements (and is capable of implementing them);
• identify the benefits to be achieved from exceeding compliance;
• identify the role of the organisation in the protection of community interests.

In addition to their customers' needs and expectations, organisations may also have a number of other 'interested parties' whose needs and expectations will also have to be addressed. For quality management purposes, these interested parties may include:

• people within the organisation;
• owners, partners, investors and shareholders;
• suppliers;
• the general public.

The needs and expectations of these interested parties will be similar to the customers **except** that they will be more directed to recognition, work satisfaction, competencies and development of knowledge. Involving motivated people in the finalisation of a product can be a key to success!

2.5.3 Section 5.3 Quality policy

Section 5.3 Quality Policy	The organisation's quality policy shall be: • controlled; • appropriate; • committed to meeting requirements; • communicated and understood throughout the organisation; • capable of continual improvement; • a framework for establishing and reviewing quality objectives; • regularly reviewed.

Quality policies and quality objectives need to be established in order to provide a general focus for the organisation. Policies and objectives determine the intended results and assist the organisation in applying its resources to achieve these results.

First step

The first step that an organisation must take is to define and document its quality management policy. That is, produce a mission statement that covers the organisation's objectives for quality and its commitment to quality. This quality policy must be relevant to the company's organisational goals and take into account the expectations and needs of the customer. The organisation then needs to ensure that its quality management policy is understood and implemented by all staff members and use it to provide confidence that the application of management (as described in the Quality Manual) is efficient, comprehensive and effective in ensuring that the organisation delivers the right product:

• on time;
• to the agreed specifications;
• within budget.

The purpose and benefits of establishing a quality policy and quality objectives

The organisation's quality policy should always be to achieve 'sustained, profitable growth by providing products which consistently satisfy the needs and expectations of its customers'. This level of quality can be achieved by adopting a system of procedures that reflect the competence of the organisation to existing customers, potential customers, and independent auditing authorities and which is aimed at:

• maintaining an effective QMS that complies with ISO 9001:2000;
• achieving and maintaining a level of quality which enhances the organisation's reputation with customers;
• ensuring compliance with all the relevant statutory and safety requirements;

- endeavouring, at all times, to maximise customer satisfaction with the products provided by the organisation.

Quality policy structure

Summarised, the quality management policy shall include the requirement that:

- clear responsibilities for each activity and development task are identified;
- each organisational activity is defined and controlled by a Quality Process, Quality Procedure (QP) or Quality Plan;
- staff are trained to the requirements listed in the company's Quality Manual;
- compliance with company procedures detailed in the Quality Manual and associated Quality Plans are audited;
- remedial action is taken whenever appropriate;
- the QPs contained in the Quality Manual and associated Quality Plans themselves are regularly reviewed.

Quality Management System review

One of the responsibilities of top management is to carry out regular systematic evaluations of their organisation's QMS to confirm its continued suitability, adequacy, effectiveness and efficiency with regard to their organisation's quality policy and objectives. This review should include the need to adapt and respond to changing needs, customer expectations, the market it serves and include details of any remedial actions that are required.

2.5.4 Section 5.4 Planning

Section 5.4 Planning	Quality planning shall be documented and shall include: • quality objectives; • resources.

Having defined its overall business objectives, the organisation is then in a position to define its quality objectives and to plan the resources etc. that they will need to meet these objectives.

2.5.4.1 Section 5.4.1 Quality objectives

Section 5.4.1 Quality objectives	Quality objectives shall: • be established; • be measurable; • be consistent with quality policy; • include a commitment for continual improvement; • cover product requirements.

The overall quality objectives of the organisation need to be firmly established during the planning stage and then circulated to all personnel involved so that they can easily translate them into individual (and achievable) contributions. These objectives should be periodically reviewed and should:

• be relevant to the various levels and functions within the organisation;
• be consistent with the organisation's quality policy;
• be capable of being measured.

They should consider:

• current and future requirements;
• the markets served;
• the output from management previous reviews;
• current product and process performance;
• the required (and anticipated) levels of satisfaction of all interested parties.

2.5.4.2 Section 5.4.2 Quality management system planning

Section 5.4.2 Quality management system planning	Quality planning shall be documented and shall: • meet the requirements contained in section 4.1; • QMS processes; • identification of resources; • requirements for continual improvement; • requirements for change control.

Having defined its quality objectives, the next step will be to plan how to meet these objectives (i.e. the processes, resources, responsibilities, methodologies, procedures etc. that will be needed). As ISO is quick to point out 'Quality planning is an integral part of the QMS' and so organisations should take into careful consideration the:

• needs and expectations of the customers;
• required product performance;
• previous experiences and lessons learned;
• improvement opportunities;
• risk assessment;

- performance indicators;
- results of reviews and the need for change control;
- the need for documentation and records.

Customer satisfaction and quality can only be achieved by operating in accordance with the documented QMS. Specific customer requirements need to be identified and documented during the contract review process and these requirements need to be communicated and achieved in order to ensure customer satisfaction.

2.5.5 Section 5.5 Responsibility, authority and communication

Section 5.5 **Responsibility, authority and communication**	Administration of the QMS shall be documented and shall cover: • responsibilities and authorities; • management representative's duties; • internal communication.

Management need to define and implement their QMS so that it provides confidence that the organisation can satisfy the needs and expectations of interested parties and in such a way that is consistent with the organisation's size, culture and products.

The following sub-sections describe how an organisation's QMS should be administered.

2.5.5.1 Section 5.5.1 Responsibility and authority

Section 5.5.1 **Responsibility and authority**	The organisation shall define and communicate throughout the organisation: • functions and their interrelationships; • responsibilities and authorities.

The QMS is effectively the organisation's rule book. As such it has to be accepted and implemented by everyone. There needs to be a feeling of involvement **and** commitment in achieving the organisation's quality objectives, from top management right down to the newest employee. Personnel need, however, to know exactly what they are responsible for and so management must clearly define functions, levels of responsibility and authority for all personnel, in order to implement and maintain their QMS effectively and efficiently.

It is essential that top management ensures that the responsibilities, authorities (and their relationship) for documenting, planning and implementing the QMS are defined and communicated throughout the organisation.

Table 2.1 Responsibilities in a typical organisation

Title	Responsibility
Managing Director	• Approval of the QMS • Management review • Design control
Quality Manager	• Internal audit • Resolution of QMS discrepancies • Control and maintenance of the QMS • Quality documentation and (quality) change control procedures • Training
General Manager	• Planning and co-ordination • Design control • Estimating • Project management • Control of contract documentation • Planning and organisation • Supplier selection and purchasing • Definition of installation, inspection, test and maintenance requirements • Training
Financial Director	• Control of budget and finance • Supplier selection and purchasing • Contract management, control and review • Management and co-ordination of sales and support functions
Business Development Manager	• Sales • Estimating • New product identification and evaluation • System design
Sales Managers	• Quotations • Contract review and order processing • Sales order processing
Support Manager	• Control of production and measuring equipment • Maintenance of support stores • Processing of sales orders • Purchasing
Engineers	• Installation, repairs, testing and maintenance activities • Control of equipment and materials allocated
Warehouse	• Stock control • Stock replenishment • Protection and preservation of stock • Receiving inspection • Packaging and despatch
Administration	• Sales database administration • Checking of sales orders • Allocation of order reference numbers

Top management should continually review the organisation's resources to ensure that adequate staff, equipment and materials are available to meet customer requirements. All staff should be allocated authority to perform their allocated responsibilities and they should have a share in the responsibility for identifying non-compliance or possible improvements and recording these instances so that that corrective action can be taken, both to rectify the immediate situation and to prevent recurrence.

Table 2.1 is an indication of the responsibilities for a typical organisational structure.

2.5.5.2 Section 5.5.2 Management representative

Section 5.5.2 Management representative	The organisation shall appoint a member who, irrespective of all other duties, is responsible for: • establishing, administering and maintaining the QMS processes; • advising top management on the performance of and improvements to the organisation's QMS; • promoting awareness of customer requirements; • liaising with external parties on all matters relating to the organisation's QMS.

Whilst top management can all agree that they going to have a QMS, they need to nominate someone from within management (and at managerial level) with responsibility and authority to see its successful implementation. This person (usually referred to as the Quality Manager) is responsible for:

• ensuring that the organisation's QMS is (at all times) relevant, effective and appropriate – usually achieved by completing internal quality audits (see 8.2.2).
• ensuring that the organisation meets the customer's quality requirements;
• ensuring that all personnel are aware and capable of meeting and (when required) administering the organisation's quality processes;
• producing and maintaining the quality documentation (i.e. procedures and instructions) required for those processes;
• managing, performing and verifying that the end product meets the company's quality requirements;
• supplying regular reports to top management on the performance of the QMS and making recommendations for its improvement;
• liaising with external parties on all matters relating to the QMS.

2.5.5.3 Section 5.5.3 Internal communication

Section 5.5.3 Internal communication	The details of the organisation's QMS processes shall be given to all those responsible for their effectivenes.

To ensure the continued effectiveness of the organisation's QMS, it is important that everyone involved in the implementation of the system is aware of the Quality Processes that have been agreed by management. It is the responsibility of the Quality Manager (as management's representative) to inform everyone about the requirements, objectives and accomplishments of and from the Quality Processes. There are no set rules about how this sort of information should be distributed; it really depends on how the organisation is set up. Choices can include (but not necessarily be restricted to) team briefings, organisational meetings, notice boards, in-house journals/magazines, audio-visual and other forms of e-information systems).

2.5.6 Section 5.6 Management review

Section 5.6 Management review	The QMS shall be regularly reviewed to ensure its continued suitability, effectiveness and adequacy. Opportunities for improvement shall be assessed and records of all reviews shall be maintained.

Although, when first written, an organisation's QMS is assumed to cover all eventualities, doubtless there are parts of the system that will need further definition.

ISO 9001:2000 has recognised this possibility and has made it a mandatory requirement for top management to complete a review of their organisation's QMS (for continued suitability and effectiveness) on a bi-annual basis. Records of these reviews should be retained and details of all actions agreed, allocated and minuted.

The objective of these management reviews is to establish that the QMS:

- is achieving the expected results;
- meets the organisation's requirements;
- conforms to the requirements of ISO 9001:2000;
- continues to satisfy the customers needs and expectations;
- is functioning in accordance with the established operating procedures;
- is capable of identifying irregularities, defects and/or weaknesses in the system (and to evaluate possible improvements).

During the review, management will also review:

- the effectiveness of previous corrective actions;
- the adequacy and suitability of the QMS for current and future operations of the organisation;
- any complaints received, identify the cause and recommend corrective action if required;
- previous internal and external audits and identify any areas of recurring problems or potential improvements;
- reports of non-conforming items and trend information to identify possible improvements.

Evaluation and auditing

When evaluating a QMS, there are four basic questions that should be asked in relation to every process being evaluated.

- is the process identified and appropriately described?
- are responsibilities assigned?
- are the procedures implemented and maintained?
- is the process effective in providing the required results?

There are three basic types of audit to choose from:

- **First-party audits** – conducted by, or on behalf of, the organisation itself for internal purposes and which can form the basis for an organisation's self-declaration of conformity.
- **Second-party audits** – conducted by customers of the organisation or by other persons on behalf of the customer.
- **Third-party audits** – conducted by external independent audit service organisations. Such organisations, usually accredited, provide certification or registration of conformity with requirements such as those of ISO 9001:2000. (See ISO 9001:2000 Section 8.2.2 Internal audit for further information).

2.5.6.1 *Section 5.6.1 General*

Section 5.6.1 General	The QMS shall be subject to regular reviews to evaluate the: • need for changes; • effectiveness of the organisation's quality policies; • effectiveness of the organisation's quality objectives.

Management need to establish a process for periodically reviewing the organisation's QMS to ensure that it continues to meet the requirements of ISO 9001:2000, agrees with the organisation's policies and objectives and continues to provide customer satisfaction. Current performance, client feedback and opportunities for improvement all need to be evaluated and possible alterations have to be made to the relevant quality documentation analysed.

It is essential that records are retained of all these management reviews and that any change that might have an effect on existing work practices is subjected to a change control procedure.

2.5.6.2 Section 5.6.2 Review input

Section 5.6.2 Review input	The input to management reviews shall include results from: • earlier management reviews (e.g. follow-up actions); • previous internal, third-party and external audits; • customer feedback; • process performance; • product conformance; • preventive and corrective actions; • changes that could affect the QMS and recommendations for improvement.

For completeness, inputs to management reviews should include everything concerned with the performance, conformance and improvement of the product. The review body should evaluate new technologies, statutory conditions, regulatory changes and environmental conditions for their affect on their product. Inputs would include, but are not restricted to:

- results from previous internal, customer and third-party audits;
- analysis of customer feedback;
- analysis of process performance;
- analysis of product conformance;
- the current status of corrective and preventive actions;
- the results of self-assessment of the organisation;
- supplier performance.

2.5.6.3 Section 5.6.3 Review output

Section 5.6.3 Review output	Management reviews shall be aimed at: • improving the organisation's overall QMS and its processes; • improving the product; • enhancing customer satisfaction; • confirming the resources required.

The aim of completing management reviews is to provide a continuing record of the organisation's capability to produce quality products that meet the quality objectives, policies and requirements (contained in their QMS) and which continue to provide customer satisfaction.

Review output should be centred on:

- improved product and process performance;
- conformation of resource requirements and organisational structure;
- meeting market needs;
- risk management;
- change control;
- continued compliance with relevant statutory and regulatory requirements.

The actual management review process should also be evaluated to confirm its continued effectiveness and a complete record of all reviews must be retained for future use.

2.6 Section 6 – Resource management

This section covers resources with regard to training, induction, responsibilities, working environment, equipment requirements, maintenance etc.

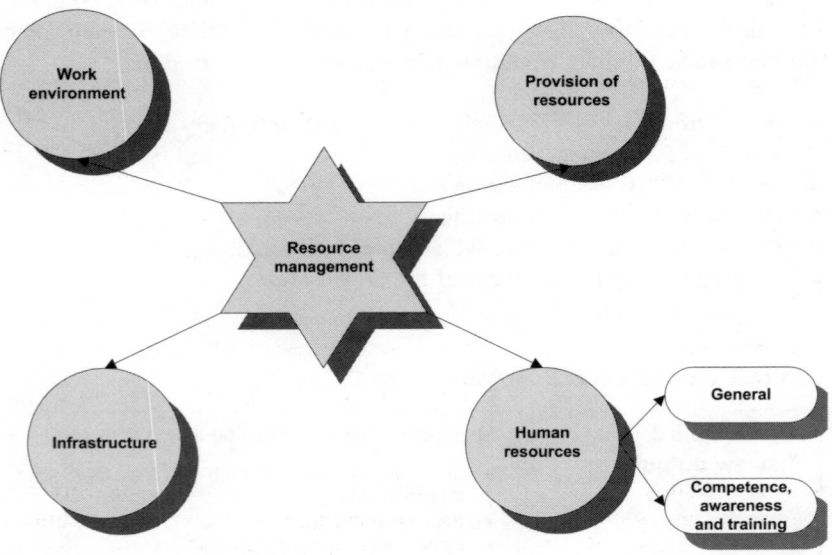

Figure 2.4 Resource management

2.6.1 Section 6.1 Provision of resources

Section 6.1 Provision of resources	The organisation shall provide resources to: • implement, maintain and continually improve their QMS and its processes; • enhance customer satisfaction; • meet customer requirements.

The organisation needs to identify and make available all the resources (e.g. information, infrastructure, people, work environment, finance, support etc.) required to implement and improve their QMS and its associated quality processes.

Resources can include (but not be limited to):

- natural resources;
- tangible resources (e.g. support facilities);
- intangible resources (e.g. intellectual property);
- future resources;
- organisational resources;
- information management systems;
- training and education;
- resources to encourage continual improvement.

Suppliers

A complete historical record should be maintained by an organisation to register any variations to the contract, any concessions made, variations allowed by the purchaser and specifications altered. The design office often carries out this activity.

In a similar manner, suppliers must provide the purchasers with an assurance that they are capable of continuing to supply logistic support for the lifetime of the product. This logistic support may include the provision of spares, updating of documentation, details of product improvement etc., depending upon the purchaser's requirements.

2.6.2 Section 6.2 Human resources

Section 6.2 Human resources	The organisation shall establish procedures for: • the assignment of personnel; • training, awareness and competency.

The organisation needs to identify and make available human resources to implement and improve their QMS and comply with contract conditions. Consideration must be given to their competency for the job that they are selected to complete and the possible requirements for additional training.

2.6.2.1 Section 6.2.1 General

Section 6.2.1 General	Assigned personnel shall be: • competent; • educated and trained: • skilled and experienced.

Human resources are the principal method of achieving product completion and customer satisfaction. The old adage 'a happy worker is a good worker' still stands true in this age of information technology and with the increased training and education opportunities currently available, highly motivated, well qualified personnel are at a premium. To employ and retain the right sort of person for the job, management must, when determining the resources required, adequately define their responsibilities and authorities, establish their individual and team objectives and encourage recognition and reward. They must also:

- consider career planning and on-the-job training (OJT);
- encourage innovation and effective teamwork;
- make use of information technology;
- measure people satisfaction.

2.6.2.2 Section 6.6.2 Competence, awareness and training

Section 6.2.2 Competence, awareness and training	The organisation shall: • identify the requirements for training personnel; • provide appropriate training; • evaluate the effectiveness of the training provided; • maintain records of all training.

The organisation is responsible for ensuring that all personnel are trained and experienced to the extent necessary to undertake their assigned activities and responsibilities effectively. Thus, whenever training needs have been identified, top management should endeavour to make the relevant training available and full records must be maintained of all training undertaken by employees.

Most organisations will recruit employees who are already well qualified and quite capable of meeting the relevant technical, skill, experience and educational requirements of the organisation. There will still, however, be a need for some additional system or contract-specific training and all staff have a responsibility for identifying and recommending the training needs of others and for ensuring that all employees allocated specific tasks are suitably qualified and experienced to execute those tasks.

It is very important that an organisation's staff receive sufficient training to enable them to carry out their functions. Organisations should, therefore, determine the competence levels required, assess the competence of its people and develop plans to close any gaps. Then, based on an analysis of the present and expected needs of the organisation (compared with the existing competence of its people and the requirements of related legislation, regulation, standards, and directives) determine the type and amount of training required.

Training plan

Training should cover the organisation's policies and objectives and, as well as having introductory programmes for new people, there should also be available periodic refresher programmes for people already trained. The training should emphasise the importance of meeting requirements and the needs of customers and other interested parties. It should also include an awareness of the consequences to the organisation and its people of failing to meet the requirements. A typical training plan would include:

- training objectives;
- training programmes and methodologies;
- the training resources needed;
- identification of necessary support;
- evaluation of training in terms of enhanced competence of people;
- measurement of the effectiveness of training and the impact on the organisation.

2.6.3 Section 6.3 Infrastructure

Section 6.3 Infrastructure	The organisation shall identify, provide and maintain the necessary: • workspace and associated facilities; • equipment, hardware and software; • supporting services.

Depending on the size of the organisation and the products that it is offering, the infrastructure (e.g. workspace and facilities) required may include plant, hardware, software, tools and equipment, communication facilities, transport and supporting services.

The organisation should define, provide, develop, implement, evaluate and consider its requirements in terms of product performance, customer satisfaction and controlled improvement.

2.6.4 Section 6.4 Work environment

Section 6.4 Work environment	The organisation shall identify and manage the work environment required to achieve conformity of product.

An organisation's work environment is a combination of human factors (e.g. work methodologies, achievement and involvement opportunities, safety rules and guidance, ergonomics etc.) and physical factors (e.g. heat, hygiene, vibration, noise, humidity, pollution, light, cleanliness and air flow). All of these factors influence motivation, satisfaction and performance of people and as they have the potential for enhancing the performance of the organisation, they must be taken into consideration by the organisation when evaluating product conformance and achievement.

2.7 Section 7 – Product realisation

This section absorbs most of the 20 elements of the old ISO 9000:1994 standard, including process control, purchasing, handling and storage, and measuring devices.

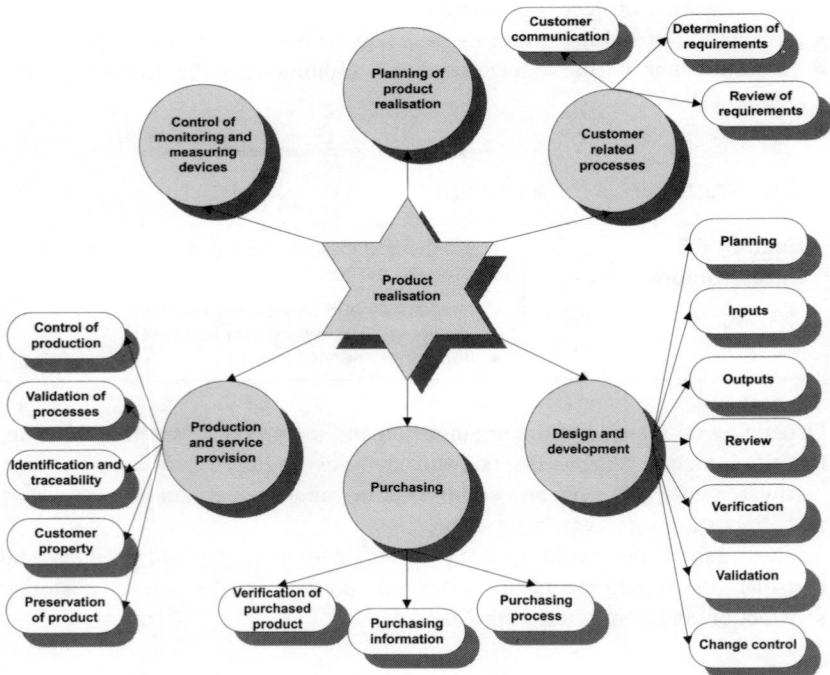

Figure 2.5 Product realisation

2.7.1 Section 7.1 Planning and realisation

Section 7.1 Planning and realisation	The organisation shall plan and develop the processes needed for product realisation. These shall include: • product, contract quality objectives and requirements; • product processes and their associated documentation, resources and facilities; • verification, validation, monitoring, inspection and test requirements; • criteria for acceptability; • details of the records that are required.

A process can be represented as a flow of activities consisting of three separate elements:

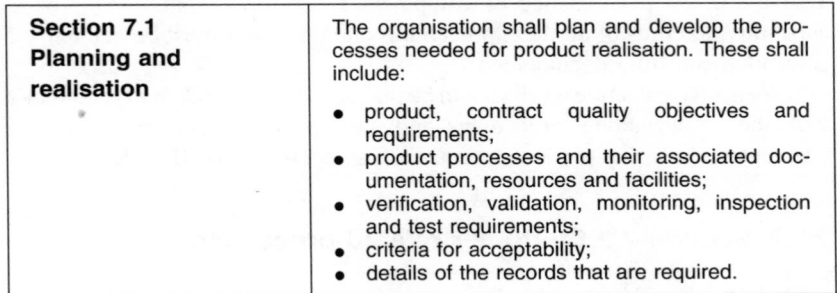

Figure 2.6 Planning realisation processes

Realisation processes result in the products of an organisation. Support processes include all the other management processes that are necessary to the organisation, but do not directly add any value. To ensure product realisation, therefore, consideration should be given to desired outputs, process steps, activities, workflow, control measures, training needs, equipment, methodologies, information, materials and other resources. In fact, anything that might have an effect on the output.

Identification of processes

The organisation needs to identify the processes required to realise products that satisfy the requirements of customers and a plan has to be defined to manage these processes, especially their input and output stages. The documentation that describes how the QMS processes are applied for a specific product, project or contract is usually contained in a separate Quality Plan.

In ISO 9001:2000 the organisation is recommended to identify and plan all of the production, installation and servicing processes that directly affect quality. Procedures should be available to ensure that these processes are completed under controlled conditions especially with respect to special processes such as those for defining work to be carried out where no previous procedure exists.

Process planning

Special equipment or environmental conditions; compliance with relevant standards (national, European and international); criteria for workmanship (e.g. written standards, representative samples or illustrations) need to be planned. Procedures must be available to ensure that there is an appropriate system for the maintenance of equipment to ensure a continuing process capability. Records of all these procedures and processes must be maintained, controlled and fully documented.

Indeed, all productive work should be planned and undertaken in accordance with the organisation's procedures and any specific documents that have been detailed for that particular contract (e.g. contract specifications).

2.7.2 Section 7.2 Customer related processes

Section 7.2 Customer related processes	The organisation shall establish procedures for the: • identification of customer requirements; • review of product requirements; • customer communication.

Before entering into a contract situation, an organisation needs to find out exactly what the customer wants in terms of product specification, availability, delivery, support etc. It also needs to confirm that it has sufficient resources to complete the contract and is capable of satisfying the customer's requirements, in full.

2.7.2.1 Section 7.2.1 Determination of requirements related to the product

Section 7.2.1 Determination of requirements related to the product	The organisation shall determine: • product requirements specified by the customer; • product requirements not specified by the customer; • regulatory and legal product requirements.

On receipt of an order and/or contract, the organisation should thoroughly review it to ensure:

- customer requirements are fully understood and documented;
- the organisation has the ability to meet the customer's requirements;
- any differences between a quotation and the order are identified and resolved.

The customer's requirements can include many elements (e.g. product, options, delivery method, terms of contract, method of payment etc.) and the organisation's ability to meet these requirements will rely on:

- people and their skills, experience and motivation;
- production tools and equipment;

- raw materials;
- stock availability;
- information, drawings and instructions.

Once the organisation has successfully proved to the customer that their QMS is acceptable (see preceding paragraphs), the next step is to commence contract negotiations.

2.7.2.2 Section 7.2.2 Review of requirements related to the product

Section 7.2.2 **Review of** **requirements related** **to the product**	Prior to submission of a tender or acceptance of a contract, the organisation shall ensure that: • product requirements have been defined; • contract requirements have been fully established; • all requirements differing from those previously expressed are resolved; • the organisation has the ability to meet defined requirements.

Most organisations will offer their standard products in a catalogue for the customer to make a selection from. These products will be identified against a design specification and normally be accompanied by a picture and/or technical description. Most organisations will also usually be willing to provide system-specific products to suit individual customer requirements. These specialist service requirements will differ from one customer to another (and from one contract to another) and will, therefore, possibly need to be covered by an individual tender, quotation and/or contract.

The contract document

The contract will specify which part of ISO 9001:2000 is to be used, what portions can be deleted and what additional conditions have to be inserted. The contract will also specify the use of quality plans, quality programs, quality audit plans and other relevant technical specifications.

Once the customer has accepted a proposal, or an order is placed, it should be recorded and reviewed in order to establish that the requirements of the order are adequately defined and documented. Any differences from the proposal should be resolved and the organisation should have established that they are fully capable of meeting and satisfying the customer's requirements. Most of the larger organisations will rely on some form of computerised order processing system to ensure rapid fulfilment of customer orders. Whilst this is a preferred method, it is not an essential ISO 9001:2000 requirement.

Contract signature

Before signature, both parties must thoroughly review the contract and be absolutely sure that:

- the QMS requirements are fully understood;
- all the requirements, clauses and provisions are complete, unambiguous, mutually acceptable (considering the economics and risks in their respective situations);
- the requirements are adequately documented and defined;
- the organisation is able to meet all the contractual requirements.

Where product requirements are changed, the organisation shall ensure that the relevant documentation is amended and that the relevant personnel are made aware of the changed requirements. Where the customer provides no documented statement of requirement, the customer requirements must be confirmed before acceptance.

Any requirement differing from those in the original enquiry or tender should be resolved at this stage and it must be confirmed that all the contractual requirements can be met.

Servicing

Most service practices will vary widely between suppliers, distributors and users. If servicing is to be provided, or is required as part of the contract, then the supplier must establish procedures for controlling and authenticating the quality of the service performed and ensure that they meet the required standards.

2.7.2.3 Section 7.2.3 Customer communication

Section 7.2.3 Customer communication	The organisation shall have procedures available to: • provide customers with product information; • handle, customer enquiries, contracts or order handling including amendments; • cover customer feedback and/or customer complaints.

The need to maintain open lines of communication with the customer cannot be over-emphasised and procedures should be put in place to ensure that the customer is kept fully up-to-date with the progress of their product/contract and that all customer comments and complaints are dealt with in a speedy and effective manner.

2.7.3 Section 7.3 Design and development

Section 7.3 Design and development	The organisation shall develop procedures for design and development: • planning; • inputs; • outputs; • review; • verification; • validation; • change control.

Design is usually meant to mean the production of something new, although it can, in many circumstances, be a variation of an existing product or service. It could, therefore, be a new product or it could be a system made up of a variety of products. Either way, a process or design plan needs to be developed that confirms:

- what the customer needs;
- what the boundaries are (e.g. customer requirements);
- how the organisation is going to achieve it;
- how long it will take;
- who will undertake the task;
- who will check and verify the product.

2.7.3.1 Section 7.3.1 Design and development planning

Section 7.3.1 Design and development planning	The organisation shall plan and control the design and development of the product through all processes. This planning shall include: • stage reviews; • verification and validation activities; • identification of responsibilities and authorities; • management of the interfaces between different groups that may be involved; • provision of effective communication; • clarity of responsibilities; • product and planning review procedures.

The best production methods cannot compensate for an inadequate or mediocre design! Quality cannot be an 'add on'; it has to be designed into a product before it is manufactured and the only way of achieving that is through careful planning and controlled documentation throughout the design stage.

Whether the responsibility for the design of a product rests purely with the supplier, the purchaser, or is a joint function, it is essential that the designer is fully aware of the exact requirements of the project and has a sound background knowledge of all the proper standards, information and procedures that will be required.

Functions of the design office

The functions of the design office are extremely important for they will not only influence the maintenance of quality throughout the manufacturing process, but also play a major part in setting the quality level of the final product. If there is no quality control in the drawing office, what chance is there of ever having quality on the shop floor? When the engineers are trying to manufacture something to a set of drawings that have countless mistakes on them, how on earth can they be expected to produce an acceptable item!

Thus, in close co-operation with the marketing, sales and manufacturing sections, the design office prepares business and performance specifications, sets target dates, provides technical specifications, reviews drawings, produces overall schemes to the estimating section, discusses these schemes with the manufacturing section and develops the design in conjunction with other supplier functions.

Design criteria

Design criteria will have to be clarified, documented and recorded in the design plan and used for reference throughout the design process. The level of detail on the design plan will vary depending upon the type and size of system, but at all times it should contain sufficient detail to control the design process in accordance with the customer's requirements. Where items require interpretation (e.g. positioning, practicality, maintainability, etc.) they will need to be reviewed prior to design finalisation.

2.7.3.2 Section 7.3.2 Design and development inputs

Section 7.3.2 Design and development inputs	Product requirement inputs shall be defined, documented and include: • functional and performance requirements; • regulatory and legal requirements; • information derived from previous similar designs; • other requirements essential for design and development.

Following initial contract approval, details of all the relevant standards, specifications and specific customer requirements that are going to be used during production will have to be identified and steps taken to ensure that they are available. Procedures will have to be established and maintained in order to make certain that the functions of the design office are in agreement with the specified requirements. Any incomplete, ambiguous or conflicting requirements must be resolved at this stage and revisions of the specification reviewed and agreed by both parties.

The design input items are documented on the design plan and reviewed by the designer prior to commencing design process. Where ambiguity exists, the designer will need to clarify this with customer and document the results.

Design input may consist of:

- national/international codes of practice;
- customer supplied documents, drawings, specifications and samples;
- statutory regulations;
- previous and/or similar designs.

Process inputs for product design and/or development can be divided into three categories:

1. **internal** – policies, standards, specifications, skill and dependability requirements, documentation and data on existing products and outputs from other processes;
2. **external** – customer or marketplace needs and expectations, contractual requirements, interested party specifications, relevant statutory and regulatory requirements, international or national standards, and industry codes of practice;
3. **other** – operation, installation and application, storage, handling, maintenance and delivery, physical parameters and environment and disposal requirements.

Staff

All staff performing productive work should be capable of undertaking their tasks correctly. Guidance concerning tasks may be available from training, experience, detailed instructions, comparison with examples; or a mixture of these. Detailed instructions are normally required where their absence could adversely affect the quality and acceptability of the product. Other items that need controlling (especially those that ensure that acceptable products are produced) include:

- tools;
- production equipment;
- production environment.

Special processes

ISO 9001:2000 requires an approved control system for 'special processes' that cannot easily be inspected on completion of the product (e.g. welding). The simplest means to ensure that they are correct each time is by experimenting, and then documenting the successful process (personnel, equipment, materials, sequence and environment). The process can then be repeated each time the product is required. Production of a reject then becomes an improbability but not, unfortunately, an impossibility!

Process control and instructions

As part of a contract, the supplier may be required to identify (and plan) any production and/or installation process that directly affects quality and (in particular) any special process that may only become apparent after production and/or when the product is used. These plans and instructions should be included in any representative samples that are provided.

Marketing implications

It would be totally unproductive for an organisation to make something (e.g. a product or a system), find that it is not required by anyone and consequently be unable to sell it! For this reason most organisations have a separate marketing section who are responsible for determining the need for a product or service and for estimating the market demand.

Customer requirements

Customer requirements will specify and detail the way the work is to be performed, the standard of workmanship and the degree of quality assurance that they require. The marketing section must be capable of translating the user requirements into technical language that will be sufficient to enable the design staff to convert the requirements into practical designs and specifications that enable production, testing, maintenance and servicing to be technically and economically possible.

The customer's technical requirements should include:

- performance and environmental characteristics – specific use, reliability etc.;
- sensory characteristics – style, colour, taste, smell;
- installation configuration or fit;
- standards, specifications and specific user requirements;
- packaging;
- quality assurance.

Market readiness

In order for the management to always be aware of their organisation's market readiness, the marketing section (in close co-operation with the design and manufacturing sections) needs to define and review market readiness, field support and production capability.

Components, parts and materials

Although the design office needs to be free to be creative, it is also imperative that they maintain a close relationship with the manufacturing section so that they can be aware of **their** exact requirements, **their** problems and **their** component preferences etc. It can be so easy for the design office to work in splendid isolation, make arbitrary decisions, select components that **they** think are suitable, but then find that the size and tolerance is completely inappropriate for the manufacture of that device.

The design office must have available complete listings of all the appropriate components, parts and materials, their reliability, availability, maintainability, safety, acceptability and adequacy. They must be aware of recent developments, new technologies and advances in both materials and equipment that are available on the market and applicable to that particular product.

Specifications and tolerances

Tolerances should never be unduly restrictive for this could create problems with respect to machine capabilities or require operator skills (and time) far beyond those, which are really essential. Tolerance specifications should also be flexible enough to allow for interchangeability of material where necessary.

Health and safety

As health and safety has now become a mandatory requirement of ISO 9001:2000, designers should be even more aware of the implications of the statutory national, European and international legal requirements for health and safety as they could well place constraints on their designs.

These regulations will not just be concerned with the condition and safety of the material but will also provide measures for overcoming the possibility of danger to persons and property when the material is being used, stored, transported or tested. All aspects of a product or service should be identified with the aim of enhancing product safety and minimising product liability. This can be achieved by:

- identifying the relevant safety standards that make a product or service more effective;
- carrying out design evaluation tests and prototype testing for safety;
- analysing instructions, warnings, labels and maintenance manuals etc. to minimise misinterpretation;
- developing a means of traceability to allow a product to be recalled if safety problems are discovered.

Computers

Nowadays, of course, most design offices have computers to record and store their information on plus disc retrieval systems that enable regular updating and amendment of data. This updated information is then available for use with standard software programs and Computer Aided Design (CAD) packages to produce accurate information either by list, graph or drawing.

2.7.3.3 Section 7.3.3 Design and development outputs

Section 7.3.3 Design and development outputs	The organisation shall ensure that: • design output meets design input requirements; • sufficient information is available for production and service operations; • product acceptance criteria have been met; • the characteristics of the product that are essential to its safe and proper use have been defined.

All documentation associated with the design output (e.g. drawings, schematics, schedules, system specifications, system descriptions, etc.) needs to:

- be produced in accordance with agreed customer requirements;
- be reviewed (by another designer who has not been associated with the initial design) to ensure that it meets the design input;
- identify all of the characteristics which are critical to the effective operation of the designed system;
- be reviewed and approved by the customer prior to use.

Design office responsibilities

Another responsibility of the design office is to maintain a link with the production department so that they can assist in the analysis of failures, swiftly produce solutions and forestall costly work stoppages. This is often referred to as 'design output' and is covered by the activities of the 'internal audit' system that is required to ensure that the design output meets the specified requirements of the design input through design control methods such as:

- undertaking qualification tests and demonstrations;
- comparing the new design with a similar proven design;
- ensuring that it conforms to appropriate regulatory (for example safety) requirements; whether or not these have been stated in the input documentation;
- identifying those characteristics of the design that are crucial and establishing that these characteristics meet the design input criteria.

Examples of the output from design and/or development activities include:

- product specifications;
- training requirements;
- methodologies;
- purchase requirements;
- acceptance criteria.

Inspection and test status

Once products have been inspected, there needs to be a method for easily identifying them as being either acceptable or unacceptable. This can be achieved in many ways, including:

- marking;
- stamping;
- labelling;
- segregating;
- associated documents;
- test reports;
- physical location.

2.7.3.4 Section 7.3.4 Design and development review

Section 7.3.4 Design and development review	The organisation shall complete systematic reviews to: • evaluate the ability of the product to fulfil requirements; • identify problems; • propose follow-up actions.

Design process control

The process of translating the design input into design and developed output is primarily controlled by the design review, which ensures that:

- adherence to contractual and statutory requirements has been fully met;
- all alternative design concepts and items have been considered;
- all potential design problems have been identified and evaluated;
- all calculations have been correctly performed and re-checked;
- the suitability of the designed item/system with respect to environmental and operating conditions has been considered;
- the compatibility with existing (or proposed) items or systems is assured;
- the designed item or system is maintainable;
- all necessary working documents (e.g. calculations, notes, sketches, etc.) accompany the design output documentation.

The majority of design activities can be verified during the design process review and a record maintained of all the items that have been considered together with their results. Whenever possible the use of computers is recommended for verifying designs and currently there are many proprietary brands being marketed.

Final verification of the design is usually completed during final inspection and test and the designer is responsible for specifying and supplying any inspections or tests that are required during system installation to practically verify the design.

Design process review

When designing and/or developing products or processes, as well as ensuring that the needs of all interested parties are satisfied, the organisation will have to take into consideration life cycle costs, environmental requirements, Reliability, Availability, Maintainability and Safety (RAMS) requirements and ergonomic considerations.

A risk assessment (using risk assessment tools such as Failure Mode and Effects Analysis (FMEA), Fault Tree Analysis (FTA), reliability assessment, simulation techniques etc.) will be needed to assess the potential for, and the effect of, possible failures in products and/or processes and the results used to define and implement preventive actions to mitigate identified risks.

Periodic reviews

Periodic reviews should be completed throughout the design process (for example, preliminary, intermediate and final) with the aim of:

- confirming design and/or development objectives are being met;
- evaluating potential hazards and/or modes of failure found in product use;
- evaluating life-cycle product performance data;
- evaluating the impact of the product on the environment;
- ensuring all other viable paths have been considered;
- confirming that all statutory requirements have been considered and are complied with;
- ensuring that there is adequate supporting documentation available to define the design and how the product or service is to be used and maintained.

The tests should include:

- the evaluation of the performance, durability, safety, reliability and maintainability of the product under expected storage and operational conditions;
- inspection procedures to verify that all design features are as they were originally intended and that all authorised design changes have been carried out and that these have been properly recorded;
- validation of computer systems and associated software.

Participants in such reviews should include representatives of functions concerned with the design and/or development stage(s) being reviewed and the results of the reviews and subsequent follow-up actions need to be recorded.

2.7.3.5 Section 7.3.5 Design and development verification

Section 7.3.5
Design and
development
verification
	The organisation shall verify that:
	• design output meets the design and develop-
	  ment inputs;
	• the results of the verification have been
	  recorded.

ISO 9001:2000 requires an organisation to verify that design outputs meet the design input specifications and that they meet the needs of the customer. In particular, verification of engineering designs (prior to construction, installation or application) software outputs (prior to installation or use) and direct customer services (prior to their widespread introduction) can prove very beneficial to an organisation! The aim should be to generate sufficient data through these verification activities to enable design and development methodologies and decisions to be reviewed.

Design verification and review is another form of periodic evaluation and uses one of the following methods:

- **alternative calculations** – to verify the precision of the original calculations and their analysis;
- **comparison** – with other similar designs;
- **third party evaluation** – to verify that the original calculations and/or other design activities have been correctly carried out;
- **feedback** – from previous designs and experience;
- **information** – gained during manufacture, assembly, installation, commissioning, servicing and field use;
- **customer** – feedback (i.e. asking the customer);
- **testing** – by model or prototype.

2.7.3.6 Section 7.3.6 Design and development validation

Section 7.3.6 Design and development validation	The organisation shall validate that the: • product is capable of meeting the requirements for its intended use; • results of the validation have been recorded.

As design work is normally performed in accordance with the customer's instructions, it is sometimes difficult for an organisation to validate the end product. In these situations, the organisation will normally only be required to validate that the design meets the customer's requirements. Installed systems will then need to be inspected and tested to ensure compliance and customer satisfaction and acceptance and it is only **then** that the design can be finally validated.

In-process inspection and testing

Items that have been produced in accordance with an organisation's documented processes generally pass through a number of stages. Rather than leaving inspection and testing to when the last stage has been completed, it is more cost effective to check the items as they progress through the various stages of their production and/or installation. These are called 'in-process inspections' and their objective is to identify rejects and inadequate processes as they happen and not at the end of a job lot.

The organisation must, therefore, establish effective stages of inspection, define the type of inspection to be performed and clarify the acceptance/rejection criteria. All the in-process inspections should be documented, and any faulty items must be identified and segregated.

Final inspection and testing

Once again, the principle of final inspection is similar to an in-process inspection, i.e. to identify acceptable products from faulty products, record the results and confirm the acceptance/rejection decision.

The tests will normally include the:

- evaluation of the performance, durability, safety, reliability and maintainability of the product under expected storage and operational conditions;
- inspection procedures to verify that all design features are as they were originally intended and that all authorised design changes have been carried out and that these have been properly recorded;
- validation of computer systems and associated software.

Note: Wherever applicable, validation should be completed prior to the delivery or implementation of the product. If this isn't possible or impractical, then partial validation should be performed to the extent applicable.

2.7.3.7 Section 7.3.7 Control of design and development changes

Section 7.3.7 Control of design and development changes	The organisation shall: • identify, document and control all design and development changes; • evaluate the effect of these changes; • verify, validate and approve these changes before implementation.

Throughout the design and development phase, there are likely to be a number of changes, alterations, modifications and improvements made to the design of the product and its development processes. It is essential that:

- these are identified, documented and controlled;
- the effect of the changes on constituent parts and delivered products is evaluated;
- the changes are verified, validated and approved before implementation.

All changes to the design criteria (input and/or output) should be subject to strict documentation control and should be reviewed and verified by the designer and/or the customer, prior to incorporation within the design. All changes need to be subject to an agreed change control procedure to ensure that the changes have been fully evaluated, agreed (or concessions made) and that only the latest versions of design documents are available in work places. It is essential that the results of the review of changes and subsequent follow up actions are always documented.

It is essential that all of the design documentation, drawing and notes etc. are retained in a design project file so that it can be made immediately available and can be produced for reviews etc. The design output should be reviewed and approved by top management before being provided to the customer for approval and use.

2.7.4 Section 7.4 Purchasing

Section 7.4 Purchasing	The organisation shall have documented procedures for: • purchasing control; • purchasing information; • verification of purchased product.

When an organisation has to purchase products, materials and/or services from suppliers who have not been previously specified in a contract or by a customer, they are normally selected on their ability to meet the organisation's requirements given due consideration to the quality, statutory obligations, timescale and cost. A list of approved suppliers and subcontractors needs to be maintained by the organisation and this should contain the following information:

- previous performance in supplying to similar specifications and requirements;
- stocking of high-volume standard items conforming to relevant national and/or international standards (or supplied with a statement of conformity);
- compliance with an approved third-party product or quality registration scheme;
- recommendation by other similar purchasers or manufacturers of equipment;
- trial order and evaluation of performance.

Purchasing process

The organisation should have available a process to ensure appropriate selection, evaluation and control of all purchased products. All supplies and subcontracts should be subject to an authorised purchase order that provides full details of the type and extent of supply.

2.7.4.1 Section 7.4.1 Purchasing process

Section 7.4.1 Purchasing process	The organisation shall have procedures to: • ensure purchased product conforms to purchase requirements; • evaluate, re-evaluate and select suppliers.

Purchasing processes and procedures

The organisation is responsible for producing purchasing processes and procedures that include:

- identification of requirements;
- selection of suppliers;
- quotations and tenders;
- purchase price;
- order forms;
- verification of purchased products;
- non-conforming purchased products;
- contract administration and associated purchase documentation;
- supplier control and development;
- risk assessment.

Suppliers

Having identified their suppliers (usually selected from previous experience, past history, test results on similar projects or published experience from other users) an organisation should establish a system by which the supplier/subcontractor is clearly advised exactly what is required, and by when. This is often achieved by use of a purchase order system.

Subcontractors

If a supplier uses subcontractors, it is important that they can be relied on to produce a quality product, have the ability to meet subcontractual requirements, (including quality assurance) and do not reduce the quality of the final product. The supplier (who is normally referred to as the prime contractor) must ensure that all items purchased from a subcontractor are covered by a purchasing document. This document will contain details of the product ordered, type, class, style, grade and the title/number/issue of the relevant standard, specification, drawing, inspection instruction etc. that it must conform to. The prime contractor should ensure that subcontractors have their own QMS and that the purchased product or service is satisfactory.

2.7.4.2 Section 7.4.2 Purchasing information

Section 7.4.2 Purchasing information	Purchasing documents shall describe: • the product to be purchased; • requirements for approval or qualification of product, service, procedure, process, equipment and personnel; • QMS requirements.

A process should be established to ensure that purchasing documents contain sufficient details about:

- the product to be purchased;
- the necessary approval and qualification requirements (i.e. procedures, processes etc.) for product, equipment and personnel;
- the QMS requirements;
- agreement on quality assurance – whether the prime contractor can completely rely on the subcontractor's quality assurance scheme or whether some (or all) of the product will have to be tested by the prime contractor or via a third party;
- agreement on verification methods by the purchaser at source or on delivery; whether this should be by sample or on a 100% basis; whether this inspection should be at the prime contractor's or the subcontractor's premises;
- settlement of quality disputes – who, how, when and where.

2.7.4.3 Section 7.4.3 Verification of purchased product

Section 7.4.3 Verification of purchased product	The organisation shall establish procedures to verify that the purchased product meets specified purchase requirements.

It is essential that all goods and services received from a third party are checked to confirm that they are those that were ordered, the delivery is on time and that they are of good quality. The amount of inspection will depend on how critical the supplied goods and service is to the end product and the amount of inspection should be compatible with the risk or inconvenience if the item is later found to be faulty.

A consumable item (e.g. low-cost items such as lights bulbs, duplicating paper etc.) are normally only checked for correct identity, correct quantity and any signs of damage. It would be unwise to perform detailed inspections on these items which, if found to be faulty, could be replaced within a short time at little comparative expense. Conversely, detailed inspections should always be performed on major components, as, if they are faulty, the rectification could be expensive and time-consuming.

It should also be appreciated that the worst possible time to identify an item as a reject is when it is handed over to the final customer. If the product (or its components) can be checked at earlier stages, it is time well spent.

In-inspection

Receiving or in-inspection should be documented to confirm that it has taken place and that the goods or services are deemed fit for use in the next stage of the process. This may often be by a completing goods received note, or marking the supplier's delivery note. The delivery should also be checked against the purchase order to ensure that it is complete. Should the inspection identify the delivery as reject, the items should be segregated, labelled or identified to avoid them being used in error.

Goods inwards

In industry there are very few suppliers who are not actually purchasers themselves. Even the largest companies have to obtain consumables, components and sometimes complete assemblies from a subcontractor at some stage or other and therefore the quality of the supplier's final product, to a considerable degree, depends on the quality of the subcontractor's goods.

To be certain that the items purchased, or obtained, from a third party are up to the required standard, the prime contractor will have to set up some kind of quality inspection, unless that is, the supplier himself operates a fully satisfactory and recognised QMS.

The term 'goods inwards' describes the procedures designed to cover this type of inspection and it is a very important quality assurance function.

Inspection and testing

It is the prime contractor's responsibility to ensure that inspection and tests are always performed on all incoming goods and that no incoming material is used or processed until it has been inspected or otherwise verified to confirm that it is up to the specified requirements.

The prime contractor will have to show in their Quality Plan exactly how this is to be achieved and precisely what inspections and tests are to be carried out to confirm quality. It is then up to the purchaser to decide if this is enough or whether they would like to see additional or supplementary inspections carried out. The amount of inspection will, of course, vary according to the degree of control exercised by the subcontractor, their past performance and records – for example, are they assessed to ISO 9001:2000, etc.

This inspection should complement and be in addition to the existing quality control procedures and must be clearly laid down. Records should detail who actually carried out the inspection that released the product, the assembly line and despatch services. The inspection must:

- consider that all incoming material where quality is unproved should remain suspect until proven as satisfactory;
- ensure that written control procedures are available to establish a product has:
  - not been inspected;
  - been inspected and approved or;
  - been inspected and rejected;
- ensure that any defective material that is received from a third party is subject to the same controls as defective material that may occur in their own production.

Inspection procedures

Ineffective or incomplete control usually leads to costly defects. The prime contractor must, therefore, ensure that all manufacturing operations are carried out under strictly controlled conditions. These conditions should be covered by work instructions that define the manufacturing process, suitable manufacturing equipment and if a special working environment is required.

Workmanship criteria will have to be fully documented using either written standards, photographs, sketches or representative samples.

Control of quality

The choice of how quality is controlled and the type of inspection is normally left up to the prime contractor who may decide on a stage inspection, sampling inspection, final inspection or perhaps even a combination of all methods as being more appropriate. The method chosen should, however, cover every phase of manufacture, assembly and installation and the instructions should include the following details:

- identification of material;
- detailed operations to be performed;
- tools or test equipment required;
- requirements for operational checks, calibration and equipment availability;
- methods of inspection;
- environmental conditions to be maintained during operation or inspection;
- criteria for passing or failing the test;
- sampling techniques and related decision criteria if applicable.

Non-compliance

Inspection and testing is normally carried out on completion of installation and maintenance activities, with results being documented. If items fail to comply with agreed contract criteria, then they should either be repaired, replaced or identified for subsequent evaluation and decision. All repaired items need to be re-inspected to ensure their acceptability prior to being used.

2.7.5 Section 7.5 Production and service provision

Section 7.5 Production and service provision	The organisation shall have procedures for the control of: • production and service operations; • validation of processes • identification and traceability; • customer property; • preservation of product.

A documented process needs to be agreed and implemented by the organisation to cover all production and service operations.

2.7.5.1 Section 7.5.1 Control of production and service provision

Section 7.5.1 Control of production and service provision	The organisation shall have the following available: • information concerning product characteristics; • appropriate work instructions; • suitable production equipment; • measuring and monitoring devices and facilities; • processes to cover the release, delivery and post-delivery activities.

The organisation should identify the requirements for product realisation and ensure that it has:

• the ability to comply with contractual requirements;
• the ability to train and have available competent people:
• a viable system for communication;
• a process for problem prevention.

2.7.5.2 Section 7.5.2 Validation of processes for production and service provisions

Section 7.5.2 Validation of processes for production and service provisions	The organisation shall define validation arrangements for: • review and approval of processes; • approval of equipment; • qualification of personnel; • use of defined methodologies and procedures; • requirements for records; • re-validation.

Where the resulting output cannot be verified by subsequent measurement or monitoring (and where deficiencies may become apparent **only** after the product is in use or the service has been delivered), the organisation needs to validate any production and/or service processes to demonstrate the ability of the processes to achieve their planned results.

The organisation should have procedures available to ensure that these processes are completed under controlled conditions especially with respect to special processes, and for defining work to be carried out where no previous procedure exists.

2.7.5.3 Section 7.5.3 Identification and traceability

Section 7.5.3 Identification and traceability	The organisation shall have procedures available for: • identification of product; • product status; • traceability.

ISO 9001:2000 recommends organisations maintain documented procedures for identifying products (hardware, software, documents and/or data) throughout all stages of production, delivery, receipt and installation. This process should be documented and reviewed for its continued applicability on a regular basis.

If required, organisations can also establish a system for identifying individual products or batches.

As previously mentioned (see **Goods inwards** in Section 2.7.4.3) all received goods should be inspected, their status defined and be located in stores. Non-conforming items should be placed in a reject area or marked as 'reject for review'. The status of work in progress should be clearly indicated by markings or associated documentation recording the inspections undertaken and their acceptability.

2.7.5.4 Section 7.5.4 Customer property

Section 7.5.4 Customer property	The organisation shall: • retain records of all customer provided material; • protect and maintain all customer provided property.

Customer supplied products are goods which have been provided by the customer (or his agent), normally free of charge, for incorporation into the product. The existence of 'free issue' products will only be relevant to certain organisations. However, it should be remembered that items returned to the organisation for repair or rectification are also within this category.

Any goods received from customers need to be visually inspected at the receipt stage and any undeclared non-conformance immediately reported to the customer.

The organisation should ensure that all property belonging to the customer (including its intellectual, property rights) is protected and that care is taken to ensure that it is well maintained, used in accordance with the manufacturer's instructions and safeguarded at all times.

Should the items become lost, damaged or unserviceable, while in the organisation's control, the problem should be recorded and the customer advised.

Purchaser supplied product

In some circumstances material, sub assemblies or components may have been supplied to the organisation by the purchaser as part of the contract. In these cases it is important that the organisation has a goods inward inspection process to assure themselves that the item they are receiving is the correct one, has not been damaged in transit and is suitable for its purpose.

Note: 'Customer property' can include intellectual property'!

2.7.5.5 Section 7.5.5 Preservation of product

Section 7.5.5 Preservation of product	The organisation shall have procedures available for identifying, handling, packaging, storing and protecting products during internal processing and delivery to their intended destination.

Part numbers and labels

A manufacturer's/supplier's part number or description label should identify any material or equipment that cannot be obviously identified. This identification can be on the packaging or on the item itself and should remain in place for as long as possible provided it does not hamper effective use of the item. If items have a serial number then this number should also be recorded.

Product protection

All materials and goods that are received, whether they are the property of the organisation or others, should, as far as practicable, be protected and their quality preserved until such time as they are transferred to a customer, disposed of to a third party or utilised. The overall objective should be to prevent deterioration and damage whilst in storage, or in the process of transportation, installation, commissioning and/or maintenance. Written instructions and procedures for the handling, identification and storage of materials, components, parts, sub assemblies and completed items will have to be established and made available. These instructions must contain details of quarantine areas or bonded stores, how they should be used, together with methods of cleaning, preserving and packaging.

Documented procedures

As previously mentioned, ISO 9001:2000 recommends organisations to maintain documented procedures for identifying products (e.g. hardware, software, documents and/or data) throughout all stages of production, delivery, receipt and installation. If required, organisations can also establish a system for identifying individual products or batches and consider the need for any special requirements (i.e. associated with software, electronic media, hazardous materials, specialist personnel and products or materials) arising from the nature of the product which are unique or irreplaceable.

In some cases (e.g. toxic contamination), in order to prevent damage and deterioration of the product (and harm to the product user!), it might even be necessary to refer to another document, regulation or standard to ensure that the items are correctly handled, stored and delivered.

Storage

All QMS standards emphasise the importance of having satisfactory storage facilities and stipulate that these must be available for **all** materials, consumables, components, sub assemblies or completed articles. In a similar manner, the standards specify that materials should always be properly stored, segregated, handled and protected during production so as to maintain their suitability.

The supplier will thus have to provide secure storage areas or stock rooms so that the materials can be isolated and protected (e.g. from harmful environments) pending use or shipment. Storage areas will have to be protected and kept tidy and the supplier must ensure that material only leaves the storage areas when it has been properly authorised.

Procedures for rotation of stock will need to be established and special consideration should always be given to items with limited shelf life and items that might require special protection during transit or storage. This is usually referred to as deterioration control. Where corrosive or toxic materials are stored in quantity, these items must be kept in a separate storage area.

Delivery

The supplier must make arrangements to ensure that the quality of the product is protected following final inspection and test. Where contractually specified, this protection can even be extended to include delivery to the final destination. Some of the factors that should be considered by suppliers when delivering their product to the purchaser are:

- the nature of the material;
- the type(s) of transport to be used;
- environmental conditions during transit;
- time in transit;
- handling methods en route;
- storage en route and at the destination.

2.7.6 Section 7.6 Control of measuring and monitoring devices

Section 7.6 Control of measuring and monitoring devices	The organisation shall ensure that all measuring and monitoring devices are: - calibrated and adjusted periodically or prior to use; - traceable to international or national standards; - safeguarded from adjustments that would invalidate the calibration; - protected from damage and deterioration during handling, maintenance and storage.

The control of measuring and test equipment (whether owned by the supplier, on loan, hired or provided by the purchaser), should always include a check that the equipment is exactly what is required, has been initially calibrated before use, operates within the required tolerances, is regularly recalibrated and that facilities exist (either within the organisation or via a third party) to adjust, repair or recalibrate as necessary.

In particular, measuring and monitoring devices that are used to verify process outputs against specified requirements need to be maintained and calibrated against national and international standards. The results of all calibrations carried out must be retained and the validity of previous results re-assessed if they are subsequently found to be out of calibration.

All production and measuring equipment that is held needs to be well-maintained, in good condition and capable of safe and effective operation within a specified tolerance of accuracy. Test and measuring equipment should be regularly inspected and/or calibrated to ensure that it is capable of accurate operation, by comparison with external sources traceable back to national standards. Any electrostatic protection equipment that is utilised when handling sensitive components should be regularly checked to ensure that it remains fully functional.

Control of inspection, measuring and test equipment

All production equipment including machinery jigs, fixtures, tools, templates, patterns and gauges should always be stored correctly and satisfactorily protected between use to ensure their bias and precision. They should be verified or recalibrated at appropriate intervals. Special attention should be paid to computers if they are used in controlling processes and particularly to the maintenance and accreditation of any related software.

Software

Software used for measuring and monitoring of specified requirements shall be validated prior to use. (Note also see ISO 10012:1992 'Quality Assurance Requirements for Measuring Equipment – Metrological confirmation system for measuring equipment'.)

Calibration

Without exception, all measuring instruments can be subject to damage, deterioration or just general wear and tear when they are in regularly use in workshops and factories. The organisation's QMS should take account of this fact and ensure that **all** test equipment is regularly calibrated against a known working standard held by the manufacturer.

Of course, calibrating against a standard is pretty pointless if that particular standard cannot be relied upon and so the 'workshop standard' must also be calibrated, on a regular basis, at either a recognised calibration centre or at the UK Physical Laboratory (or similar) against one of the national standards.

The supplier's QMS will thus have to make allowances for:

- the calibration and adjustment of all inspection, measuring and test equipment that can affect product quality;
- the documentation and maintenance of calibration procedures and records;
- the regular inspection of all measuring or test equipment to ensure that they are capable of the accuracy and precision that is required;
- the environmental conditions being suitable for the calibrations, inspections, measurements and tests to be completed.

The accuracy of the instrument will depend very much on what items it is going to be used to test, the frequency of use of the test instrument, industry standards of acceptability, etc. and the organisation will have to decide on the maximum tolerance of accuracy for each item of test equipment.

Calibration methods

There are various possibilities, such as:

- send all working equipment to an external calibration laboratory;
- send one of each item (i.e. a 'workshop standard') to a calibration laboratory, then sub-calibrate each working item against the workshop standard;

- testing by attributes – i.e. take a known 'faulty' product, and a known 'good' product; and then test each one to ensure that the test equipment can identify the faulty and good product correctly.

Calibration frequency

The calibration frequency depends on how much the instrument is used, its ability to retain its accuracy and how critical the items being tested are. Infrequently used instruments are often only calibrated prior to their use whilst frequently used items would normally be checked and re-calibrated at regular intervals depending, again, on product criticality, cost, availability etc. Normally 12 months is considered as about the maximum calibration interval.

Calibration ideals

- Each instrument should be uniquely identified, allowing it to be traced.
- The calibration results should be clearly indicated on the instrument.
- The calibration results should be retained for reference.
- The instrument should be labelled to show the next 'calibration due' date to easily avoid its use outside of the period of confidence.
- Any means of adjusting the calibration should be sealed, allowing easy identification if it has been tampered with (e.g. a label across the joint of the casing).
- If the instrument is found to be outside of its tolerance of accuracy, any items previously tested with the instrument must be regarded as suspect. In these circumstances, it would be wise to review the test results obtained from the individual instrument. This could be achieved by compensating for the extent of inaccuracy to decide if the acceptability of the item would be reversed.

2.8 Section 8 – Measurement, analysis and improvement

This section absorbs the former inspection and measurement control sections of ISO 9001:1994.

2.8.1 Section 8.1 General

Section 8.1 General	The organisation shall define the activities needed to measure and monitor: • product conformity; • product improvement.

Under ISO 9001:2000 the organisation is required to determine and implement procedures to ensure product and QMS conformity and improvement.

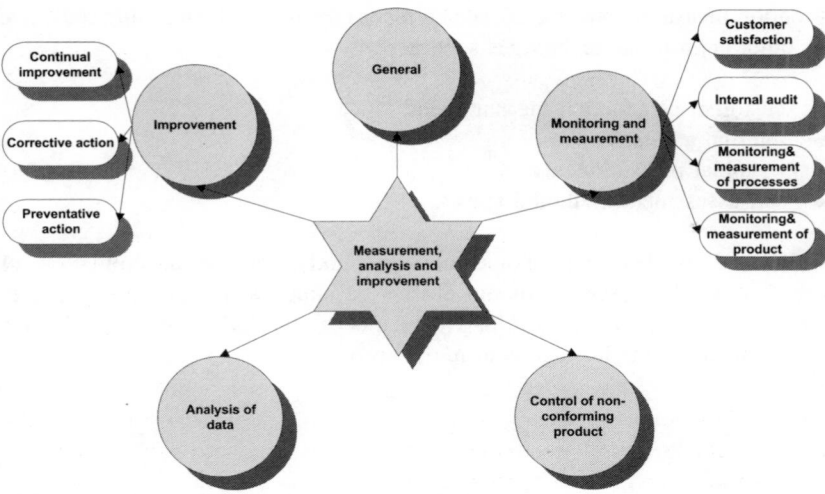

Figure 2.7 Measurement, analysis and improvement

The use of statistical techniques can help to understand the variability of a product and in so doing, help organisations to solve problems and improve efficiency. Basically, statistical techniques:

- make better use of available data to assist in decision making;
- help to measure, describe, analyse, interpret and model variability;
- help to provide a better understanding of the nature, extent and causes of variability;
- help to solve and even prevent problems that may result from such variability;
- promote continual improvement.

Details of the application of statistical techniques are given in ISO TR 10017:1999 – Guidance on Statistical Techniques for ISO 9001:1994.

2.8.2 Section 8.2 Monitoring and measurement

Section 8.2 Monitoring and measurement	The organisation shall have procedures available to: • ensure customer satisfaction; • control internal audits; • ensure effective monitoring and measurement of product and processes.

To enable an organisation to measure customer satisfaction, evaluate its product and the efficiency of its processes, they need to establish a method to monitor, measure, collect, analyse and record the relevant data using statistical or other appropriate techniques such as:

- customer satisfaction measurement;
- internal audits;
- financial measurements;
- self-assessment methodologies.

Collection of this data should not be purely for the accumulation of information. This process should always be aimed at progressive improvement of the organisation's QMS. The results of this analysis will then be one of the inputs to the management review process.

2.8.2.1 Section 8.2.1 Customer satisfaction

Section 8.2.1 Customer satisfaction	The organisation shall monitor customer satisfaction and/or dissatisfaction.

The organisation should establish processes to gather, analyse and make effective use of all customer-related information as one of the measurements of performance of their QMS. This information can come from many sources such as:

- customer requirements and contract information;
- feedback from the delivery of a product;
- market needs;
- service delivery data;
- information relating to competition.

The organisation's process should address conformance to requirements, meeting the needs and expectations of customers, price and delivery of product and overall customer satisfaction. Examples of sources of information on customer satisfaction include:

- customer complaints;
- direct communication with customers;
- questionnaires and surveys;
- focus groups;
- reports from consumer organisations;
- reports in various media;
- sector studies.

2.8.2.2 Section 8.2.2 Internal audit

Section 8.2.2 Internal audit	The organisation shall plan and conduct periodic internal audits to determine whether the QMS: • continues to conform to the requirements of ISO 9001:2000; • has been effectively implemented and maintained. The organisation shall plan the audit programme taking into account: • the status and importance of the activities and areas to be audited; • the results of previous audits. The organisation shall have a documented procedure which includes: • the responsibilities and requirements for conducting audits; • the scope, frequency, methodologies used; • the method for recording results and reporting to management.

An organisation should establish an internal audit process to assess the strengths and weaknesses of its QMS, to identify potential danger spots, eliminate wastage and verify that corrective action has been successfully achieved. The internal audit process should also be used to review the efficiency and effectiveness of other organisational activities and support processes including:

- existence of adequate documentation;
- effective implementation of processes;
- identification of non-conformance;
- documentation of results;
- competence of personnel;
- opportunities for improvement;
- capability of processes;
- use of statistical techniques;
- use of information technology;
- analysis of quality cost data;
- assigned responsibilities and authorities;
- performance results and expectations;
- adequacy and accuracy of performance measurement;
- improvement activities;
- relationships with interested parties, including internal customers.

To be effective, an 'internal audit' must be completed by trained personnel and where possible by members of the quality control staff – provided, that is, that they are not responsible for the quality of that particular product and they are **not** associated with the activity being audited. In addition to documenting non-conformances, internal audit reporting should also indicate areas for improvement (with recommendations), as well as areas of outstanding performance.

There are three basic types of audit to choose from:

- **First-party audits** – conducted by, or on behalf of, the organisation itself for internal purposes and can form the basis for an organisation's self-declaration of conformity.
- **Second-party audits** – conducted by customers of the organisation or by other persons on behalf of the customer.
- **Third-party audits** – conducted by external independent audit service organisations. Such organisations, usually accredited, provide certification or registration of conformity with requirements such as those of ISO 9001:2000.

It is essential that management shall take timely corrective action on all deficiencies found during the audit. Follow-up actions should include the verification of the implementation of corrective action, and the reporting of verification results.

Financial approach

As part of their overall management system, organisations should establish a methodology for linking financial considerations with the QMS. This could include:

- prevention, appraisal and failure costs analysis;
- costs of conformance and non-conformance;
- life-cycle approach.

Self-assessment

Organisations should consider establishing and implementing a self-assessment process. The range and depth of the assessment should be planned in relation to the organisation's objectives and priorities. Self-assessment can be a very useful tool to evaluate improvement and ISO 9004:2000 helps organisations by providing an annex containing 'Guidelines for self-assessment'. For the assistance of small businesses, I have also included a section (see Part Seven) on 'self assessment' which includes check sheets against the requirements of ISO 9001:2000 and examples of Stage Audit checklists.

2.8.2.3 Section 8.2.3 Monitoring and measurement of processes

Section 8.2.3 Monitoring and measurement of processes	The organisation shall measure and monitor QMS processes to ensure they: • meet customer requirements; • satisfy their intended purpose.

The organisation should identify measurement methodologies, perform measurements to evaluate their process performance and use the results obtained to improve the product realisation process. Examples where process performance measurements can be used to improve processes include:

- timeliness;
- dependability;
- reaction time of processes and people to special internal and external requests;
- cycle time or throughput;
- effectiveness and efficiency of people;
- utilisation of technologies;
- cost reduction.

2.8.2.4 Section 8.2.4 Monitoring and measurement of product

Section 8.2.4 Monitoring and measurement of product	The organisation shall: • monitor and measure the characteristics of a product; • document evidence of conformity with the acceptance criteria; • indicate the authority responsible for release of product; • not release the product until all the specified activities have been satisfactorily completed.

The organisation should establish, specify and plan their measurement requirements (including acceptance criteria) for its products taking into consideration the:

- location of each measurement point in its process sequence;
- characteristics to be measured at each point;
- documentation and acceptance criteria to be used;
- equipment and tools required;
- inspections and tests that need to be witnessed or performed by the customer, statutory and/or regulatory authorities;
- possible requirements for qualified third parties to perform type testing, in-process inspections, product verification and/or product validation;

- necessary qualification requirements of material, product, process, people or the QMS;
- requirements for final inspection;
- outputs of the measurement process of the product;
- conformance to customer, statutory and regulatory requirements.

Typical examples of product measurement records include:

- inspection and test reports;
- material release notices;
- certificates as required;
- electronic data.

To be of any use it is very important that the inspection and test status of a product is immediately clear. The QMS will have to show exactly how this will be achieved (using such methods as markings, stamps, tags, labels, routing cards, inspection records, test software, physical location or other suitable means) to indicate the conformance or non-conformance of the product, and whether it has been inspected and approved, or inspected and rejected.

Production control

To reduce the possibility of manufacturing or design errors causing production line and product delays, the quality status of the product, process, material or environment must be checked at various stages during the production sequence. The use of control charts, statistical sampling procedures and plans are some of the techniques that are used for production and process control.

Product testing

Product testing (i.e. final inspection and testing), are methods of testing whether the product is acceptable or not. These methods have to be developed by the supplier in conjunction with the purchaser and should be included in the suppliers QMS, Quality Manual and/or Quality Plan. These methods would normally contain:

- confirmation that all the relevant inspections and tests have been carried out during manufacture, are fully documented and are recorded in accordance with the Quality Plan or agreed procedure;
- details of the acceptance and rejection criteria that are to be used;
- the measurement and acceptance criteria;
- the quantity to be inspected;
- the sampling plan;
- who is to complete the inspection processes;
- details of the equipment that requires statistical analysis.

Special processes

Occasionally during manufacture, the supplier will be required to perform an inspection on components or activities that cannot normally be verified or inspected at a later stage. The purpose of these inspections is to detect, at an early stage, non-conforming material. If these inspections are required, then the prime contractor will have to establish 'special manufacturing processes' (such as welding, forging, plastic and wood fabrication, heat treatment and the application of protective treatments) and inspection and testing processes (such as temperature and humidity cycling, vibration, radiography, magnetic particle inspection, penetrant inspection, ultrasonic inspection, pressure testing, chemical and spectrographic analysis and salt spray tests).

2.8.3 Section 8.3 Control of non-conforming product

Section 8.3 Control of non-conforming product	The organisation shall define procedures to ensure that: <ul><li>products which do not conform to requirements are prevented from unintended use or delivery;</li><li>non-conforming products that have been corrected are re-verified to demonstrate conformity;</li><li>non-conforming products detected after delivery or use are either corrected or removed from service.</li></ul>

Material control and traceability

To ensure that a non-conforming or hazardous product is not delivered by mistake to a customer, the organisation must establish and maintain procedures for identifying the product (from drawings, specifications or other documents), during all stages of production, delivery and installation. This also ensures that all parts of the product are capable of being traced and recalled if necessary.

Control of non-conformity

To cover the possibility of confusing an acceptable quality product with a defective, non-conforming or unacceptable product (and accidentally using this material or despatching it to the purchaser!), all non-conforming articles **must** be clearly identified and kept completely separate from **all** other acceptable (conforming) products. Non-conforming products can then be:

- documented and steps taken to see that they do not occur again;
- reworked so that they meet the specified requirement;
- accepted with or without repair by concession;
- regraded for possible use elsewhere;
- rejected or scrapped.

Since most production processes inevitably yield some kind of defective material, the organisation must investigate methods for preventing this from happening again and arrange for their immediate disposal. The most obvious method of disposing of a non-conforming material is to scrap it. First making sure, of course, that it cannot be confused with any other material or accidentally used again!

Whatever the choice, details about the non-conformance must be fed back into the system so that action (where economically feasible) can be taken to establish and correct the cause of the non-conformance and hopefully prevent its recurrence.

Supplier responsibility

BS 6143–2:1990 'Guide to the Economics of Quality – Prevention, appraisal and failure model' provides detailed information concerning the procedures that should be adopted. In précis form they stipulate that the supplier must:

- investigate the cause of any non-conforming product and have a corrective course of action available to prevent its recurrence;
- analyse all processes, work operations, concessions, quality records, service reports and customer complaints to eliminate the causes of non-conforming products;
- initiate preventive actions;
- change any designs, specifications or work methods that may be unsatisfactory; ensure that the responsibilities for corrective action are clearly assigned to personnel and that these responsibilities are carried out correctly;
- apply controls to ensure that corrective actions are taken and that the existing (as well as the modified) work, methods and designs are effective and suitable;
- implement and record changes in procedures that result from this corrective action.

BS 6143–2:1990 emphasises that this control of quality is not only limited just to the design, manufacture or installation facilities under the supplier's direct control. They also extend to those services, parts, materials or products that are provided by subcontractors. In some circumstances, if a subcontractor's work is found to be unsatisfactory this could mean dispensing with that particular subcontractor and having to find another one. This can, however, cause additional problems such as finding another one capable of supplying the same service and the materials before the lack of those materials (or service) causes product delays.

Permanent changes

If there are any permanent changes resulting from this corrective action, then they should be recorded in work instructions, manufacturing processes, product specifications and in the organisation's QMS. In some cases it might even be necessary to revise the procedures used to detect and eliminate potential problems.

2.8.4 Section 8.4 Analysis of data

Section 8.4 Analysis of data	The organisation shall collect data for the analysis of: • customer satisfaction; • conformance to product requirements; • characteristics and trends (and opportunities) for preventive action.

Customers may often require confirmation that the organisation is capable of continuing to produce a quality article or process. One of the methods frequently used to provide this sort of confirmation is statistical analysis. Nowadays there are many methods of statistically analysing whether the product is:

- what the market requires;
- the correct design;
- derived from a reliable specification and one that can be relied upon to last the test of time (i.e. durability);
- subject to the correct process control and capabilities;
- covered by relevant quality standards, specifications and plans.

Statistical analysis

Statistical analysis can also include data analysis, performance testing and defect analysis. Other forms of analysis are design process review and design verification. Statistical analysis is, of course, a subject on its own and vast amounts of information about statistical methods, reliability and maintainability data are readily available. An exceedingly good overview of Statistical Analysis is provided in *Statistical Process Control* and other sources of information such as *Quality and Standards in Electronics* (details of which are provided in the reference section.

With the use of statistical methodologies, the organisation should analyse data in order to assess, control, and improve the performance of processes and products and to identify areas for improvement. Analysis of data can help determine the cause of many problems and the results of this analysis can be used to determine:

- trends;
- operational performance;
- customer satisfaction and dissatisfaction;
- satisfaction level of other interested parties;

- effectiveness and efficiency of the organisation;
- economics of quality and financial and market-related performance;
- benchmarking of performance.

Records

In order that the statistical significance of a failure can be properly assessed and that the correct retrospective action may be taken, it is essential that the design section has access to all the records and other pertinent data failure reports gathered in the design office and on the shop floor.

The storage, maintenance and analysis of reliability data will require the design section to follow the progress of the product throughout its productive life cycle, through its many maintenance cycles and take due note of any customer comments. The compilation and retention of design office reliability data is not only very important, but essential to the reliability of the product and the manufacturing facility.

Storage of records

Storage facilities should be available to ensure that all stored records are identifiable and retrievable and that the storage areas are free from damp and other agents which could cause premature deterioration. If records are maintained on computer magnetic media, then these should be subject to 'back-up' at regular intervals, with the 'back-up' information being stored in a protected location to ensure security from loss or damage of active data. All records are normally retained for a minimum of two years after contract completion.

2.8.5 Section 8.5 Improvement

Section 8.5 Improvement	The organisation shall have procedures available for: • planning for continual improvement; • corrective action; • preventive action.

The organisation shall plan and manage the processes, policies and objectives that are required for the continual improvement of their QMS as well as their products using audit results, analysis of data, corrective and preventive action and management reviews.

Non-conformity

Once non-conforming items have been recognised, they should be identified by location, associated documents, or specific markings in order to prevent their inadvertent use. All non-conforming items and customer complaints should be subject to review and rectification by nominated personnel. The type and extent of non-conformity needs to be documented in order to establish trends and identify possible areas for improvement.

Corrective action

The corrective action required to prevent recurrence should be evaluated, documented, and its effective implementation monitored. All rectification should subsequently be re-inspected to ensure complete customer satisfaction.

Preventive action

All employees should be encouraged to suggest improvements in methods, materials, suppliers and subcontractors and organisations should have an established procedure for review of all activities in order to identify and evaluate all possible improvements in methods/materials and its procedures.

2.8.5.1 Section 8.5.1 Continual improvement

Section 8.5.1 Continual improvement	The organisation shall plan, manage and ensure the continual improvement of their QMS.

The organisation should continually seek to improve its processes and procedures (rather than just waiting for a problem to come along) and have available documented procedures to identify, manage and improve them. Such actions would include the following:

- defining, measuring and analysing the existing situation;
- establishing the objectives for improvement;
- searching for possible solutions;
- evaluating these solutions;
- implementing the selected solution;
- measuring, verifying, and analysing results of the implementation;
- formalising changes.

2.8.5.2 section 8.5.2 Corrective action

Section 8.5.2 Corrective action	The organisation shall have documented procedures for: - identifying non-conformities (including customer complaints); - determining the causes of non-conformity; - evaluating the need for action to ensure non-conformities do not recur; - implementing corrective action; - recording results; - reviewing corrective action taken.

The organisation should plan and establish a process for corrective action, the results of which shall be included in the management review process. The input information for this activity can derive from a number of sources such as:

- customer complaints;
- non-conformance reports;
- outputs from management review;
- internal audit reports;
- outputs from data analysis;
- relevant QMS records;
- outputs from satisfaction measurements;
- process measurements;
- results of self-assessment.

The corrective action process should include:

- a definition of the causes of non-conformances and defects;
- elimination of causes of non-conformances and defects;
- appropriate actions to avoid recurrence of problems;
- a record of the activity and results.

The necessity for corrective action should be evaluated in terms of the potential impact on operating costs, costs of non-conformance, performance, dependability, safety and customer satisfaction.

Concessions and approvals

No matter how much an organisation may pay attention to the control of quality and no matter how hard they try to avoid problems with both manpower and the product, all too often things go wrong. There could, for instance, be a problem in the production shop, an accident could happen, piece-part material could be damaged or a mistake could be made by an engineer when reading a drawing or setting up an electrical or electronic machine. Or the print shop could print the deliverable incorrectly or leave out sections.

In all of these cases there has to be a recognised method of accepting the problem instead of just trying to hide the blunder through either unofficial 'modifications' or, even worse, trying to cover it up! As the saying goes 'honesty is always the best policy' and in any case, 'Murphy's Law' says that more than likely the hidden 'repairs' will be found out and the manufacturer will consequently lose his customer's trust and any chance of follow on orders.

Concession scheme

The machinery for overcoming these problems is called the 'concession scheme'. This will normally consist of a form that has to be completed by the manufacturer/supplier **and** the customer. Details of each document, component, sub assembly, defect or mistake that is identified has to be recorded together with the action that was taken to rectify, scrap, modify or accept the problem.

The Quality Plan will indicate the acceptance or rejection criteria that will be adopted. It will describe compulsory methods that must be taken to mark imperfect or faulty material and indicate how they should be separated from any other material before it is scrapped, reworked or repaired.

If the problem is the result of a faulty design or specification that originated from the purchaser any problems must of course be referred back to them. If the fault is found to be the fault of the purchaser (e.g. unsatisfactory design) the manufacturer/supplier may, of course, be able to insist on having an ex-gratia payment to overcome the problem. If the problem originated from the manufacturer/supplier, then the purchaser is perfectly within his rights to insist on a reduction in the agreed price.

In cases where a subcontractor requests a concession, then the prime contractor has to carry out a full investigation and agree to the subcontractor's proposal before asking the purchaser to consider the request.

A concession system is a very important part of the supplier/purchaser relationship. It also promotes better discipline within the factory, shows up re-occurring problem areas and ensures that the supplier's standard of workmanship is maintained.

Defects and defect reports

One of the requirements of the QMS is that signatures shall be required from inspectors at each stage of the production to show that the product is of the required standard and assured quality.

When an item fails to meet these criteria, then the inspector must submit a defect report, showing exactly what is defective, how it affects the product and, where possible, what steps can be taken to overcome these failures in future productions.

Bonded store

Owing to the possibility of having unacceptable goods inside their premises, the manufacturer must also set up some kind of 'bonded store' where all incoming material is placed pending inspection.

Even when goods have left the bonded store it is still necessary to have some form of marking (e.g. labels or tags) to distinguish between those awaiting inspection, those inspected and accepted, and those rejected and awaiting return.

2.8.5.3 Section 8.5.3 Preventive action

Section 8.5.3 Preventive action	The organisation shall have documented procedures for: • identifying potential non-conformities; • implementing preventive action; • recording and reviewing all preventive action taken.

The organisation should use preventive methodologies such as risk analysis, trend analysis, statistical process control, fault tree analysis, failure modes and effects and criticality analysis to identify the causes of potential non-conformances. Examples of sources are:

• customer needs and expectations;
• market analysis;
• management review output;
• outputs from data analysis;
• satisfaction measurements;
• process measurements;
• systems that consolidate many sources of customer information;
• relevant QMS records;
• results of self-assessment;
• processes that provide early warning of approaching out-of-control operating conditions.

Preventive actions should be considered for inclusion in the management review process.

Part Two has provided a complete overview and explanation of the various sections and subsections making up ISO 9001:2000.

In Part Three we shall look at some of the benefits of Quality Control and Quality Assurance from the point of view of the manufacturer, supplier, purchaser and/or end user.

Part Three

The Importance of Quality Control and Quality Assurance

In Parts One and Two of this book, the recommendations, background and the various uses of ISO 9001:2000 were explained. In Part Three the reader is introduced to the requirements and benefits of quality control and quality assurance from the point of view of the manufacturer and the supplier as well as the purchaser and/or end user.

The significance and the types of specifications are explained, manufacturer's and purchaser's responsibilities are defined and a thorough review of quality during a product's life cycle enables the reader to appreciate the costs and associated benefits of quality.

Although I have written Part Three from the point of view of a manufactured product, it is equally applicable for the production of a document, report or other forms of deliverable.

3
Quality control and quality assurance

The international definition of 'Quality' as stated in ISO 9000:2000 is 'the degree to which a set of inherent characteristics fulfils requirements.'

But what of quality assurance and quality control?

Although the terms 'quality assurance' and 'quality control' are both aimed at ensuring the quality of the end product, they are in fact two completely separate processes.

3.1 Quality control

The definition of quality control (QC) is 'that part of quality management focussed on fulfilling quality requirements' (ISO 9000:2000). In other words, the operational techniques and activities that are used to fulfil the requirements for quality.

It is the amount of supervision that a product is subjected to so as to be sure that the workmanship associated with that product meets the quality level required by the design. In other words, it is the control exercised by the manufacturer to certify that **all** aspects of their activities during the design, production, installation **and** in-service stages are to the desired standards.

Control and Supervision

To meet specified requirements

Figure 3.1 Quality control

Quality control is exercised at all levels, and, as all personnel are responsible for the particular task they are doing, they are **all** quality controllers to some degree or other.

Section Heads, because of their positions and responsibilities, have more control over their own particular process and therefore have more control over the final quality. It is true, therefore, to say that all personnel are quality controllers and that Section Heads are the Principal Quality Controllers, within their own particular organisation.

3.2 Quality assurance

Quality assurance (QA) is 'that part of quality management focussed on providing confidence that quality requirements are fulfilled' (ISO 9000:2000). In other words, all those planned and systematic actions necessary to provide adequate confidence that a product or service will satisfy given requirements for quality.

- 'Quality': is fitness for intended use;
- 'Assurance': is a declaration given to inspire confidence in an organisation's capability;
- 'Quality assurance': in a product (or service), by consistently achieving stated objectives is, therefore, a declaration given to inspire confidence that a particular organisation is capable of consistently satisfying need as well as being a managerial process designed to increase confidence.

Quality assurance ensures that a product has achieved the highest standards and that its production, modification or repair (in the case of a manufactured item) has been completed in an efficient and timely manner.

Control and Supervision

**To provide Guaranteed
System Quality**

Figure 3.2 Quality assurance

The purpose of quality assurance is, therefore:

- to provide assurance to a customer that the standard of workmanship within a contractor's premises is of the highest level and that all products leaving that particular firm are above a certain fixed minimum level of specification;
- to ensure that production standards are uniform between divisions/sections and remain constant despite changes in personnel.

In a nutshell, quality assurance is concerned with:

- an agreed level of quality;
- a commitment within a company to the fundamental principle of consistently supplying the right quality product;
- a commitment from a customer to the fundamental principle of only accepting the right quality product;
- a commitment within all levels of (contractor and or customer) to the basic principles of quality assurance and quality control.

The main benefits of quality assurance are:

- an increased capability of supplying a product which consistently conforms to an agreed specification;
- a reduction in manufacturing and production costs because of less wastage and fewer rejects;
- a greater involvement and motivation within an organisation's workforce;
- an improved customer relationship through fewer complaints, thus providing increased sales potential.

3.3 Specifications

Without proper specifications it is impossible to expect a manufacturer or supplier to produce an article, equipment or system that completely satisfies the purchaser's requirements. Equally, if the manufacturer and/or supplier does not work within laid down specifications they will be unable to produce something that comes up to the purchaser's required standard.

If a manufacturer does not meet required specifications, then the part, equipment or system will not work as expected or the components will be the wrong dimensions and not fit properly etc. Worst of all, the article will not be exactly what the purchaser wanted.

The importance of specifications is, therefore, very much the responsibility of the purchaser **as well as** the manufacturer/supplier.

3.3.1 The significance of specifications

Specifications always form the basis of a contract and as such they need to be a comprehensive and precise description of exactly what the purchaser requires. The document must, therefore, avoid ambiguous words, mixed systems of units (e.g. metric and imperial) and, in particular, avoid over specification such as listing extremely close tolerances with respect to dimensions, colour, surface finishes and/or performance which are liable to increase the cost of the product unnecessarily.

Specifications can be very simple and just covered by a few words, or they can be extremely rigid and run into many volumes. It all depends on the size of the assignment and the level of accuracy that the purchaser requires.

3.3.2 Types of specification

There are three main ways in which the purchaser's requirements can be specified: general specifications, overall performance specifications and standard specifications. Although slightly different in content, each of these specifications closely examines the procedures used by the manufacturer.

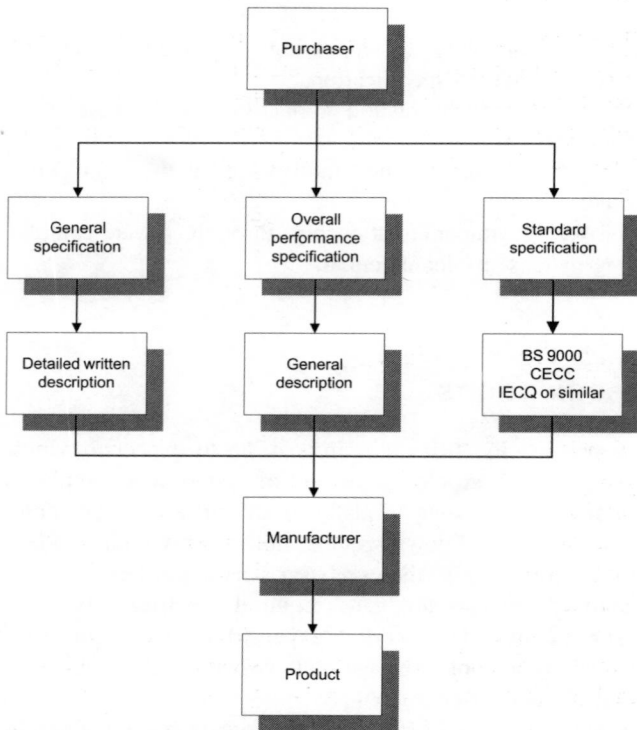

Figure 3.3 Types of specification

3.3.2.1 General specification

A general specification requires the purchaser to produce a detailed written description of the article, its construction, the materials to be used and the level of performance that it is required to provide. It is usually written by a member of the design team and then passed to an experienced engineer (independent of that particular design team) for final vetting and approval.

To avoid any problems later on, specifications must always guard against using such words as 'suitable', 'appropriate' or 'conventional'. In a similar manner, inclusion of 'possible alternatives' and 'by agreement' clauses should also be avoided.

If in-house specifications are produced in quantity, it is essential that any amended specification is published and immediately issued to all concerned. To make life simpler and avoid future problems, it is equally important that these amendments are numbered, dated and the recipients are made to destroy all previous copies and issues.

3.3.2.2 Overall performance specification

An overall performance specification tells the manufacturer in comprehensive terms exactly what the purchaser is looking for. The obvious disadvantage of this method is that it leaves the design of the product completely up to the manufacturer. This can often lead to arguments later on especially when the purchaser realises that the product is either too big, too small, the wrong shape, not up to (or exceeding) his engineering requirements and, as frequently happens, is far more expensive than the purchaser really intended.

3.3.2.3 Standard specification

A standard specification is a list that describes, **in detail**, the items or materials that are to be used in the manufacture of the product.

Obviously, without any real experience it would take a purchaser a long time to compile such a list or even be able to express – in technical terms – exactly what he wants. To overcome these problems, National Standards Organisations (NSOs) publish lists of all the materials and sub assemblies commonly used by manufacturers.

In The United Kingdom (UK) the British Standards Institution (BSI) have produced these lists in the BS 9000 series (**not** to be confused with ISO 9000!). In Europe they are made available by the CENELEC Electronic Components Committee (CECC) and internationally by the Quality Assessment System for Electronic Components (IECQ).

3.3.3 Manufacturer's responsibilities

The manufacturer's prime responsibility must always be to ensure that anything **and everything** leaving their factory conforms to the specific requirements of the purchaser – particularly with regard to quality.

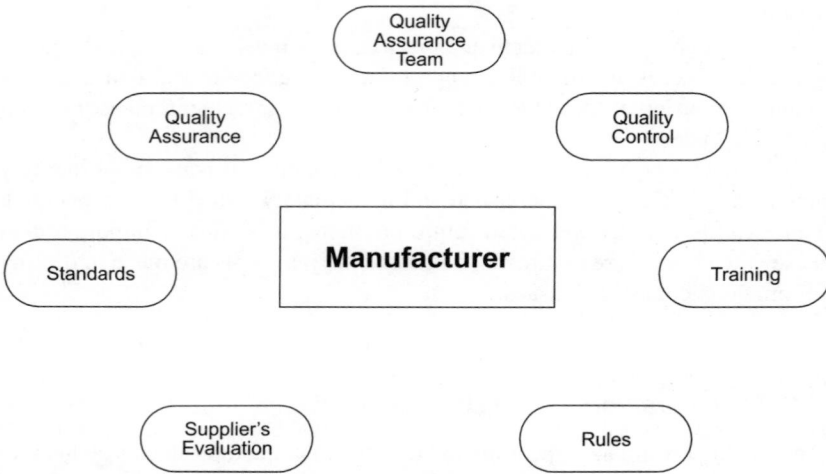

Figure 3.4 Manufacturer's responsibilities

The simplest way of doing this is for the manufacturer to ensure that their particular office, production facility or manufacturing outlet fully complies with the requirements of the quality standards adopted by the country in which they are manufacturing and the country to whom they intend supplying the component, equipment or system.

To do this they must of course first be aware of the standards applicable to that country, know how to obtain copies of these standards, how to adapt them to their own particular environment and how to get them accepted by the relevant authorities.

Although an organisation can set out to abide by accepted standards, unless they achieve this aim they will fail in their attempt to become a recognised manufacturer of quality goods. The main points that they should note are:

- that all managerial staff, from the most junior to the most senior, must firmly believe in the importance of quality control and quality assurance and understand how to implement them;
- that managerial staff **must** create an atmosphere in which quality assurance rules are obeyed and not simply avoided just because they are inconvenient, time consuming, laborious or just too boring to bother with;

- that there has to be an accepted training scheme to ensure that all members of the firm are regularly brought up to date with the ongoing and the latest requirements of quality assurance;
- that there must be a quality assurance team available to oversee and make sure that quality control and quality assurance are carried out at all times and **at all levels**, within their premises.

In addition, the manufacturer will have to provide proof that they are supplying a quality product. This is actually a 'measurement of their quality control' and usually takes the form of a supplier's evaluation, surveillance and/or audit.

National and international QMSs will also require the manufacturer to establish and maintain a fully documented method for the inspection of their system for quality control. Procedures must be developed and identified for classifying lots, cataloguing characteristics, selecting samples and rules for acceptance and/or rejection criteria, together with procedures for segregating and screening rejected lots.

3.3.4 Purchaser's responsibilities

Quite a number of problems associated with a product's quality are usually the fault of the purchaser! Obviously the purchaser can only expect to get what he ordered. It is, therefore, extremely important that the actual order is not only correct, but also provides the manufacturer with all the relevant (and accurate) information required to complete the task.

There is little point in trying to blame the manufacturer when an article doesn't come up to expectation because of an unsatisfactory design provided

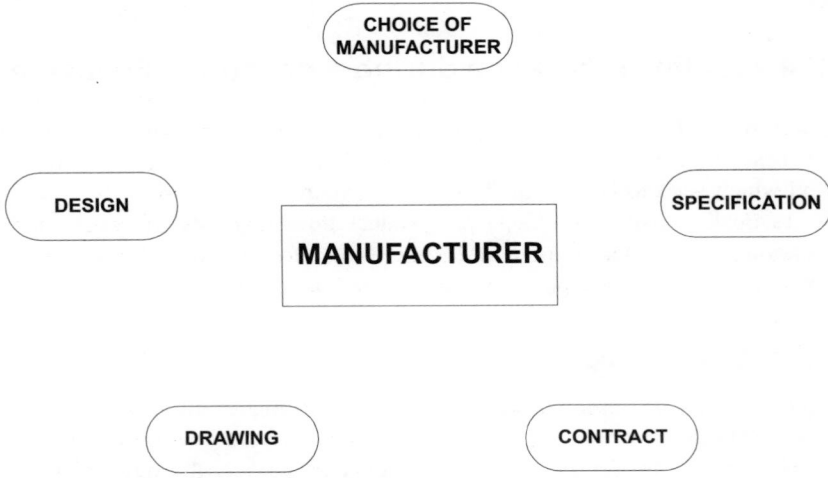

Figure 3.5 Purchaser's responsibilities

by the purchaser. In certain cases (for example when the requirements of the item cannot easily be described in words), it could be very helpful if the purchaser was to provide a drawing as a form of graphic order. In such cases, this drawing should contain all the relevant details such as type of material to be used, the material's grade or condition, the specifications that are to be followed and, where possible, the graphic order/drawing should be to scale.

If this approach proves impractical, then the order would have to include all the relevant dimensional data, sizes, tolerances etc., or refer to one of the accepted standards.

Having said all that, it must be appreciated that the actual specification being used is also very important for it sets the level of quality required and, therefore, directly affects the price of the article. Clearly, if specifications are too demanding then the final cost of the article will be too high. If specifications are too vague or obscure, then the manufacturer will have difficulty in assembling the object or may even be unable to get it to work correctly.

The choice of manufacturer is equally important. It is an unfortunate fact of life that purchasers usually consider that the price of the article is the prime and (in some cases), even the only consideration. Buying cheaply is obviously **not** the answer because if a purchaser accepts the lowest offer all too often he will find that delivery times are lengthened (because the manufacturer can make more profit on other orders), the article produced does not satisfy his requirements and worst of all, the quality of the article is so poor that he has to replace the device well before its anticipated life cycle has been completed.

If a manufacturer has received official recognition that the quality of his work is up to a particular standard, then the purchaser has a reasonable guarantee that the article being produced will be of a reasonable quality – always assuming that the initial order was correct!

3.4 Quality assurance during a product's life cycle

As shown in Figure 3.6, the life of a product is made up of five stages. Each of these stages has specific requirements that need to be correctly managed and which need to be regulated by quality controls.

As quality assurance affects the product throughout its life cycle, it is important that quality assurance procedures are introduced for design, manufacturing and acceptance stages, as well as in service utilisation.

3.4.1 Design stage

'Quality must be designed into a product before manufacture or assembly' (ISO 9004:2000).

Throughout the design stage of a product or service, the quality of that design must be regularly checked. Quality procedures have to be planned,

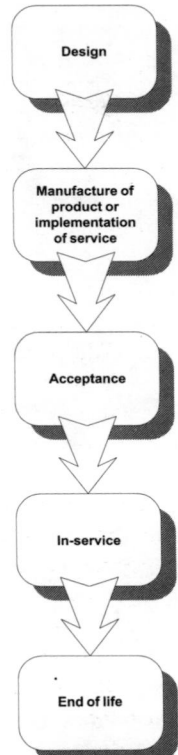

Figure 3.6 Quality assurance life cycle

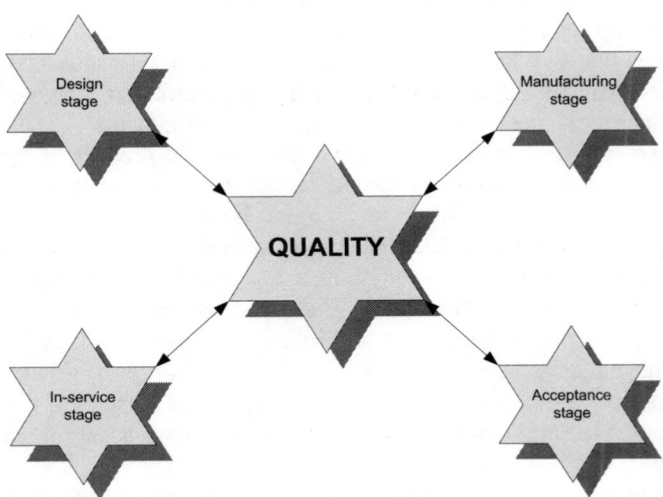

Figure 3.7 Quality assurance during a product's life cycle

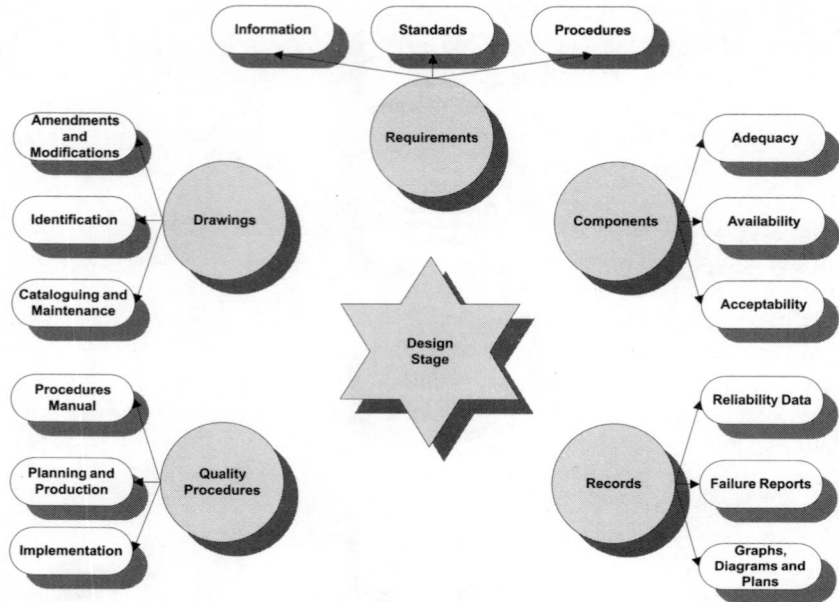

Figure 3.8 Design stage

written and implemented so as to predict and evaluate the fundamental and intrinsic reliability of the proposed design.

It doesn't matter whether the responsibility for the design of a product rests purely with the supplier, the purchaser, or is a joint function. It is essential that the designer is fully aware of the exact requirements of the project and has a sound background knowledge of the relevant standards, information and procedures that will have to be adopted during the design stages.

This is extremely important, because the actions of the design office not only influence the maintenance of quality during manufacture, but also play a major part in setting the quality level of the eventual product. If there is no quality control in the drawing office, there is little chance of there ever being any on the shop floor. When the engineers are trying to manufacture something (or a technician is attempting to assemble a system or module) to a set of drawings that have countless mistakes on them, what chance is there of them ever being able to produce an acceptable item!

These problems, although not specifically stipulated in ISO 9001:2000 should, nevertheless be addressed. The design office (or team) should produce some sort of 'Procedures Manual' which lists and describes the routine procedures that are required to turn a concept into a set of functional drawings.

These procedures will cover such activities as the numbering of drawings, authorisation to issue amendments and modifications, how to control changes to drawings, the method of withdrawing obsolete drawings and the identification, cataloguing and maintenance of drawings.

In addition to these procedures, the design office will also have to provide a complete listing of all the relevant components, availability, acceptability and adequacy and be aware of all the advances in both materials and equipment that are currently available on today's market which are relevant to the product.

It is imperative that the design team maintains a close relationship with the manufacturing division throughout these initial stages so as to be aware of their exact requirements, their problems, their choice of components etc., assist in the analysis of failures, swiftly produce solutions and forestall costly work stoppages. One of the main problems to overcome is the ease with which the design office can make an arbitrary selection, but then find that the size and tolerance is completely inappropriate for the manufacturing or assembly process.

In order that the statistical significance of a particular failure can be assessed and correct retroactive action taken, it is essential that the design team has access to all the records, failure reports and other data as soon as it is available within the design office or shop floor.

The storage, maintenance and analysis of reliability data will require the design team to follow the progress of the product throughout its productive life cycle, its many maintenance cycles and to take due note of customers' comments.

The compilation and retention of design office reliability data is not only very important, but also essential to the reliability of the product and the manufacturing facility.

Nowadays, of course, most large design offices are computerised and use processors to store their records on discs so that these records can be continually updated and amended. This information (data) can then be used with standard software such as Computer Aided Design (CAD) programs and computer aided design facilities to produce lists, graphs and drawings. The possibilities are almost endless but there are associated problems such as security against virus attack and computer crashes.

3.4.2 Manufacturing stage

'Manufacturing operations must be carried out under controlled conditions' (ISO 9004:2000).

During all manufacturing processes (and throughout early in-service life), the product must be subjected to a variety of quality control procedures and checks in order to evaluate the degree of quality.

One of the first things that must be done is to predict the reliability of the product's design. This involves obtaining sufficient statistical data so as to be able to estimate the actual reliability of the design before a product is manufactured.

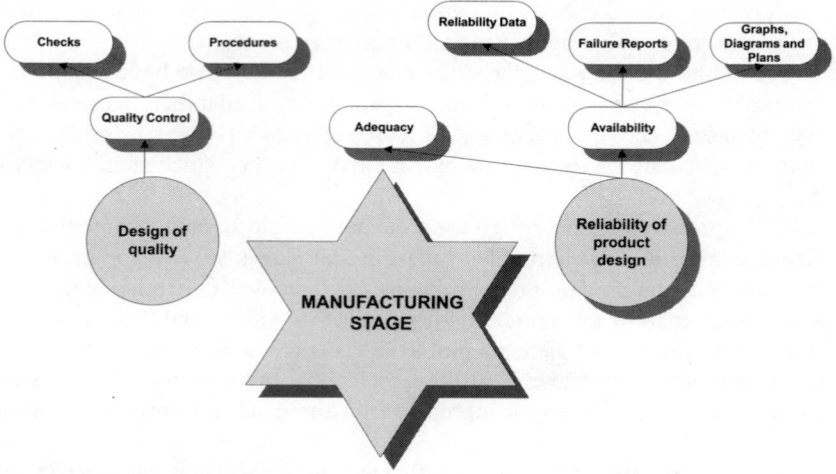

Figure 3.9 Manufacturing stage

All the appropriate engineering data has to be carefully examined, particularly the reliability ratings of recommended parts and components. The designer then extrapolates and interpolates this data and uses probability methods to examine the reliability of a proposed design.

Design deficiencies such as assembly errors, operator learning, motivational or fatigue factors, latent defects and improper part selection are frequently uncovered during this process.

3.4.3 Acceptance stage

'The Quality of a product must be proved before being accepted' (ISO 9004:2000).

During the acceptance stage, the product is subjected to a series of tests designed to confirm that the workmanship of the product fully meets the levels of quality required, or stipulated by the user and that the product performs the required function correctly. Tests will range from environmental tests of individual components to field testing complete systems.

Three mathematical expressions are commonly used to measure reliability and each of these expressions can be applied to a part, component assembly or an entire system. They are, Probability Function (PF), Failure Rate (FR) and Mean Time Between Failures (MTBF).

3.4.4 In-service stage

'Evaluation of product performance during typical operating conditions and feedback of information gained through field use improves product capability' (ISO 9004:2000)

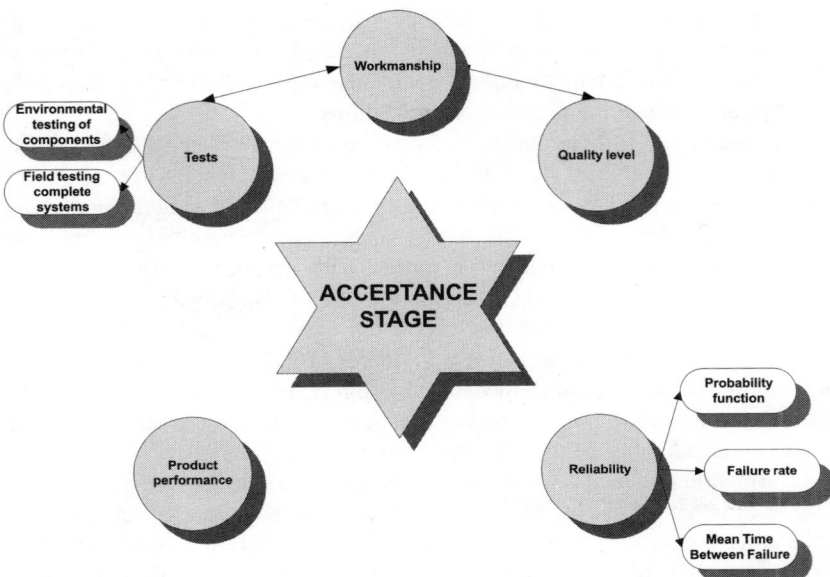

Figure 3.10 Acceptance stage

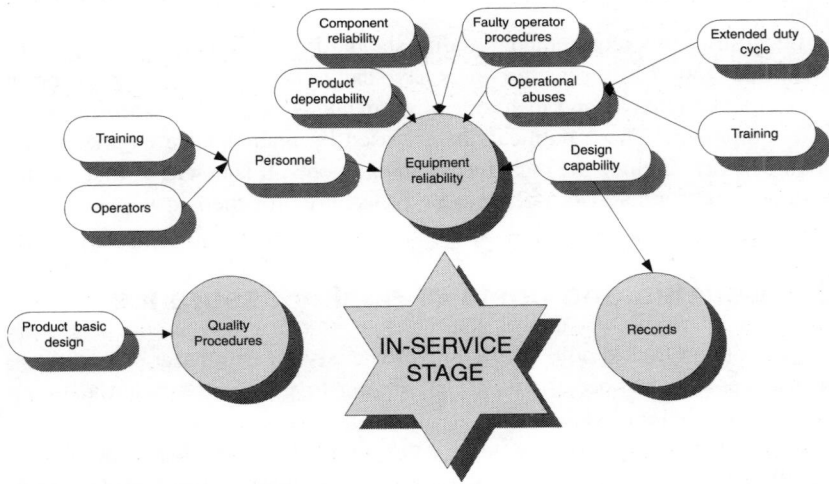

Figure 3.11 In-service stage

During the in-service stage the equipment user is, of course, principally concerned with system and equipment reliability.

Although reliability is based on the product's generic design (and can be easily proved by statistics), its practical reliability is often far less design dependent. This difference can be due to poor or faulty operating procedures, operating the system beyond its design capability or operational abuses (e.g. personal, extended duty cycles, neglected maintenance, training etc.). Each of these hazards can damage individual components and sub assemblies and each will, in turn, reduce the product's dependability.

It is interesting to note that according to studies completed by the British Institute of Management in 1998, the maintenance technician (or engineer) still remains the primary cause of reliability degradations during the in-service stage. The problems associated with poorly trained, poorly supported, or poorly motivated maintenance personnel with respect to reliability and dependability requires careful assessment and quantification.

The most important factor that affects the overall reliability of a modern product, nevertheless, is the increased number of individual components that are required in that product. Since most system failures are actually caused by the failure of a single component, the reliability of each individual component must be considerably better than the overall system reliability.

Information obtained from in-service use and field failures are enormously useful (always assuming that they are entirely accurate, of course!) in evaluating a product's performance during typical operating conditions. But the main reason for accumulating failure reports from the field is to try to improve the product. This can be achieved by analysing the reports, finding out what caused the failure and taking steps to prevent it from recurring in the future.

Because of this requirement, quality standards for the maintenance, repair and inspection of in-service products have had to be laid down in engineering standards, handbooks and local operating manuals (written for specific items and equipment). These publications are used by maintenance engineers and should always include the most recent amendments. It is **essential** that quality assurance personnel also use the same procedures for their inspections.

3.5 Benefits and costs of quality assurance

'An effective QMS should be designed to satisfy the purchaser's conditions, requirements and expectations whilst serving to protect the manufacturer's best interests' (ISO 9004: 2000).

In practice, some quality assurance programmes can be very expensive to install and operate, particularly if inadequate quality control methods were used previously. If the purchaser requires consistent quality he must pay for it, regardless of the specification or order which the manufacturer has accepted. However, against this expenditure must always be offset the savings in scrapped material, rework and general problems arising from lack of quality.

From a manufacturer's point of view there is a business requirement to obtain and maintain the desired quality at an optimum cost. The following represent some of the additional expenses that can be incurred:

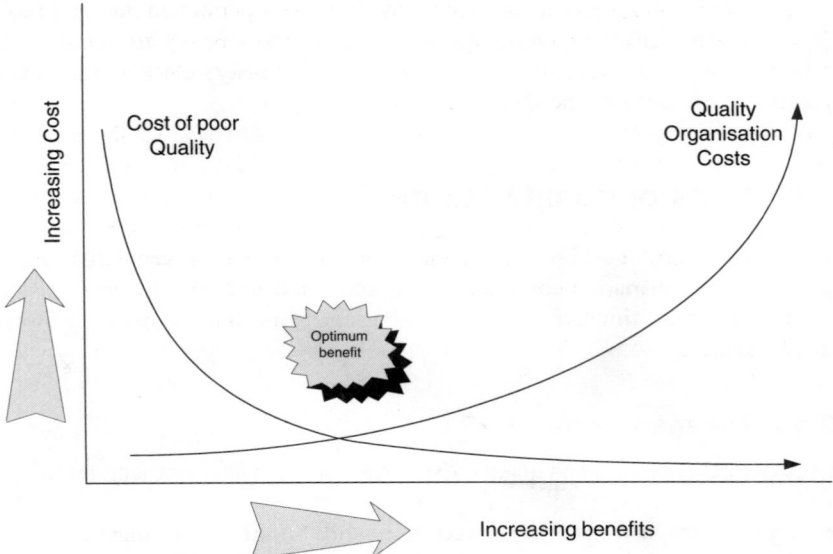

Figure 3.12 Quality Management System costs

- salaries for the quality assurance team, planners, quality supervisors, calibration/test equipment staff and Quality Managers;
- training for the quality assurance team;
- visits by the quality assurance staff to other companies, subcontractors and the eventual consumer, for evaluation and audit of their facilities and products;
- test equipment of a recognised type, standard and quality; regularly maintained and calibrated by an accredited calibration centre;
- better storage facilities.

But why bother with 'quality assurance'?! It is all very expensive to set up and extremely expensive to run – is it really worth it?!

The short answer is, '**yes**'.

In order to be part of this enormous European and world market, manufacturers, suppliers **and** sole traders must not merely be aware of the requirements and need for quality assurance, they must also be able to prove that they are capable of constantly producing a quality product that is as good as, if not better, than any others available.

Hopefully they will take pride in producing an item of equipment or system that operates correctly and which will fully satisfy the purchaser – as opposed to something that goes wrong as soon as it is switched on. There will not be many reorders for that model!

Insisting on an assurance of quality has got to save money in the long run. It ensures that manufacturing design features are more dependable and efficient, and built-in quality at every stage will obviously reduce wastage and increase customer satisfaction.

3.6 Costs of quality failure

With an effective QMS in place, the manufacturer will achieve increased profitability and market share and the purchaser can expect reduced costs, improved product fitness for role, increased satisfaction and, above all, growth in confidence.

3.6.1 The manufacturer

Lack of quality control and quality assurance can cause the manufacturer to:

- replace scrapped material or have to rework unsatisfactory material;
- re-inspect and reprocess material returned as unsatisfactory by the purchaser;
- lose money by having to send staff to the purchasers premises to sort out their complaints of unsatisfactory labour;
- lose money through a major quality failure halting production;
- lose money through field repairs, replacements and other work having to be carried out under warranty;
- lose money by having to carry out investigations into claims of unsatisfactory work;
- lose money by having to investigate alternative methods of producing an article without quality failures;
- lose their image and reputation;
- lose market potential;
- have to acknowledge complaints, claims, liabilities and be subject to waste of human and financial resources;

But most of all . . .

- lose customers!

3.6.2 The purchaser

By not insisting that the manufacturer abides by a set of recognised quality standards, the purchaser can be involved in:

- delays in being able to use the product and the possibility of the purchaser losing orders because of it;

- possible increases in their organisation, operation, maintenance downtime and repair costs;
- dissatisfaction with goods and services;
- health and safety aspects (now a mandatory requirement of ISO 9001:2000);
- lack of confidence in the manufacturer.

So far we have detailed some of the requirements and benefits of quality control and quality assurance from the point of view of the manufacturer, supplier, purchaser and the end user. Terms have been explained and specifications defined.

Having discussed the pros and cons of an efficient quality system, in Part Four we will see how by adopting a properly structured Quality Management System we can meet these requirements.

Part Four _____

Quality Management System

In Part Four, the basic requirements of a Quality Management System are discussed and the reader is shown how an organisation's Quality Management System becomes the documented proof of a firm's commitment to quality management. The reader is shown how a Quality Management System can be structured to an organisation's particular type of business and how a Quality Management System will cover such functions as customer liaison, design, purchase, subcontracting, manufacturing, training and installation.

4
Quality Management System

4.1 Quality Management System – requirements

'A Quality Management System is a management system to direct and control an organisation with regard to quality.' (ISO 9000:2000).

It is an organisational structure of responsibilities, activities, resources and events that together provide procedures and methods of implementation to ensure the capability of an organisation to meet quality requirements.

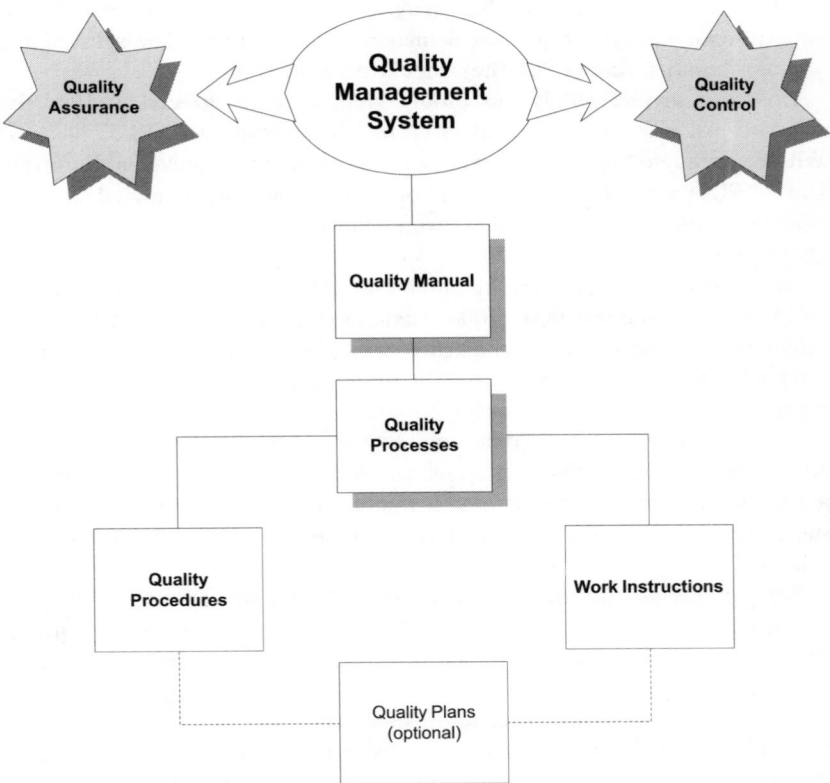

Figure 4.1 Quality Management System

Having seen in Part Three the advantages and benefits of quality control and quality assurance, what about the Quality Management System (QMS) that needs to be set up so as to adapt and instigate these procedures?

4.1.1 Basic requirements of a Quality Management System

To be successful, an organisation, large and small, must:

- be able to offer services that satisfy a customer's expectations;
- agree with the relevant standards and specifications of a contract;
- be available at competitive prices; **and**
- supply at a cost that will still bring a profit to that organisation.

They must, above all, provide a quality product that will promote further procurement and recommendations.

So how can your organisation become a quality organisation? Well, I can assure you that it is not just a case of simply claiming that you are a reliable organisation and then telling everyone that you will be able to supply a reliable product or service! Nowadays, especially in the European and American markets, purchasers are demanding proof of these claims. Proof that you are the organisation that **they** should be dealing with.

How can anyone supply this proof? Well, up until the end of 1994 the standard that was most often called up in UK contracts was BS 5750:1987. Within the Single European Market, tenders required the equivalent European Union (EU) standard EN 29000:1987 or the equivalent International standard (ISO 9000:1987). In America these were (and still are) included in the ASQC Q90 series.

Nowadays, of course, these requirements are covered under the common ISO 9001:2000 and ISO 9004:2000 standards (see Part One). These standards provided the requirements and guidelines for organisations wishing to establish their own QMS and in doing so control the quality of their organisation – from within their organisation.

You may also find that some contracts stipulate that the product 'must comply with the requirements of (such and such) a standard' (for example, for a British component manufacturer it might be BS 3934:1992 'Mechanical standardisation of semiconductor devices', or ANSI A137–1:1988 'Ceramic Tiles').

But perhaps we are moving on too fast. Before an organisation is even **qualified** to tender for a contract to produce something, they must first **prove** their organisation capability by showing that they can operate a Quality Management System.

To satisfy these requirements an organisation's QMS has to encompass all the different levels of quality control that are required during the various stages of design, manufacture and acceptance of a product and be capable of guaranteeing quality acceptance.

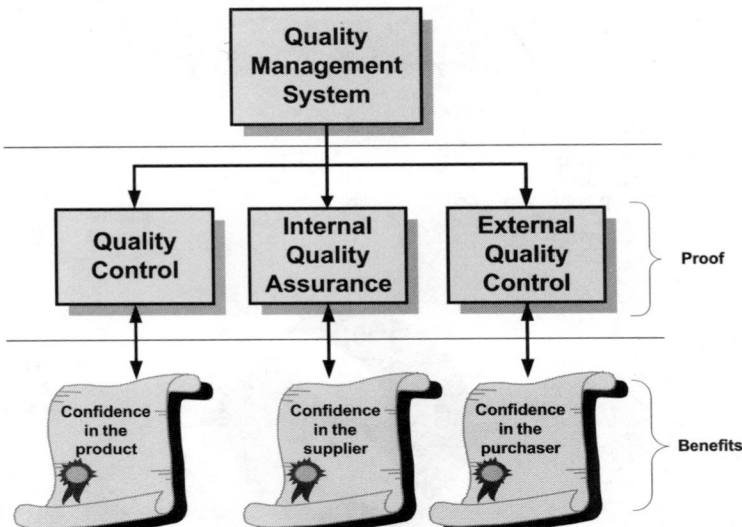

Figure 4.2 Quality Management System – organisational structure

These requirements are covered by national, European and international standards. But although these standards may vary slightly from country to country, basically they are very similar and cover the following topics:

- organisational structure;
- measurement of quality assurance;
- the contract;
- design control;
- purchasing and procurement;
- production control;
- product testing;
- handling, storage, packaging and delivery;
- after sales service.

4.2 Quality Management System principles

The first thing that ISO 9000 requires is for an organisation to set up and fully document their position with regard to quality assurance. These documents comprise the organisation QMS and describe the organisation's capability for supplying goods and services that will comply with laid down quality standards. It contains a general description of the organisation's attitude to quality assurance and specific details about the quality assurance and quality control within that organisation.

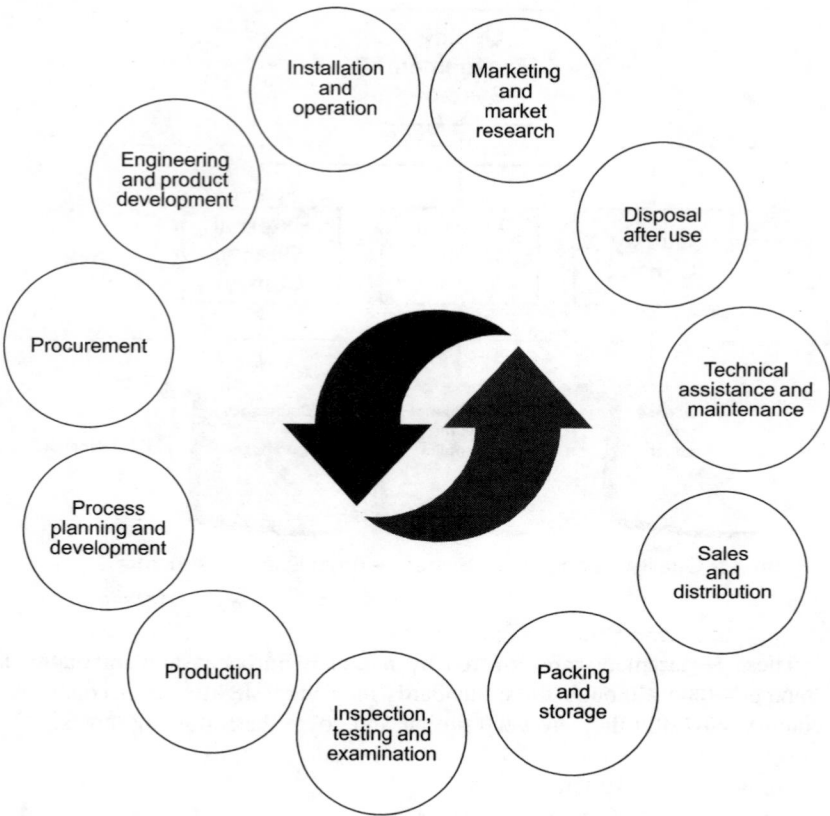

Figure 4.3 Quality loop

To be successful an organisation must be able to prove that they are capable of producing the component, product or service to the customer's complete satisfaction so that it conforms exactly to the purchaser's specific requirements and that it is always of the desired quality.

An organisation's QMS is, therefore, the organisational structure of responsibilities, procedures, processes and resources for carrying out quality management and as such must be planned and developed in order to be capable of maintaining a consistent level of quality control.

The QMS must be structured to the organisation's own particular type of business and should consider all functions such as customer liaison, designing, purchasing, subcontracting, manufacturing, training, installation, updating of quality control techniques and the accumulation of quality records. In most organisations this sort of information will normally be found in the organisation Quality Manual.

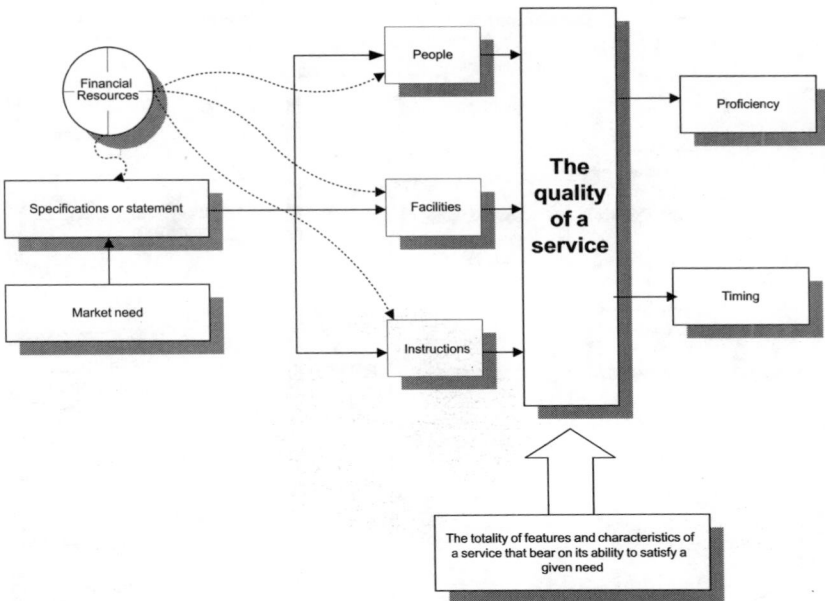

Figure 4.4 Some of the determinants and measurements of the quality of a service. (Figures 4.4 and 4.5 are extracts from BS 4778:1979 which have been reproduced with the kind permission of BSI. Although the 1979 edition has been superseded these figures are included here since they illustrate the concept.)

The type of QMS chosen will, of course, vary from organisation to organisation depending upon its size and capability. There are no set rules as to exactly how these documents should be written. However, they should – as a minimum requirement – be capable of showing the potential customer exactly how the manufacturer or supplier is equipped to achieve and maintain the highest level of quality throughout the various stages of design, production, installation and servicing.

As an example, some of the determinants and measures of the quality of a service are shown in Figure 4.4 whilst those effecting the quality of a product are shown in Figure 4.5.

4.3 Quality Management System approach

Customers require products that continually meet their needs and expectations and in order to be profitable, an organisation must be able to offer products that continually achieve customer satisfaction and satisfy their customers' requirements. As well as providing a framework for providing customer

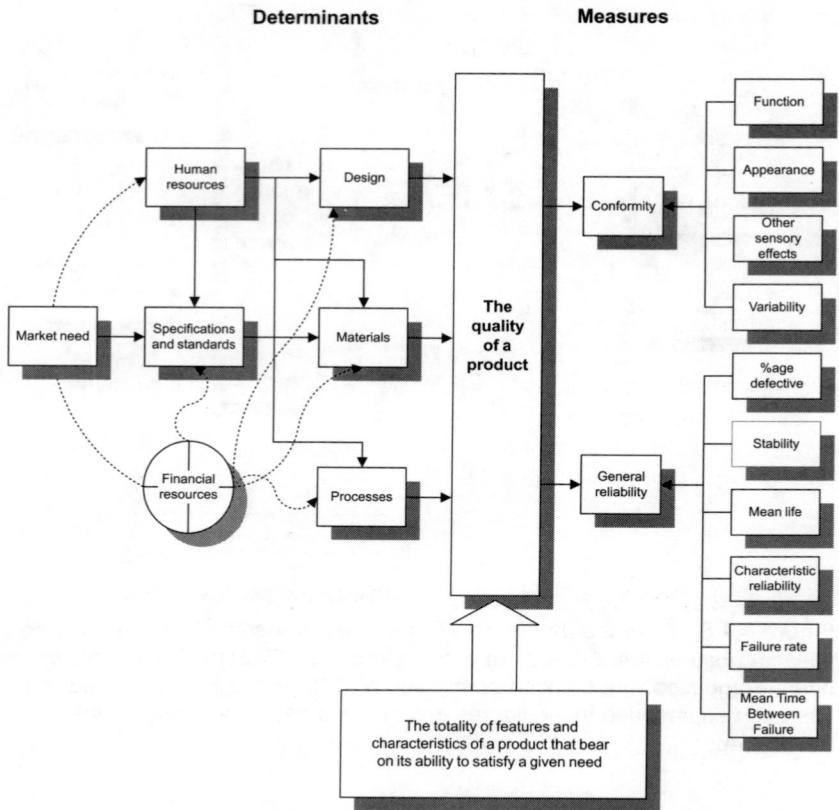

Figure 4.5 Some of the determinants and measurements of the quality of a product

satisfaction, a QMS also provides confidence (to the organisation and to its customers) that the organisation is capable of providing products that consistently fulfil requirements. This is achieved by:

- determining the needs and expectations of the customer;
- establishing the quality policy and quality objectives of the organisation;
- determining the processes and responsibilities necessary to attain the quality objectives;
- establishing measures for the effectiveness of each process towards attaining the quality objectives;
- applying the measures to determine the current effectiveness of each process;
- determining means of preventing non-conformities and eliminating their causes;

- looking for opportunities to improve the effectiveness and efficiency of processes;
- determining and prioritising those improvements which can provide optimum results;
- planning the strategies, processes and resources to deliver the identified improvements;
- implementing the plan;
- monitoring the effects of the improvements;
- assessing the results against the expected outcomes;
- reviewing the improvement activities to determine appropriate follow-up actions.

Any organisation that adopts the above approach will create confidence in the capability of its processes and the reliability of its products. It will also provide a basis for continual improvement and can lead to increased customer satisfaction.

4.4 Quality Management System reliability

For an organisation to derive any real benefit from a QMS, everyone in the organisation must:

- fully appreciate that quality assurance is absolutely essential to their future;
- know how they can assist in achieving quality;
- be stimulated and encouraged so to do.

In addition, their organisation's QMS must be fully documented and it must be capable of providing an adequate and uninterrupted control over all internal and external activities that affect the quality of a service or product. This QMS must emphasise the preventive actions that are required to avoid problems recurring and working systems will have to be developed, issued and maintained.

These regulations and requirements are usually found in the organisation's Quality Manual.

4.5 Quality Manual

This is the main policy document that establishes the QMS and how it meets the requirements of ISO 9001:2000. It provides general information on the system (i.e. objectives, goals, roles, organisation and responsibilities).

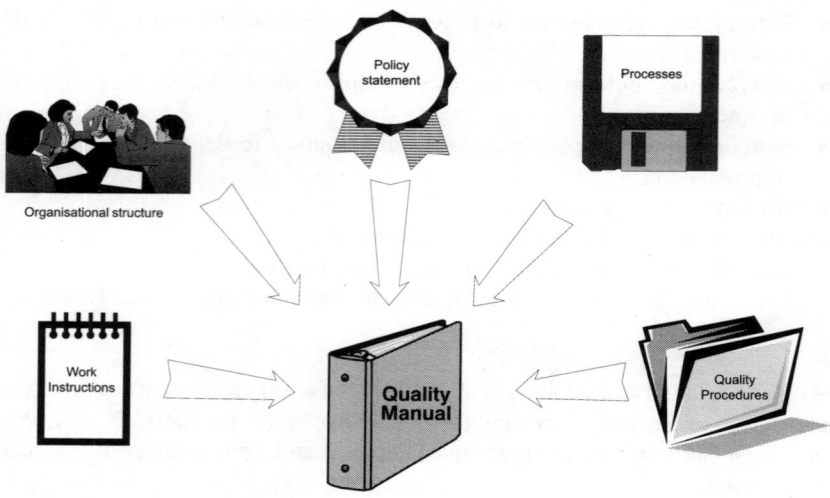

Figure 4.6 Quality Manual

The Quality Manual (see example in Part Six) is the formal record of that organisation's QMS. It:

- is a rule book by which an organisation functions;
- is a source of information from which the client may derive confidence;
- provides consistent information, both internally and externally, about the organisation's QMS;
- is a means of defining the responsibilities and inter-related activities of every member of the organisation;
- is a vehicle for auditing, reviewing and evaluating the organisation's QMS.

To be effective, the Quality Manual:

- the Quality Manual will have to include a firm statement of the organisation's policy towards quality control;
- must contain details of their quality assurance section, its structure and organisation, together with a description of their responsibilities;
- must indicate quality assurance training programmes etc.

The Quality Manual will describe how the organisation:

- documents and records inspections;
- how their goods inwards facility operates;
- how they monitor quality.

The Quality Manual will identify the organisation's business-critical processes and their associated Quality Procedures (QPs) and Work Instructions (WIs). The Quality Manual will also provide examples of the various forms and documentation used by the manufacturer – such as production control forms, inspection sheets and documents used to purchase components from subcontractors.

For a complete description and guidance on how to develop a Quality Manual, the reader is referred to ISO 10013 – Guidelines for developing Quality Manuals.

4.6 Processes

Processes describe the activities required to implement the QMS and to meet the policy requirements made in the Quality Manual. Core Business Processes describe the end-to-end activities involved in project management and are supplemented by a number of supporting processes.

4.7 Quality Procedures

QPs are formal documents that describe the method by which the Core Business and supporting processes are managed. They describe how the policy objectives of the Quality Manual can be met in practice and how these processes are controlled. They contain the basic documentation used for planning and controlling all activities that impact on quality.

4.8 Work Instructions

WIs describe in detail how individual tasks and activities are to be carried out, e.g. what is to be done, by whom and when it has to be completed.

4.9 Quality Plan

When complex assemblies or multi-part contracts are required, separate instructions may have to be included in the Quality Manual in order to cover individual parts of the contract. These types of instructions are called Quality Plans.

The accepted definition (as provided in ISO 9000:2000) of a Quality Plan is that it is '. . . a document specifying which procedures and associated resources shall be applied, by whom and when to a specific project, product, process or contract'. In setting out the specific quality practices, resources and sequence of activities a Quality Plan, therefore, ensures that specific

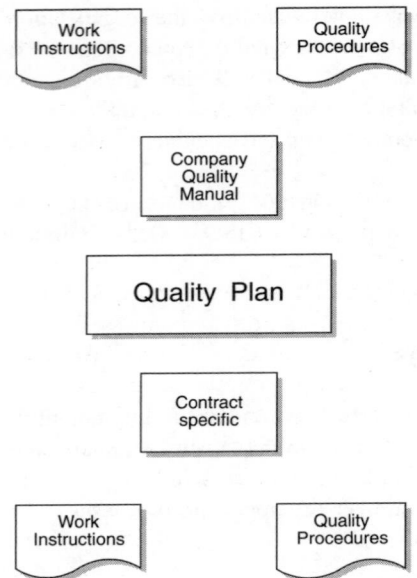

Figure 4.7 Quality Plan

requirements for quality are appropriately planned and addressed. It should state its purpose, to what it applies its quality objectives (in measurable terms), specific exclusions and, of course, its period of validity.

Quality Plans describe how the QMS is applied to a specific product or contract. They may be used to demonstrate how the quality requirements of a particular contract will be met, and to monitor and assess adherence to those requirements. While a Quality Plan usually refers to the appropriate parts of the Quality Manual, it can be used in conjunction with a QMS or as a stand-alone document.

Quality Plans provide a collated summary of the requirements for a specific activity. They include less information than the organisation's QMS but, with all the detail brought together, the requirement for performance should be more readily understandable and the risk of non-conformance and mis-interpretation of intentions should be reduced.

Quality assurance for the manufacture of complex assemblies can be very difficult to stipulate in a contract especially if the most important inspections have to be left until the assembly is almost complete – and by which time many of the sub assemblies and components will have become almost inaccessible! In these cases it is essential for the organisation's Quality Manager to develop and produce a Quality Plan that details all the important information that has to be provided to the shop floor management.

The Quality Plan will cover all of the quality practices and resources that are going to be used, the sequence of events relevant to that product, the specific allocation of responsibilities, methods, QPs and WIs, together with the details of the testing, inspection, examination and audit programme stages.

The Quality Plan should, nevertheless, be flexible and written in such a way that it is possible to modify its content to reflect changing circumstances.

At all work places, QPs and WIs must be readily available. These will include the specifications that must be obeyed, particulars of the drawings, documentation, tools and gauges that are going to be used, the sampling method, the tests which have to be made, the test specifications and procedures, the acceptance/rejection criteria – and so on.

The main requirement of a Quality Plan, however, is to provide the customer (and the workforce) with clear, concise instructions and guidance as well as the appropriate inspection methods and procedures; the results of inspections (including rejections) and details of any concessions issued for rework or repair. All these must be clearly recorded and available for a purchaser's future (possible) examination.

A well thought out Quality Plan will divide the project, service, product or assembly work into stages, show what type of inspection has to be completed at the beginning, during, or end of each stage and indicate how these details should be recorded on the final document. The Quality Plan should be planned and developed in conjunction with design, development, manufacturing, subcontract and installation work and ensure that all functions have been fully catered for.

One of the main objectives of quality planning is to identify any special or unusual requirements, processes, techniques including those requirements that are unusual by reason of newness, unfamiliarity, lack of experience and/or absence of precedents. As ISO 9004:2000 points out, if the contract specifies that Quality Plans are required, then these Quality Plans should fully cover the following areas and ensure that:

- design, contract, development, manufacturing and installation activities are well documented and adequate;
- all controls, processes, inspection equipment, fixtures, tooling, manpower resources and skills that an organisation must have to achieve the required quality, have been identified, recorded and the necessary action taken to obtain any additional components, documentation etc. that is required;
- quality control, inspection and testing techniques (including the development of new instrumentation) have been updated;
- any new measurement technique (or any measurement involving a measurement capability that exceeds the known state of the art) that is required to inspect the product, has been identified and action taken to develop that capability;
- standards of acceptability for all features and requirements (including those which contain a subjective element) have been clearly recorded;

- compatibility of design, manufacturing process, installation, inspection procedures and applicable documentation have been assured well before production begins;
- as each special requirement is identified, the means for testing and being able to prove successfully that the product or service is capable of successfully complying with the requirements has to be considered.

The integration of special or unusual requirements into the QMS must be carefully investigated, planned and documented.

As a Quality Plan is effectively a sub set of the actual Quality Manual. The layout of the Quality Plan is very similar to that of the Quality Manual and refers (other than system-specific QPs and WIs) normally to the QPs and Work Instructions contained in that Quality Manual.

The following briefly describes how each of the ISO 9000 elements is covered in a Quality Plan.

4.9.1 Management responsibility

The Quality Plan should show who is responsible for:

- ensuring activities are planned, implemented, controlled and monitored;
- communicating requirements and resolving problems;
- reviewing audit results;
- authorising exemption requests;
- implementing corrective action requests.

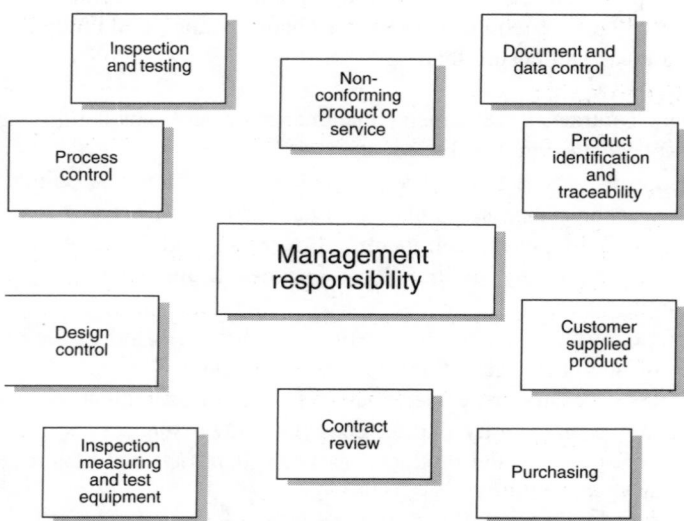

Figure 4.8 Management responsibility

Where the necessary documentation already exists under the present QMS, the Quality Plan need only refer to a specific situation or specification.

4.9.2 Contract review

Contract review should cover:

- when, how and by whom the review is made;
- how the results are to be documented;
- how conflicting instructions or ambiguities are resolved.

4.9.3 Design control

Design control should indicate:

- when, how and by whom the design process, validation and verification of the design output is carried out, controlled and documented;
- any customer involvement;
- applicable codes of practice, standards, specifications and regulatory requirements.

4.9.4 Document and data control

Document and data control should refer to:

- what is provided and how it is controlled;
- how related documents will be identified;
- how and by whom access to the documents can be obtained;
- how and by whom the original documents are reviewed and approved.

4.9.5 Purchasing

Under the heading of purchasing the following should be indicated:

- the important products to be purchased;
- the source and requirements relating to them;
- the method, evaluation, selection and control of subcontractors;
- the need for a subcontractor's Quality Plan in order to satisfy the regulatory requirements applicable to purchase products/services.

4.9.6 Customer supplied product

Customer supplied products should refer to:

- how they are identified and controlled;
- how they are verified as meeting specified requirements;
- how non-conformance is dealt with.

4.9.7 Product identification and traceability

If traceability is a requirement then the plan should:

- define its scope and extent (including how services/products are identified);
- indicate how contractual and regulatory authority traceability requirements are identified and incorporated into working documents;
- indicate how records are to be generated, controlled and distributed.

4.9.8 Process control

Process control may include:

- the procedures/instructions;
- process steps;
- methods to monitor and control processes;
- service/product characteristics.

The plan could also include details of:

- reference criteria for workmanship;
- special and qualified processes;
- tools, techniques and methods to be used.

4.9.9 Inspection and testing

Inspection and testing should indicate:

- any inspection and test plan;
- how the subcontractors' product shall be verified;
- the location of inspection and test points;
- procedures and acceptance criteria;
- witness verification points (customers as well as regulatory);
- where, when and how the customer requires third parties to perform:
  - type tests;
  - witness testing;
  - service/product verification;
  - material, service/product, process or personnel certification.

4.9.10 Inspection, measuring and test equipment

Inspection, measuring and test equipment should:

- refer to the identity of the equipment;
- refer to the method of calibration;

- indicate and record calibration status and usage of the equipment;
- indicate specific requirements for the identification of inspection and test status.

4.9.11 Non-conforming service/product

Under the heading of non-conforming service/product, an indication should be given:

- of how such a service/product is identified and segregated;
- the degree or type of rework allowed;
- the circumstances under which the supplier can request concessions.

Details should also be provided with respect to:

- corrective and preventive action;
- handling, storage, packaging, preservation and delivery.

4.9.12 Other considerations

Quality Plans should:

- indicate key quality records (i.e. what they are, how long they should be kept, where and by whom);
- suggest how legal or regulatory requirements are to be satisfied;
- specify the form in which records should be kept (e.g. paper, microfilm or disc);
- define liability, storage, retrievability, disposition and confidentiality requirements;
- include the nature and extent of quality audits to be undertaken;
- indicate how the audit results are to be used to correct and prevent recurrence of deficiencies;
- show how the training of staff in new or revised operating methods is to be completed.

Where servicing is a specified requirement, suppliers should state their intentions to assure conformance to applicable servicing requirements, such as:

- regulatory and legislative requirements;
- industry codes and practices;
- service level agreements;
- training of customer personnel;
- availability of initial and ongoing support during the agreed time-period;
- statistical techniques, where relevant.

Note: For further information I would recommend looking at ISO 10005:1995 which provides the reader with guidance on how to produce Quality Plans as well as including helpful suggestions on how to maintain an organisation's quality activities.

4.10 Quality records

Quality records provide objective evidence of activities performed or results achieved.

Records of QMS inspections and tests concerning the design, testing, survey, audit and review of a product or service are the evidence that a supplier is capable of and is indeed meeting the quality requirements of the customer.

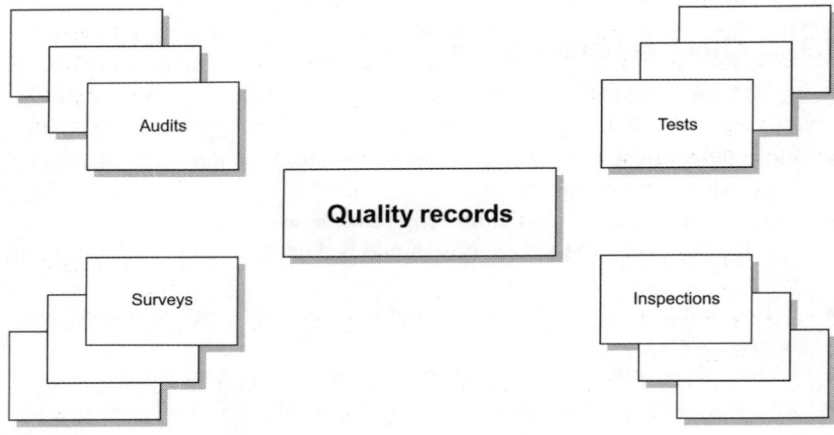

Figure 4.9 Quality records

Records such as QMS audit reports, calibration of test and measuring equipment, inspections, tests, approvals, concessions, etc., ensure that an organisation is capable of proving the effectiveness of their QMS.

Records, therefore, are important parts of quality management and the QMS will have to identify exactly what type of record is to be made, at what stage of the production process they should be made and who should make them etc. To be of any real value it is essential that these records are covered by clear, concise instructions and procedures. Above all, the storage of records should be systematic and capable of being easily and quickly accessed.

Having agreed and decided on the necessity for records, the next step is to:

- establish methods for making changes, modifications, revisions and additions to these records;
- establish methods for accounting for the documents;
- show their retention time;
- lay down methods for the disposal of those that are superseded or become out of date;
- show how they should be stored.

These procedures would be written up as QPs and will normally form part of the Quality Manual. WIs should also be available to show how important it is to keep records of defects, diagnosis of their causes and details of the corrective action that was carried out together with the success or failure of this corrective action.

If this information is stored in a computer, then it is essential that the integrity of that system **must** also be satisfactorily assured.

The retention of records is an aspect that is far too often overlooked by organisations. Records are very important, not only from an historical point of view, but also as a means to settling disputes about bad workmanship, identifying faults and settling production problems whether this be internally, by the supplier, or externally, by the organisation.

In Part Four of this book we have addressed the basic requirements for a structured Quality Management System and shown how ISO 9000 can be structured to suit a particular business or profession.

In Part Five, quality control techniques, the organisational structure and the duties of quality assurance personnel plus their resources are discussed.

Part Five

Quality Organisational Structure

Having seen the basic requirements for a Quality Management System, Part Five will cover quality control techniques, organisational structure and duties of quality staff.

Then in Part Six a complete example of a Quality Manual is provided which can be easily customised to suit any organisation's business.

5
Quality organisational structure

5.1 Management

The main requirement of the organisation's management is that they establish, define and document their organisation's policy, objectives and commitments to quality. This documented system is then presented as a Quality Manual, quality programme, or as a controlled documented system.

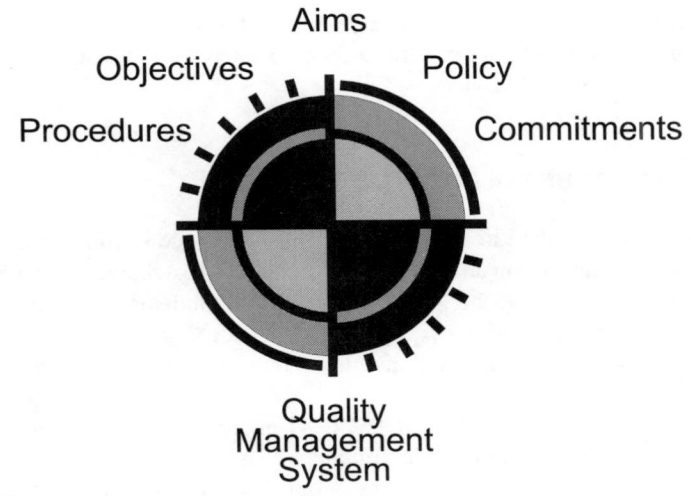

Figure 5.1 Quality organisational requirements

Whatever system is chosen, the document must include details of the organisation's Quality Management System (QMS) and the aims, policies, organisation and procedures that are essential to demonstrate that they agree with the requirements of ISO 9001:2000.

Suppliers having difficulty in establishing their own particular level of managerial responsibility with regard to organisation quality assurance should obtain a copies of BS 6143:1992 'Guide to the economics of quality' Parts 1 and 2. These standards are available from the BSI and are a user-friendly guide to:

- the costs for continuous improvement and Total Quality Management (TQM) (Part 1);
- the costs of defect prevention and a study of the various activities and losses due to internal or external failures (Part 2).

Having established their overall position, the management will then have to:

- develop, control, co-ordinate, supervise and monitor their corporate quality policy and ensure that this policy is understood and maintained throughout the organisation;
- ensure that the organisation's QMS always meets the requirements of the national, European or international standard that that particular organisation has chosen to work to and where this fails to happen, see that corrective actions are carried out;
- define objectives such as fitness for use;
- ensure that the performance, safety and reliability of a product or service is correct and make sure that the costs associated with these objectives are kept to a reasonable figure.

5.2 Quality assurance personnel

As previously described in Part Three, quality assurance is concerned with a consistency of quality and an agreed level of quality. To achieve these aims the organisation must be firmly committed to the fundamental principle of consistently supplying the right quality product. Equally, a purchaser must be committed to the fundamental principle of only accepting the right quality product.

Thus, a commitment within all levels of an organisation (manufacturer, supplier or purchaser), to the basic principles of quality assurance and quality control is required. It is, therefore, essential that a completely separate and independent division is formed to deal solely with quality matters. The organisation and duties of this section would usually look something like that shown in Figure 5.2.

5.2.1 Quality Manager

The first requirement is for the organisation to nominate an individual who will be solely responsible to top management for the implementation and maintenance of the QMS. This person is called the 'Quality Manager'.

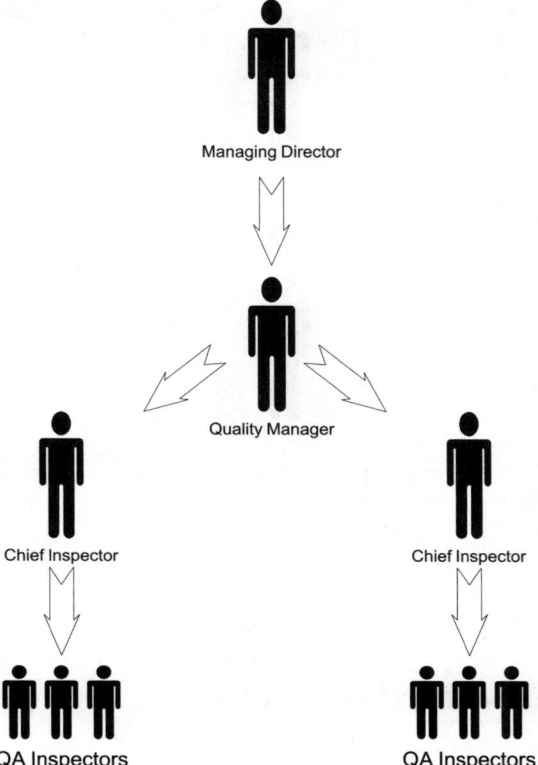

Figure 5.2 Quality assurance – typical organisation structure

The Quality Manager will answer directly to the Managing Director and will be responsible for all matters regarding the quality of the end product together with the activities of **all** sections within the organisation's premises.

In small organisations this requirement might even be part of the General Manager's duties, but regardless of who it may be, it is essential that this person must be someone who is completely independent of any manufacturing or user function and has a thorough working knowledge of the requirements and recommendations of ISO 9000.

In addition, owing to the importance of quality assurance, it is essential that the Quality Manager is fully qualified (both technically and administratively) and can quickly exert (show) his position and authority.

As can be seen from Figure 5.3, the Quality Manager's job is usually a very busy one (even in a small organisation!) and the Quality Manager's responsibilities are spread over a wide area which covers all of the organisation's operations.

Figure 5.3 Responsibilities of the Quality Manager

5.2.1.1 General functional description

The Quality Manager is responsible for ensuring that the organisation's QMS is defined, implemented, audited and monitored in order to ensure that the organisation's deliverables comply with both the customer's quality and safety standards together with the requirements of ISO 9001:2000.

5.2.1.2 Tasks

The Quality Manager reports directly to the General Manager and his tasks will include:

- ensuring the consistency of the organisation QMS;
- ensuring compliance of the organisation QMS with ISO 9001:2000;
- maintenance and effectiveness of the organisation QMS;
- ensuring that the quality message is transmitted to and understood by everyone.

5.2.1.3 Responsibilities

The Quality Manager is responsible for:

- ensuring that the Quality Manual and individual Quality Plans are kept up to date;
- assisting and advising with the preparation of organisation procedures;
- producing, reviewing and updating the organisation's QMS;
- ensuring compliance with the organisation's QMS by means of frequent audits;
- maintaining organisation quality records;
- producing, auditing and maintaining division, section and project Quality Plans;
- identifying potential/current problem areas within the organisation's life cycle through analysis of organisation error reports;
- holding regular division quality audits.

5.2.1.4 Co-ordination

The Quality Manager shall:

- act as the focal point for all organisation quality matters within the organisation;
- co-ordinate and verify that all internal procedures and instructions are in accordance with the recommendations of ISO 9001:2000;
- operate the QMS as described in the Quality Manual and ensure that its regulations are observed.

Above all the Quality Manager must always ensure that the customer's interests are protected. Even if this means, at times, that he and his division become very unpopular with the rest of the organisation and sometimes they even have to assume the mantel of organisation 'scapegoat'!

5.2.2 Chief Quality Assurance Inspector

There may be more than one Chief Quality Assurance Inspector (QAI) in an organisation depending upon its size and activities.

The duties of the Chief QAI are to:

- plan, co-ordinate and supervise all pre-shop, in-process, and out-going inspections within their area of responsibility;
- ensure that the product or service is in agreement with the customers' requirements and conform to the established quality standards and specifications;

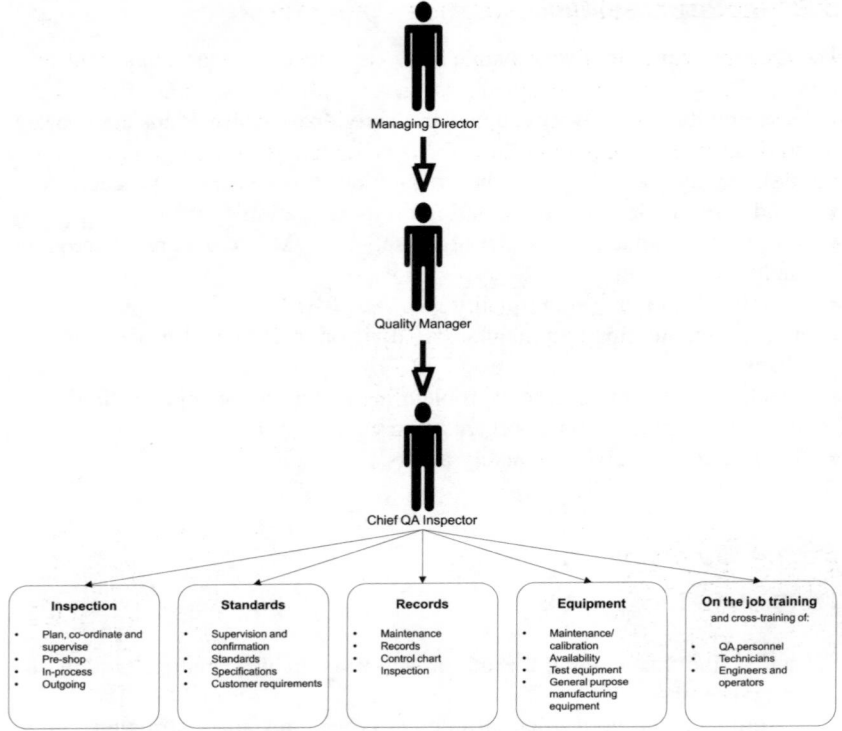

Figure 5.4 Responsibilities of the Chief Quality Assurance Inspector

- be responsible for scheduling and controlling inspections, designating inspection stations, setting up local inspection procedures and statistical inspection controls;
- oversee the maintenance of inspection records, control charts and the preparation of inspection reports;
- ensure that all test equipment is maintained, properly calibrated and readily available at all inspection stations;
- be responsible for reviewing the maintenance of quality inspection stations;
- co-ordinate on-the-job and cross training within sections;
- establish and maintain inspection systems and controls to determine the acceptability of a completed product;
- be responsible for detecting deficiencies during manufacture, initiate corrective actions where applicable and prevent defects;
- compile quality and feedback data, quality history and statistical results to help quality control development, refinement and management;
- advise management and key maintenance personnel on all aspects concerning quality trends.

5.2.3 Section Quality Assurance Inspectors

Two assurers are normally nominated for each section, a principal and an alternate. The principal is always the assurer, the alternate assumes the duties when asked to do so by the principal and during the absence of the principal. When not engaged on QA duties, the QAIs are employed on normal everyday activities.

Figure 5.5 Responsibilities of the Section Quality Assurance Inspectors

The task of the Section QAI is to:

- review (and make recommendations) to the Chief QAI on all things concerning engineering change proposals, waivers, deviations and substitution of parts, materials, equipment and processes;
- compile quality feedback data and quality history sheets;
- supply technical data and assistance to the design office.

5.2.4 Quality assurance personnel

Quality assurance personnel are members of the organisation judged competent to carry out quality assurance duties. They are nominated by the Quality Manager in consultation with the QAIs and are directly responsible to the Quality Manager when engaged in QA work.

Quality assurance personnel are:

- not to allow their own judgement to be influenced by others;
- not to allow equipment to leave the premises below the desired standard;
- to ensure – by close liaison with Section Heads – that a section's work is not unreasonably delayed because of quality assurance;
- to ensure that when a job (system, module or equipment etc.) fails their inspection that the respective Section QAI is informed and that the Section Head (and engineer responsible) are made fully aware of the reasons for the failure;
- to advise the Section QAI of any problems associated with quality assurance, particularly anything that is likely to effect production or harmony between any of the sections and the quality assurance division.

5.2.5 Quality assurance resources

It is not enough for management to supply just the personnel for a quality assurance section. Resources, appropriate for the implementation of the quality policies, must also be available.

These shall include:

- management budget;
- design and development equipment;
- manufacturing equipment;
- inspection, test and examination equipment;
- instrumentation and computer software.

Parts One to Five have provided complete details of the background and requirements of ISO 9001:2000. Having understood this material, it is now time to move on to the next stage – to design your own Quality Management System!

Part Six contains a complete example of a Quality Management System which can be used as a template to design your own Quality Management System.

Part Six ——————————

Example Quality Manual

In Part Six of the book I have provided an example of a complete Quality Management System consisting of a Quality Manual and associated Quality Processes, Quality Procedures and Work Instructions.

A copy of this Quality Management System is available (by email) at no extra cost from the author, in Rich Text format or Word 95-2000 format. He can be contacted at stingray@herne.demon.co.uk to enable organisations to quickly produce their own customised versions of this manual.

Herne European Consultancy Ltd

Quality Management System

Part 1 - Quality Manual

This Quality Manual has been issued on the authority of the Managing Director of Herne European Consultancy Ltd for the use of all staff, subcontractors, clients or regulatory bodies to whom Herne European Consultancy Ltd may be required to provide such information to.

Managing Director
Herne European Consultancy Ltd

File No:	**H-QMS-029RLT00**
Version No:	**00.05**
Date:	**31.12.00**

Document Control Sheet

Title	This version	Date
Herne European Consultancy Ltd - Part 1 - Quality Manual	00.05	31.12.00
	File Number	No of Pages
	H-QMS-029RLT00	63

Abstract

The Herne European Consultancy Ltd Quality Management System is divided into four parts. This Quality Manual is Part 1 and describes the policies adopted by Herne European Consultancy Ltd. It defines:

- the overall Quality Management System adopted by Herne European Consultancy Ltd;
- the organisation that has been developed to implement that Quality Management System;
- the associated documentation (e.g. Quality Processes, Quality Procedures and Work Instructions) that have been designed to enable Herne European Consultancy Ltd to carry out the Quality Management System.

The Quality Processes designed to meet these policies are contained in Part 2 and the details of the Quality Procedures and Work Instructions are in Parts 3 and 4.

Name	Function	Level
	Quality Manager	Prepare
	Managing Director	Agree
	Managing Director	Approve

Keywords

Core Business Process, ISO 9001:2000, Policy, Quality, Quality Management System, Quality Manager, Quality Manual, Quality Procedure, Supporting Process, Work Instruction.

Approved

_____ Date:_____

(Managing Director)

Amendments

Changes in the organisation of Herne European Consultancy Ltd or the environment in which it operates, may necessitate modifications, amendments, insertions and/or deletions to the overall quality management adopted by Herne European Consultancy Ltd and its associated documentation (e.g. Quality Procedures and Work Instructions). The contents of this Quality Manual may, therefore, be altered on an as required basis. All changes shall be subject to QP/8 - Change Control. Changes shall be deemed operational following approval by the authorised person/persons and published as updated sections of the Quality Manual.

No	Chapter	Amendment details	Date
01.00	All	First issue	28.06.93
02.00	3	Complete restructure	05.04.94
03.00	Annex B	New annex	21.09.95
03.01	4.3	Revised and reworded	23.12.95
04.00	All	Editorial revisions of all sections and annexes	30.07.96
05.00	All	Revised to conform to ISO 9001:2000	31.12.00

Distribution List

1. Managing Director
2. Quality Manager
3. Company Secretary
4. Section Manager - Quality Management Systems
5. Section Manager - Environmental
6. Section Manager - Fuels
7. Section Manager - Projects
8. Spare

Contents

5.4 Planning (ISO 9001:2000-5.4)
5.4.1 Quality objectives (ISO 9001:2000-5.4.1)
5.4.2 Quality management system planning (ISO 9001:2000-5.4.2)

5.5 Responsibility, authority and communication (ISO 9001:2000-5.5)
5.5.1 Responsibility and authority (ISO 9001:2000-5.5.1)
5.5.2 Management representative (ISO 9001:2000-5.5.2)
5.5.3 Internal communication (ISO 9001:2000-5.5.3)

5.6 Management review (ISO 9001:2000-5.6)
5.6.1 General (ISO 9001:2000-5.6.1)
5.6.2 Review input (ISO 9001:2000-5.6.2)
5.6.3 Review output (ISO 9001:2000-5.6.3)

6 Resource management (ISO 9001:2000-6)
6.1 Provision of resources (ISO 9001:2000-6.1)
6.2 Human resources (ISO 9001:2000-6.2)
6.2.1 General (ISO 9001:2000-6.2.1)
6.2.2 Competence, awareness and training (ISO 9001:2000-6.2.2)
6.3 Infrastructure (ISO 9001:2000-6.3)
6.4 Work environment (ISO 9001:2000-6.4)

7 Product realisation (ISO 9001:2000-7)
7.1 Planning of product realisation (ISO 9000:2000-7.1)
7.2 Customer-related processes (ISO 9000:2000-7.2)
7.2.1 Determination of requirements related to the product (ISO 9001:2000-7.2.1)
7.2.2 Review of requirements related to the product (ISO 9000:2000-7.2.2)
7.2.3 Customer communication (ISO 9000:2000-7.2.2)
7.3 Design and development (ISO 9000:2000-7.3)
7.3.1 Design and development planning (ISO 9001:2000-7.3.1)
7.3.2 Design and development inputs (ISO 9001:2000-7.3.2)
7.3.3 Design and development outputs (ISO 9001:2000-7.3.3)
7.3.4 Design and development review (ISO 9001:2000-7.3.4)
7.3.5 Design and development verification (ISO 9001:2000-7.3.5)
7.3.6 Design and development validation (ISO 9001:2000-7.3.6)
7.3.7 Control of design and development changes (ISO 9001:2000-7.3.7)
7.4 Purchasing (ISO 9001:2000-7.4)
7.4.1 Purchasing process (ISO 9001:2000-7.4.1)
7.4.2 Purchasing information (ISO 9001:2000-7.4.2)
7.4.3 Verification of purchased product (ISO 9001:2000-7.4.3)

Abbreviations and acronyms

Abbreviation	Definition
CP	Core Business Process
DCS	Document Control Sheet
HEC	Herne European Consultancy Ltd
HSE	Health & Safety Executive (UK)
ISO	International Standards Organisation
IT	Information Technology
QM	Quality Manual
QMS	Quality Management System
QP	Quality Procedure
SP	Supporting Process
SQP	Section Quality Plan
TQM	Total Quality Management
WI	Work Instruction

References

Ref.	Abbreviation	Title	Issue date
1.	ISO 9001	Quality Management Systems - Requirements	2000
2.	3042940	Herne European Consultancy Ltd's Memorandum and Articles of Association	1994
3.	ACP 8	Directions for the organisation and direction of work	1995
4.	ACP 9	Documentation manual (draft) for the Aircraft Industry	1995

Herne European Consultancy Ltd - Quality Policy

Within Herne European Consultancy Ltd we are committed to provide products and services which meet the customers' specified contractual and project requirements. We are totally committed to setting and achieving quality standards that are capable of meeting, in **all** respects, the specified requirements and reasonable expectations of our customers.

Herne European Consultancy Ltd shall develop and maintain a Quality Management System that conforms to the requirements of ISO 9001:2000 so that we can provide and maintain a consistently high quality in all work we undertake. Our Quality Management System shall ensure that proper communication, work control and accountable records are generated for all work undertaken.

All members of Herne European Consultancy Ltd staff are charged with promoting these aims and are required to familiarise themselves with the contents of this Quality Manual which defines the Quality Management System that has been established and adopted as the means for achieving these declared objectives. Everyone connected with Herne European Consultancy Ltd shall be supported according to their individual needs for personal development, training and facilities.

The Quality Manager based at the Herne European Consultancy Ltd main office is my appointed management representative responsible for monitoring and ensuring the correct and effective implementation of Herne European Consultancy Ltd Quality Management System as a whole.

Total Quality Management **shall** be applied to every aspect of our activity and quality **shall** be the responsibility of everyone, in every activity, throughout Herne European Consultancy Ltd.

Managing Director
Herne European Consultancy Ltd

1 Introduction

1.1 Background

Herne European Consultancy Ltd (HEC) specialises in Quality Management Systems that meet the requirements, recommendations and the specifications contained in the year 2000 ISO 9001 standard.

HEC provides advice and guidance on all quality matters. We can produce either complete Quality Management Systems, Quality Manuals, Quality Processes, Quality Procedures, Work Instructions or technical books to suit individual customer requirements.

Nothing is considered too small. Indeed HEC have become renowned for assisting the smaller company (who rarely possess a quality infrastructure) in establishing their own Quality Management System in accordance with ISO 9001:2000 and working towards becoming an ISO 9001:2000 certified company.

HEC's aim is to produce everything that you want in support of your company's Quality Management System. Specifically we believe in developing a good relationship with every client at every level.

We take pride in being reliable and friendly in day-to-day dealings with the client and many long relationships have developed over the years.

At HEC, we believe that it is important to develop a good working relationship with the client. Only in this way can we consider, discuss and develop the customer's requirements as opposed to setting a whole raft of restrictive practices.

HEC also provides qualified advice on environmental requirements (particularly those for the electronics industry) and are experts in fuel conservation, management and safety issues.

1.2 Costs

Each contract budget is carefully prepared to suit the circumstances. The type and style of the contract is carefully analysed and accurate costings programmed accordingly. A financial breakdown is always provided and it is only by mutual consent that any deviation is allowed from the agreed budget.

We believe in being honest. If from our experience and knowledge it is felt that a source of action is inappropriate, we will tell the client. We will not just take the money and settle for a sub standard result. From the first brief to the final event, production, or programme every contract is overseen and carefully controlled through the many production stages.

1.3 Scope

This Quality Manual defines:

- the overall quality policy adopted by HEC;
- the organisation that has been developed to implement this quality policy;
- the documentation (i.e. Quality Processes, Quality Procedures and Work Instructions) that has been designed to enable HEC to carry out that policy.

Other than the permissible exclusions shown in the relevant parts of the text, HEC's Quality Manual conforms to the requirements of ISO 9001:2000 (Ref. 1). It takes into consideration the requirements of HEC's Memorandum and Articles of Association (Ref. 2), together with all other applicable national, European and international standards and procedures - e.g. ACP8 and ACP9 (Refs. 3 & 4) written for the aircraft industry. If there are any discrepancies between the HEC Quality Manual and these other directives/ standards, the requirements of the HEC Quality Manual shall prevail.

Changes in HEC organisation or the environment in which HEC organisation is operating, may necessitate modifications, amendments, insertions and deletions to HEC Quality Procedures and associated responsibilities. The contents of this Quality Manual may, therefore, be altered on an as required basis. Changes shall be deemed operational following approval by the authorised person/persons and published as updated sections of the Quality Manual.

Certain technical terms and usage in this Quality Manual, although only reflecting the masculine gender, are, in fact, the parlance of the field and should be interpreted to apply equally to both sexes.

1.4 Herne European Consultancy Ltd - organisational chart

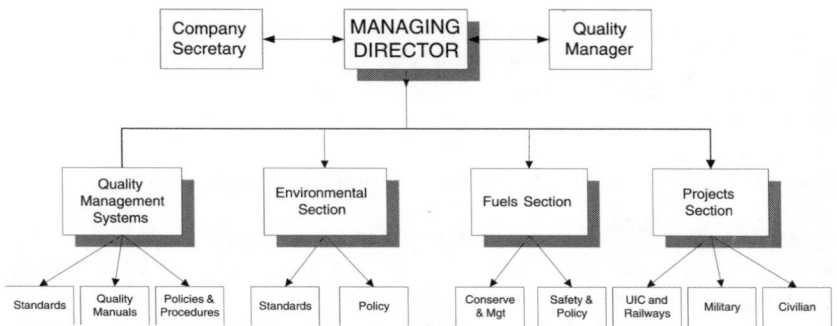

Figure 1 Herne European Consultancy Ltd – organisational chart

1.5 Quality policy and objectives

1.5.1 Policy

HEC shall define and manage the processes necessary to ensure that all project deliverables conform to customer requirements. As a means of continually improving project performance, HEC shall establish a Quality Management System covering the requirements of ISO 9001:2000. This QMS shall be implemented, maintained, continually improved and have the full support of top management.

HEC shall prepare procedures that describe the processes required to implement the Quality Management System. These shall include:

- Core Business Processes and supporting processes;
- Quality Procedures that describe the methods adopted to manage the Core Business Process and supporting processes;
- Work Instructions that describe the operating methods, practice and control of the Core Business Process and supporting processes.

1.5.2 Objectives

The main objective of the HEC Quality Management System is to ensure that company activities, whether they are organisational (e.g. management and organisation) or technical (e.g. specification work, testing, simulation) comply with the Quality Manual and the Quality Plans.

In cases of non-compliance (e.g. if part of the specification work is not carried out in accordance with those agreements), a problem solving process shall be executed by the first line manager. This process shall include the location of root causes, remedial action, review of HEC procedures and Section Quality Plans and, if necessary, their adjustment and modification.

The Quality Manager plays an important part in this process. His role shall be to suggest alternative solutions and help the first line manager to take the necessary remedial action. If no effective corrective action is taken, the Quality Manager has the duty to inform the Managing Director.

Summarised, the Quality Management System shall include:

- clear responsibilities for each activity and development task;
- confirmation that each activity is defined and controlled by a Quality Procedure or a Section Quality Plan;
- confirmation that staff are trained to the requirements listed in the Quality Manual and Section Quality Plans;
- confirmation that compliance with the processes and procedures detailed in the Quality Manual and Section Quality Plans are audited;
- confirmation that remedial action is taken whenever appropriate;
- confirmation that the Quality Processes, Quality Procedures and Work Instructions contained in the Quality Manual and Section Quality Plans are regularly reviewed.

1.5.3 Implementation

Quality management in HEC is based on the Quality Management System described in ISO 9001:2000. The purpose of the quality system is to define the policy, organisation and responsibilities for the management of quality within HEC.

The most important aspects of HEC's Quality Management System are to be found in the HEC Quality Manual (i.e. this document) which describes, in detail, how the main elements of ISO 9001:2000 are catered for. The Quality Manual is then supported by individual Quality Plans for each section or major contract/document, Quality Processes, Quality Procedures and Work Instructions.

All HEC personnel shall be issued with a copy of this Quality Manual and the objectives of the manual shall be explained to them by the HEC Quality Manager as part of their introduction to HEC.

1.5.4 Overall responsibility

All those who have a leading role within HEC have a day-to-day responsibility for ensuring conformance to the requirements and rules stated in this Quality Manual.

However, the responsibility of ensuring that HEC has a quality policy and for ensuring that an organisation with the necessary resources is in place to implement the policy shall always lie with the Managing Director.

1.5.5 Responsibility for contract quality

The responsibility for the development of contract quality rests with HEC's Managing Director through his individual Section Managers.

The responsibility for ensuring that the product conforms to the defined quality requirements in this manual lies with **all** HEC personnel.

Specialised areas of operation and technical expertise may be required to meet the needs of HEC. In many cases these will have to be provided externally via a subcontractor. In **all** cases these subcontractors shall be required to supply and prove that their Quality Management System is in accordance with the principles of ISO 9001:2000.

1.5.6 Responsibility for the Quality System

The Quality Management System forms an integral part of the overall HEC management and the role of the Quality Manager within the company is to provide confidence that application of contract management (as described in this Quality Manual) is efficient, comprehensive and effective in ensuring that HEC - and every section - delivers the right product:

- on time;
- to the agreed specifications;
- within budget.

The Managing Director has appointed the Quality Manager to implement and maintain HEC's quality system. The Quality Manager has the responsibility and the authority to ensure that adequate procedures, plans and instructions are drawn up so as to provide a common approach to quality assurance throughout HEC and to ensure that the quality system is continuously monitored and improved by means of internal audits and management reviews.

2 Quality Management System

2.1 Requirements

HEC's Quality Management System (QMS) is the organised structure of responsibilities, activities, resources and events that together provide procedures and methods of implementation to ensure the capability of HEC meets the quality requirements of our customers.

HEC has to develop, establish and implement a QMS in order to ensure that the overall objectives and policies stated in HEC's Memorandum of Articles and Association are met.

To achieve these requirements, HEC involves all phases of the well known quality loop (see Figure 2) from the initial identification of the requirement to the final satisfaction of the customer's requirements and expectations.

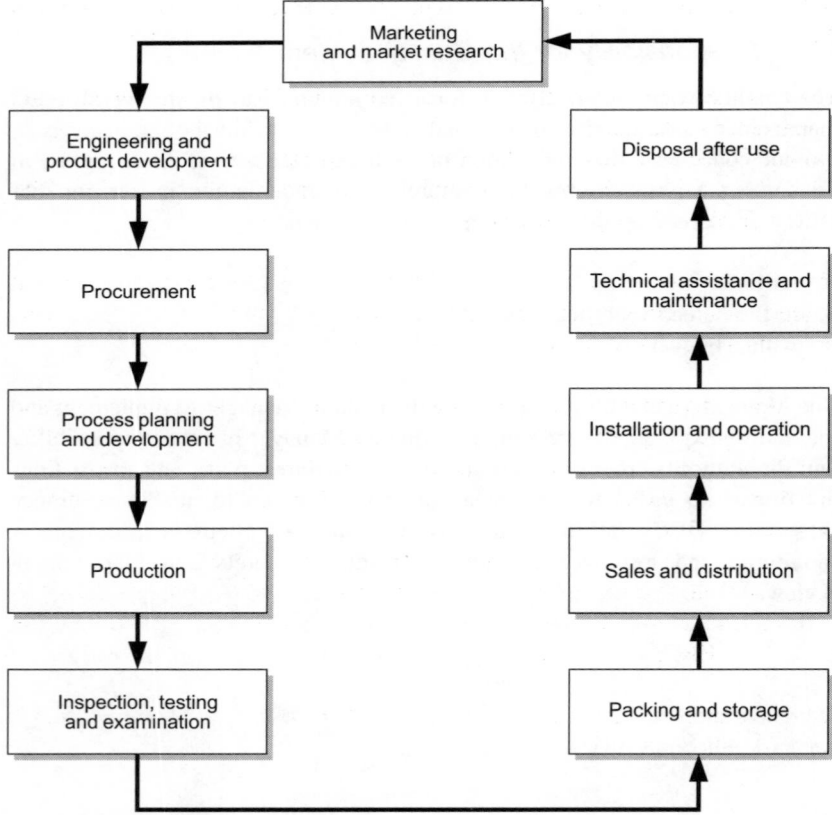

Figure 2 Quality loop

Within HEC an effective QMS ensures that all activities are fully understood, controlled and documented and that everyone knows exactly what they are supposed to be doing and how they should be doing it.

There are four main requirement sections making up the ISO 9001:2000 standard ranging from how to control a design process to how to audit an activity - but the most important element is the first one which demands that **everyone** shall be involved in quality in order for it to succeed and that it **must** be management led and that there **must** be a commitment to quality - **at the highest level**.

Within HEC we have this commitment. It stems from HEC's decisions in this respect and manifests itself throughout HEC's management, at all levels.

2.2 Organisational goals

The primary goal of HEC shall, at all times, be the quality of the end product and service. To succeed, HEC must be able to offer products and services that:

- meet the need, use and purpose as defined in HEC's Memorandum and Articles of Association;
- satisfy the customer's requirements and expectations;
- comply with applicable international, European and national quality standards and specifications.

In order to meet these objectives, HEC has to organise itself in such a way that the technical, administrative and human factors affecting the quality of HEC products and services are always under control.

It is **imperative** that this control is orientated to the reduction, elimination and - of paramount importance - the prevention of quality deficiencies. An HEC QMS, therefore, has to be developed and implemented for the purpose of accomplishing the objectives set out in HEC's Memorandum and Articles of Association.

Above all, and to achieve maximum effectiveness, it is essential that this QMS is designed so that it is appropriate to the type of contract and services being offered by HEC.

Demonstration of the continued success of the QMS shall be achieved via regular audits and reviews.

2.3 Purpose

The purpose of a QMS is to ensure that the end product (i.e. the deliverable) conforms to the customer's (i.e. user's), contractual requirements.

HEC's QMS, therefore, involves all HEC's functions, wherever and however instigated (e.g. Director level, Section Manager, etc.) that directly, or indirectly, affects HEC deliverables and contracts.

In essence, this QMS essentially consists of the documented rules, procedures and instructions prepared in accordance with ISO 9001:2000. These are stated in this Quality Manual (QM) as well as the associated Core Business Process (CP), Supporting Processes (SPs) Quality Procedures (QPs) and Work Instructions (WIs). The HEC audit team (consisting of the Managing Director, Quality Manager and Company Secretary) plus Section Manager may decide if additional documents are required for individual sections. In these cases, the requirement for an additional document shall be clearly stated and rules developed. This following section of the manual describes HEC's QMS and demonstrates how it meets the requirements of ISO 9001:2000.

2.4 Documentation

A QMS can only be effective if it is fully documented, understood and followed by all. Within HEC's QMS there are four levels of documentation, and these are structured as shown in Table 1.

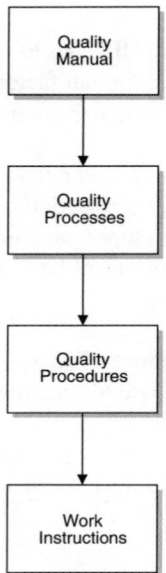

Figure 3 Quality Management System

Table 1 Herne European Consultancy Ltd's Quality Management System - documentation

Part 1	Quality Manual	The main policy document that establishes the HEC's QMS and how it meets the requirements of ISO 9001:2000.
Part 2	Quality Processes	The Core Business Process plus Supporting Processes that describe the activities required to implement the QMS and to meet the policy requirements made in the QM.
Part 3	Quality Procedures	A description of the method by which quality system activities are managed.
Part 4	Work Instructions	A description of how a specific task is carried out.

2.4.1 The Quality Manual

Management within HEC is based on the quality system described in ISO 9001:2000. The purpose of the HEC QMS is to define the policy, organisation, and responsibilities for the management of quality within HEC.

The most important aspects of the HEC QMS are to be found in the HEC QM which describes, in detail, how the sections of ISO 9001:2000 are catered for using CPs, SPs, QPs, WIs and individual Section Quality Plans (SQPs) for each section or major deliverable that support the QM.

HEC's QM provides a definitive statement of the policy, objectives, operating systems and procedures established by HEC for use in all projects managed by our organisation.

The QM describes a number of systematic controls and procedures for the staff in fulfilling their duties and responsibilities. It defines the lines of traceable accountability and responsibility and exists primarily as an internal management control document. It recognises the established elements of modern formalised quality management as expressed in national and international standards and as appropriate to the nature of the work undertaken.

The QM also stands as a formal statement of HEC's QMS, which has been established in response to the specified system requirements. As such, it provides a statement of commitment to customers (or external approval and/or regulatory bodies) to which HEC may be required to provide such information.

2.4.2 Quality Processes

The HEC QMS relies on the eight quality management principles contained in ISO 9001:2000 to enable a continual improvement of our business, our overall efficiency and to make us capable of responding to customer needs and expectations. These eight principles are:

- **Customer focused organisation** - HEC depends on our customers and is committed to understanding, anticipating and responding to every customer's requirements with product and service excellence.
- **Leadership** - Leaders establish unity of purpose, direction, and create the environment in which people can become fully involved in achieving HEC's objectives.
- **Involvement of people** - HEC have created an environment which makes every employee a team member and encourages participation in achieving our goals.
- **Process approach** - The desired result is achieved by relating resources and activities to managed processes.
- **System approach to management** - Identifying, understanding and managing a system of interrelated processes for a given objective contributes to the effectiveness and efficiency of HEC.
- **Continual improvement** - Continual improvement is a permanent objective of HEC.
- **Factual approach to decision making** - Effective decisions are based on the logical and intuitive analysis of data and information.
- **Mutually beneficial supplier relationships** - Mutually beneficial relationships between HEC and its suppliers enhance the ability of both organisations to create value.

The organisational processes making up the HEC QMS comprise a Core Business Process (CP) (describing the end to end activities involved in HEC project management and the production of contract deliverables) supplemented by a number of Supporting Processes (SPs) which describe the infrastructure required to complete HEC projects on time and within budget.

To ensure achievement of process objectives, a process owner with full responsibility and authority for managing the process and achieving process objectives shall be nominated.

Current HEC processes are listed in Part 2 (Quality Processes) of the QM.

2.4.3 Quality Procedures

Quality Procedures (QPs) form the bulk of the QMS and describe how the policy objectives of the QM can be met in practice and how these processes are controlled.

QPs contain the basic documentation used for planning and controlling all activities that impact on quality. This, for example, could be procedures for customer complaints, project review, etc.

Each QP is unique as it contains details of procedures directly applicable to HEC. The QPs must, of course, cover the specific requirements contained in ISO 9001:2000, although in reality they often cover more as they are an efficient method of controlling every aspect of HEC business.

These documented procedures can be made available and used in either hard copy or electronic format and may be used as separate documents outside the QM in places of work.

Some procedures may contain data or information, the knowledge of which must remain restricted to HEC. These procedures are not included in the QM, beyond their title and reference number.

Current HEC Quality Procedures are listed in Part 3 to the QMS.

2.4.4 Work Instructions

Work Instructions (WIs) describe how to perform specific operations and are produced for all of the relevant activities of HEC so as to ensure that the whole company can work to the same format. They describe how individual tasks and activities are to be carried out.

WIs describe in detail, procedures such as what is to be done, who should do it and when it has to be completed. They can, for example, cover simple issues such as making travel and hotel arrangements to more complex issues such as the structure of HEC reports.

They are produced for all of HEC's relevant activities so as to ensure that the whole company can work to the same format. Current HEC WIs are listed in Part 4 of the QMS.

2.4.5 Records

Records provide objective evidence of and demonstrate conformance to specified requirements contained in the QMS. Normally records are retained for five years - except as required by law.

2.4.6 Project Quality Plans

For larger and more complex projects/contracts, project-specific Quality Plans may have to be produced. These are effectively a subset of the QM and describe additional procedures and controls that will have to be applied. The production of these Quality Plans shall be co-ordinated with the Project/ Contract Manager concerned.

3 Customer satisfaction

From the customer's point of view, HEC's QMS **must** provide them with a level of confidence in the ability of HEC to deliver the desired quality as well as the consistent maintenance of that quality.

To be effective, HEC's QMS shall need to ensure:

- that objective evidence is provided (in the form of information and data) concerning the quality of the system and the quality of HEC's products and services;
- consideration has been given to the risks related to deficient products and services;
- consideration has been given to the risks pertaining to the health and safety of people;
- costs due to design deficiencies (including rework, re-processing and loss of production) have been considered.

HEC's QMS shall be designed and structured so that:

- it meets the customers' needs and expectations;
- it provides an effective management resource in the optimisation and control of quality in relation to risk, cost and benefit considerations;
- the system is well understood and effective;
- emphasis is placed on problem prevention rather than dependence on detection after occurrence.

4 Conformance with ISO 9001:2000

Subsequent sections of this QM describe the arrangements or systems that have been established to meet the specified requirements and are presented as far as possible in similar order to those in ISO 9001:2000. Not all requirements specified in ISO 9001:2000 are addressed in the HEC QM because in certain cases there is no relevance to the operation of HEC and its work (see Annex B - QMS to ISO 9001:200 cross-check for further details).

Amendments

Changes in the HEC organisation or the environment in which the HEC organisation is operating may necessitate modifications, amendments, insertions and deletions to the overall QMS adopted by HEC and as described in this QM. The contents of QM and its associated documentation (i.e. CPs, SPs, QPs and WIs) may, therefore, be altered as necessary and on an as required basis. All changes shall be subject to a formal review and agreement process (see QP/8 - Change Control). Changes shall be deemed operational following approval by the authorised person/persons and published as updated sections/ annexes of the QM.

Quality Manual administration

The Quality Manager shall review the effectiveness and suitability of QMS at least twice a year. As well as the QMS documentation, the whole scope of this manual shall also be reviewed. Where the system is found to be ineffective as a result of the changing needs of HEC's business operations and its stakeholders, amendments shall be made to the QM.

Amendments shall be circulated to all registered holders of controlled copies who shall be responsible for updating their copies. When the sum of the amendments involve changing more than ten pages of the manual, the Managing Director shall authorise the re-issue of the whole QM. Every issue replaces and cancels all previous issues and amendments. A number in accordance with QP/1 - Document Control shall identify each issue and revision. These issue/amendment numbers shall be clearly shown on the front cover of all of HEC's quality documentation and included in the Document Control Sheet (DCS).

Confidentiality

This QM is the intellectual property of HEC and may not be copied in whole or part, or transmitted to any third party without the express written permission of the Quality Manager.

The following sections of this QM are modelled on ISO 9001:2000 and each section, sub-section, etc. directly corresponds (in terms of number and content) with the ISO equivalent number.

4.1 General requirements (ISO 9001:2000-4.1)

HEC shall manage and define the processes necessary to ensure that all project deliverables conform to customer requirements.

As a means of continually improving project performance, HEC shall:

- establish a QMS covering the requirements of ISO 9001:2000;
- prepare procedures that describe the processes required to implement the QMS.

4.2 Documentation requirements (ISO 9001:2000-4.2)

4.2.1 General (ISO 9001:2000-4.2.1)

HEC QMS documentation shall include:

- statements regarding Quality Policy and Quality Objectives;
- documented procedures that clearly describe the sequence of processes necessary to ensure conformance with ISO 9001:2000;
- documented instructions to ensure the effective generation and control of processes and quality records.

4.2.2 Quality Manual (ISO 9001:2000-4.2.2)

1. HEC policy and objectives

HEC shall establish and maintain a QM which shall include:

- details of any ISO 9001:2000 exclusions;
- details of associated documented procedures;
- their sequence and interaction.

2. Responsibilities

The Quality Manager is responsible for operating the QMS, ensuring that the QM is fully and effectively implemented and for co-ordinating the writing availability of the necessary processes, procedures and instructions.

3. Implementation

QP/5 - Quality Management System Review.

4.2.3 Control of documents (ISO 9001:2000-4.2.3)

1. HEC policy and objectives

HEC shall establish QMS level procedures for controlling documents required for the operation of the QMS. These procedures shall ensure that:

- documents are approved for adequacy prior to release;
- documents are reviewed, updated as necessary and re-approved;
- the relevant versions of documents are available at locations where activities essential to the effective functioning of the QMS are performed;
- obsolete documents are removed from all points of issue and use, or otherwise controlled to prevent unintended use;
- any obsolete documents retained for legal or knowledge-preservation purposes are suitably identified.

A master list identifying the current revision status of documents, shall be established and be readily available to preclude the use of invalid and/or obsolete documents.

Documents shall be legible, readily identifiable and retrievable. Applicable documents of external origin shall be identified and recorded (see 5.5.7).

2. Responsibilities

The Company Secretary is responsible for the overall planning of document control procedures throughout HEC.

3. Implementation

QP/1 - Document Control.

4.2.4 *Control of quality records (ISO 9001:2000-4.2.4)*

1. HEC policy and objectives

HEC shall maintain quality records appropriate to the company to demonstrate conformance to the requirements and the effective operation of the QMS. HEC shall establish and maintain QMS level procedures for the identification, storage, retrieval, protection, retention time, and disposition of quality records.

2. Responsibilities

The Quality Manager is responsible for maintaining quality records demonstrating conformance to the requirements and the effective operation of the QMS.

3. Implementation

SP/5 - Documentation
QP/5 - Quality Management System Review.

5 Management Responsibility (ISO 9001:2000-5)

5.1 Management commitment (ISO 9001:2000-5.1)

1. HEC policy and objectives

HEC top management (Managing Director, Quality Manager and Company Secretary) shall demonstrate their commitment by:

- carrying out regular management reviews of the QMS and its associated documentation aimed at ensuring the continual improvement of the system (also see 5.6);
- establishing the quality policy and quality objectives (also see 5.3 and 5.4.1);
- ensuring the availability of necessary resources (also see 6.1);
- ensuring adequate focus on customer requirements throughout HEC;

- ensuring that all staff are aware of the importance of meeting customer, regulatory and legal requirements.

2. Responsibilities

The HEC Executive Board is responsible for demonstrating their commitment to quality and for supporting management in achieving that commitment.

3. Implementation

The HEC QM sections 5-8 together with its supporting annexes.

5.2 Customer focus (ISO 9001:2000-5.2)

1. HEC policy and objectives

With the overall aim of achieving customer satisfaction, HEC shall ensure that:

- customer needs and expectations are determined and converted into requirements;
- customer requirements are fully understood and met (also see 7.2.1);
- customer satisfaction is enhanced.

2. Responsibilities

Top management has overall responsibility for establishing, implementing and maintaining this activity.

3. Implementation

HEC QMS Part 1 (i.e. this Quality Manual).

5.3 Quality policy (ISO 9001:2000-5.3)

1. HEC policy and objectives

HEC shall establish its quality policy and ensure that it:

- is appropriate for the needs of HEC and its customers;
- includes a commitment to meeting requirements and continual improvement;
- provides a framework for establishing and reviewing quality objectives;
- is communicated, understood and implemented throughout HEC;
- is regularly reviewed for continuing suitability.

2. Responsibilities

Top management has overall responsibility for establishing, implementing and maintaining this activity.

3. Implementation

HEC QM Section 1.5.

5.4 Planning (ISO 9001:2000-5.4)

5.4.1 Quality objectives (ISO 9001:2000-5.4.1)

1. HEC policy and objectives

HEC shall establish quality objectives at each relevant function and level. These quality objectives shall be consistent with the quality policy and the commitment to continual improvement. Quality objectives shall include those needed to meet product and service requirements.

2. Responsibilities

Top management has overall responsibility for establishing, implementing and maintaining this activity.

3. Implementation

HEC QM Section 1.5.

5.4.2 Quality management system planning (ISO 9001:2000-5.4.2)

1. HEC policy and objectives

HEC shall identify and plan the activities and resources needed to achieve quality objectives. This planning shall be consistent with other requirements of the QMS and the results shall be documented.

Planning shall cover the:

- processes required in the QMS (and any reduction in scope of this international standard);
- realisation processes and resources needed, identifying quality characteristics at different stages, to achieve the desired results;
- verification activities, criteria for acceptability and the quality records needed.

Planning shall ensure that organisational change is conducted in a controlled manner and that the QMS is maintained during this change.

2. Responsibilities

Top management has overall responsibility for establishing, implementing and maintaining this activity.

3. Implementation

HEC QM Sections 1.5, 2.1 and 2.2.

5.5 Responsibility, authority and communication (ISO 9001:2000-5.5)

5.5.1 Responsibility and authority (ISO 9001:2000-5.5.1)

1. HEC policy and objectives

HEC shall define the roles and their interrelations, responsibilities and authorities in order to facilitate effective quality management and this information shall be communicated throughout HEC. Organisational freedom necessary to perform tasks that affect quality shall be defined.

2. Responsibilities

Top management has overall responsibility for establishing, implementing and maintaining this activity.

3. Implementation

HEC QM, Annex A - HEC organisation and responsibilities.

5.5.2 Management representative (ISO 9001:2000-5.5.2)

1. HEC policy and objectives

The Managing Director shall appoint a member of the management who, irrespective of other responsibilities, shall have defined authority that includes:

- ensuring that the HEC QMS is implemented and maintained in accordance with the requirements of this international standard;
- reporting to top management on the performance of the QMS, including needs for improvement;
- ensuring awareness of customer requirements throughout HEC;
- liaising with external parties on matters relating to the HEC QMS.

2. Responsibilities

The Quality Manager reports to the Managing Director and is independent of all contractual and project responsibilities that may adversely affect quality performance. He is responsible for ensuring that the QM and its associated CPs, SPs, QPs and WIs (making up the HEC QMS) are kept up-to-date and are administered and implemented correctly and efficiently according to the quality policy laid down by the Managing Director.

The Quality Manager has the overall responsibility for ensuring that the policies set out in this QMS are understood, implemented and maintained at all levels in the organisation and that the company works towards achieving its vision and key objectives.

The Quality Manager represents HEC in all matters relevant to the QMS as established by customer, regulatory and ISO 9001:2000 requirements. He/she is responsible for ensuring that the system is effectively implemented and maintained, and reports on the performance of the QMS at management review meetings.

The Quality Manager is the prime point of liaison with certification bodies and customers' quality management representatives.

3. Implementation

Details of the Quality Manager's duties and responsibilities are included at Annex A to the QM.

5.5.3 Internal communication (ISO 9001:2000-5.5.3)

1. HEC policy and objectives

HEC shall establish and maintain procedures for internal communication between the various levels and functions regarding the QMS and its effectiveness.

2. Responsibilities

The Quality Manager has overall responsibility for establishing, implementing and maintaining this activity.

3. Implementation

QP/10 - Training.

5.6 Management review (ISO 9001:2000-5.6)

5.6.1 General (ISO 9001:2000-5.6.1)

1. HEC policy and objectives

HEC shall establish a process for the periodic review of the QMS. It shall be reviewed to ensure its continuing suitability, adequacy and effectiveness. The review shall evaluate the need for changes to HEC's QMS, including policy and objectives and continues to provide customer satisfaction.

2. Responsibilities

The Quality Manager is responsible for ensuring that quality records are maintained in a systematic and presentable form.

All staff are responsible for ensuring that they provide the necessary records as required from their involvement in implementing the quality systems.

3. Implementation

QP/5 - Quality Management System Review.

5.6.2 Review input (ISO 9001:2000-5.6.2)

1. HEC policy and objectives

The review input of the QMS shall include (but not be limited to):

- results and follow-up actions from earlier management reviews;
- results of previous internal, customer and third party audits;
- self-assessment results;
- analysis of customer feedback;
- analysis of process performance;
- analysis of product conformance;
- the current status of preventive and corrective action;
- supplier performance;
- changes that could affect the QMS;
- recommendations for improvement.

2. Responsibilities

The Quality Manager is responsible for ensuring that quality records are maintained in a systematic and presentable form.

All staff are responsible for ensuring that they provide the necessary records as required from their involvement in implementing the quality systems.

3. Implementation

QP/5 - Quality Management System Review.

5.6.3 Review output (ISO 9001:2000-5.6.3)

1. HEC policy and objectives

The output of the management review shall include:

- improved product and process performance;
- confirmation of resource requirements and organisational structure;
- market needs;
- risk management;
- change control;
- continued compliance with the relevant statutory and regulatory requirements.

Results of management reviews shall be recorded (see 4.2.4).

2. Responsibilities

The Quality Manager is responsible for ensuring that quality records are maintained in a systematic and presentable form.

All staff are responsible for ensuring that they provide the necessary records as required from their involvement in implementing the quality systems.

3. Implementation

QP/5 - Quality Management System Review.

6 Resource Management (ISO 9001:2000-6)

6.1 Provision of resources (ISO 9001:2000-6.1)

1. HEC policy and objectives

HEC shall determine and provide in a timely manner, the resources needed to establish and maintain (and continually improve) their QMS so as to enhance customer satisfaction by meeting customer requirements.

2. Responsibilities

The Managing Director has overall responsibility for establishing, implementing and maintaining this activity.

3. Implementation

SP/1 - Human Resources
SP/3 - Budget and Finance.

6.2 Human resources (ISO 9001:2000-6.2)

6.2.1 General (ISO 9001:2000-6.2.1)

1. HEC policy and objectives

HEC shall only assign personnel who are competent (e.g. education, training, skills and experience, etc.). Their responsibilities shall be defined in Annex A to the Quality Manual.

2. Responsibilities

The Managing Director has overall responsibility for establishing, implementing and maintaining this activity.

3. Implementation

SP/1 - Human Resources.

6.2.2 Competence, awareness and training (ISO 9001:2000-6.2.2)

1. HEC policy and objectives

HEC shall establish and maintain system level procedures to:

- determine competency and training needs;
- provide training to address identified needs;

- evaluate the effectiveness of training at defined intervals;
- maintain appropriate records of education, training, skills, and experience (see 4.2.4);
- ensure that the necessary expertise and levels of skills, etc. are available to handle the expected workload and range of activities.

HEC shall establish and maintain procedures to make its employees at each relevant function and level aware of:

- the importance of conformance with the quality policy, and with the requirements of the Quality Management System;
- the significant impact of their work activities on quality, actual or potential;
- the benefits of improved personal performance;
- their roles and responsibilities in achieving conformance with the quality policy and procedures and with the requirements of the Quality Management System;
- the potential consequences of departure from specified procedures.

2. Responsibilities

Section Managers are responsible for ensuring that appropriate training is carried out and that all staff involved in their projects are aware of the requirements, rules and procedures to which they are to conform and against which they will be audited.

The Quality Manager is responsible for providing internal training in the QMS.

3. Implementation

QP/10 - Training.

6.3 Infrastructure (ISO 9001:2000 6.3)

1. HEC policy and objectives

HEC shall determine, provide and maintain the infrastructure to achieve product requirements regarding (but not limited to) the following:

- buildings, workspace and associated facilities;
- hardware and software;
- tools and equipment;
- communication facilities;
- supporting services.

2. Responsibilities

The Company Secretary has overall responsibility for establishing, implementing and maintaining this activity.

3. Implementation

QP/5 - Quality Management System Review
SP/3 - Budget and Finance
SP/6 - Audits.

6.4 Work environment (ISO 9001:2000-6.4)

1. HEC policy and objectives

HEC shall define and manage those human and physical factors of the work environment needed to achieve conformity of product.

This shall include:

- health and safety conditions;
- work methods;
- work ethics;
- ambient working conditions.

2. Responsibilities

Section Managers have overall responsibility for establishing, implementing and maintaining this activity.

3. Implementation

HSE relevant documents.

7 Product Realisation (ISO 9001:2000-7)

7.1 Planning of product realisation (ISO 9000:2000-7.1)

1. HEC policy and objectives

Processes that are necessary to realise the required product and their sequence and interaction shall be determined, planned and implemented taking into consideration the outputs from quality planning (see 5.4.2).

HEC shall ensure these processes are operated under controlled conditions and produce outputs, which meet customer requirements. HEC shall determine how each process affects the ability to meet product requirements and shall:

- establish methods and practices relevant to these processes, to the extent necessary, to achieve consistent operation;
- determine and implement the criteria and methods to control processes, to the extent necessary, to achieve product conformity with the customer requirements;
- verify and validate that processes can be operated to achieve product conformity with customer requirements;
- determine and implement arrangements for measurement, monitoring and follow-up actions, to ensure processes continue to operate to achieve planned results and outputs (see 8);
- ensure the availability of the information and data necessary to support the effective operation and monitoring of the processes;
- maintain as quality records the results of process control measures, to provide evidence of effective operation and monitoring of the processes (see 4.4.2).

2. Responsibilities

Top management has overall responsibility for establishing, implementing and maintaining this activity.

3. Implementation

CP/1 - Core Business Process
SP/1 - Human Resources
SP/2 - Quality
SP/3 - Budget and Finance
SP/4 - Corrective and Preventive Action
SP/5 - Documentation
SP/6 - Audits.

7.2 Customer-related processes (ISO 9000:2000-7.2)

7.2.1 Determination of requirements related to the product (ISO 9001:2000-7.2.1)

1. HEC policy and objectives

HEC shall establish a process for identifying customer requirements that determine the:

- completeness of the customer's product and/or service requirements;
- requirements not specified by the customer but necessary for fitness for purpose;
- statutory, regulatory and legal requirements;
- customer requirements for availability, delivery and support of product and/or service.

2. Responsibilities

The Managing Director, assisted by the Section Managers, has overall responsibility for establishing, implementing and maintaining this activity.

3. Implementation

CP/1 - Core Business Process
QP/6 - Customer Feedback.

7.2.2 Review of requirements related to the product (ISO 9000:2000-7.2.2)

1. HEC policy and objectives

The customer requirements, including any requested changes, shall be reviewed before a commitment to supply a product is provided to the customer (e.g. submission of a tender, acceptance of a contract or order) to ensure that:

- customer requirements are clearly defined for product and/or service;
- where the customer provides no written statement of requirement, the customer requirements are confirmed before acceptance;
- contract or order requirements differing from those previously expressed, (e.g. in a tender or quotation), are resolved;
- HEC has the ability to meet the customer requirements for the product and/or service.

The results of the review and subsequent follow-up actions shall be recorded (see 4.2.4) and the information disseminated to all the relevant personnel.

2. Responsibilities

Section Managers have overall responsibility for establishing, implementing and maintaining this activity.

3. Implementation

CP/1 - Core Business Process
SP/5 - Documentation.

7.2.3 Customer communication (ISO 9000:2000-7.2.2)

1. HEC policy and objectives

HEC shall determine and implement arrangements for customer communication with the overall aim of meeting customer requirements. HEC shall define communication requirements relating to:

- product information;
- enquiries and order handling, including amendments;
- customer complaints and actions relating to non-conforming product (see 8.3 and 8.5.2);
- customer responses relating to product performance (see 7.3.2 and 8.2.1).

2. Responsibilities

The Managing Director has overall responsibility for establishing, implementing and maintaining this activity.

3. Implementation

CP/1 - Core Business Process
SP/4 - Corrective and Preventive Action
QP/6 - Customer Feedback.

7.3 Design and development (ISO 9000:2000-7.3)

7.3.1 Design and development planning (ISO 9001:2000 7.3.1)

1. HEC policy and objectives

HEC shall plan and control the design and development of a product which shall include:

- stages of the design and development process;
- required review, verification and validation activities;
- responsibilities and authorities for design and development activities.

Interfaces between different groups involved in design and development shall be managed to ensure effective communication- and clarity of responsibilities.

Planning output shall be updated, as the design and development progresses.

2. Responsibilities

Section Managers have overall responsibility for establishing, implementing and maintaining this activity.

3. Implementation

CP/1 - Core Business Process
SP/4 - Corrective and Preventive Action
SP/5 - Documentation
SP/6 - Audits.

7.3.2 Design and development inputs (ISO 9001:2000-7.3.2)

1. HEC policy and objectives

HEC shall define and record the requirements to be met by the product and/or service (see 4.2.4). These shall include:

- functional and performance requirements from customer or market;
- applicable statutory, regulatory and legal requirements;
- applicable environmental requirements;
- requirements derived from previous similar designs;
- any other requirements essential for design and development.

These inputs shall be reviewed for adequacy and incomplete, ambiguous or conflicting requirements shall be resolved.

2. Responsibilities

Section Managers have overall responsibility for establishing, implementing and maintaining this activity.

3. Implementation

CP/1 - Core Business Process
SP/4 - Corrective and Preventive Action
SP/5 - Documentation
SP/6 - Audits.

7.3.3 Design and development outputs
(ISO 9001:2000-7.3.3)

1. HEC policy and objectives

Design and development output shall:

- meet the design and/or development input requirements;
- contain or make reference to product and/or service acceptance criteria;
- define the characteristics of the product that are essential to its safe and proper use;
- be approved before being released.

2. Responsibilities

Section Managers have overall responsibility for establishing, implementing and maintaining this activity.

3. Implementation

CP/1 - Core Business Process
SP/4 - Corrective and Preventive Action
SP/5 - Documentation
SP/6 - Audits.

7.3.4 Design and development review
(ISO 9001:2000-7.3.4)

1. HEC policy and objectives

At suitable stages, systematic reviews of design and development shall be conducted to:

- evaluate the ability of a product to fulfil requirements for quality;
- identify problems;
- propose follow-up actions.

Participants of the reviews shall include representatives of functions concerned with the design stage being reviewed.

Results of the reviews and subsequent follow-up actions shall be recorded (see 4.2.4).

2. Responsibilities

Section Managers have overall responsibility for establishing, implementing and maintaining this activity.

3. Implementation

CP/1 - Core Business Process
SP/4 - Corrective and Preventive Action
SP/5 - Documentation
SP/6 - Audits.

7.3.5 Design and development verification (ISO 9001:2000-7.3.5)

1. HEC policy and objectives

A verification process shall be planned and implemented to ensure that the design and development output meets the design and development input. The results of the verification and subsequent follow-up actions shall be recorded (see 4.2.4).

2. Responsibilities

Section Managers have overall responsibility for establishing, implementing and maintaining this activity.

3. Implementation

CP/1 - Core Business Process
SP/4 - Corrective and Preventive Action
SP/5 - Documentation
SP/6 - Audits.

7.3.6 Design and development validation (ISO 9001:2000-7.3.6)

1. HEC policy and objectives

Prior to the delivery and implementation of the product and/or service, design and development validation shall be performed to confirm that resultant product and/or service is capable of meeting the particular requirements for a specific intended customer use.

Wherever applicable, validation shall be defined, planned and completed prior to the delivery or implementation of the product and/or service. Where it is impossible to undertake full validation prior to delivery or implementation, partial validation of the design or development outputs shall be undertaken to the maximum extent practical.

The results of the validation and subsequent follow-up actions shall be recorded (see 4.2.4).

2. Responsibilities

Section Managers have overall responsibility for establishing, implementing and maintaining this activity.

3. Implementation

CP/1 - Core Business Process
SP/4 - Corrective and Preventive Action
SP/5 - Documentation
SP/6 - Audits.

7.3.7 Control of design and development changes (ISO 9001:2000-7.3.7)

1. HEC policy and objectives

HEC shall identify, document and control all design and development changes and shall evaluate the effect of these changes and/or modifications on:

- the interaction between the elements of the design and/or development;
- the interaction between the component parts of the resulting product and/or service;
- existing products and/or services and upon post delivery product operations;
- the need for carrying out re-verification or re-validation for all or part of the design and development outputs.

The results of the review of changes and subsequent follow-up actions shall be recorded (see 4.2.4).

2. Responsibilities

Section Managers have overall responsibility for establishing, implementing and maintaining this activity.

3. Implementation

CP/1 - Core Business Process
SP/4 - Corrective and Preventive Action
SP/5 - Documentation
SP/6 - Audits.

7.4 Purchasing (ISO 9001:2000-7.4)

7.4.1 Purchasing process (ISO 9001:2000-7.4.1)

1. HEC policy and objectives

Although the majority of purchases only concern stationery and the maintenance/improvement of IT facilities, HEC, nevertheless, needs to control its purchasing processes to ensure that the purchased product conforms to HEC's requirements. The type and extent of methods to control these processes shall be dependent on the effect of the purchased product upon the final product.

HEC shall evaluate and select suppliers based on their ability to supply products in accordance with HEC's requirements. Evaluation, re-evaluation and selection criteria for suppliers shall be established. The results of evaluations and subsequent follow-up actions shall be recorded (see 4.2.4).

The HEC system for control of all purchased goods or subcontracted services shall ensure those products or services purchased and received conform to specified requirements and include provision for the assessment of suppliers and subcontractors. It shall also establish rules for the specification of requirements for purchased documents and the verification of goods and services received.

2. Responsibilities

The Company Secretary, (assisted by the Section Managers and the Quality Manager), has overall responsibility for establishing, implementing and maintaining this activity.

3. Implementation

Individual (i.e. Sectional) subcontract assessment procedures according to product and/or contract.

7.4.2 Purchasing information (ISO 9001:2000-7.4.2)

1. HEC policy and objectives

Purchasing documents shall contain information clearly describing the product and/or service ordered, including where appropriate:

- requirements for approval or qualification of product and/or service, procedures, processes, equipment and personnel;
- any QMS requirements.

HEC shall ensure the adequacy of specified purchase requirements prior to release.

2. Responsibilities

The Company Secretary (assisted by the Section Managers and the Quality Manager), has overall responsibility for establishing, implementing and maintaining this activity.

3. Implementation

Individual (i.e. Sectional) subcontract assessment procedures according to product and/or contract.

7.4.3 Verification of purchased product (ISO 9001:2000-7.4.3)

1. HEC policy and objectives

HEC shall determine and implement the procedures necessary for verification of purchased product (see 8.2.4).

Where HEC or its customer proposes to perform verification activities at the supplier's premises, HEC shall specify the required verification arrangements and method of product release in the purchasing documents.

2. Responsibilities

The Company Secretary, (assisted by the Section Managers and the Quality Manager), has overall responsibility for establishing, implementing and maintaining this activity.

3. Implementation

Individual (i.e. Sectional) subcontract assessment procedures according to product and/or contract.

7.5 Production and service provision (ISO 9001:2000-7.5)

7.5.1 Control of production and service provision (ISO 9001:2000-7.5.1)

1. HEC policy and objectives

HEC shall plan and control production and service operations, including those undertaken after initial delivery, through:

- the availability of information and specifications that clearly define the characteristics of the product that is to be achieved;
- the availability of work instructions for those activities where they are necessary for the achievement of conformity of products;
- the use and maintenance of suitable production, installation, and maintenance equipment (see 6.3);
- the availability of monitoring and measuring equipment;
- the implementation of suitable monitoring and measurement activities (see 8.2.3 and 8.2.4);
- suitable methods for release and delivery and/or installation of product and/or service.

2. Responsibilities

Top management, assisted by Section Managers, has overall responsibility for establishing, implementing and maintaining this activity.

3. Implementation

HEC QMS Part 3 - Quality Procedures
HEC QMS Part 4 - Work Instructions
SP/1 - Human Resources
SP/5 - Documentation.

7.5.2 Validation of processes for service provision (ISO 9001:2000-7.5.2)

1. HEC policy and objectives

As HEC's product is exclusively management system documents and reports this section is not applicable to HEC's business.

7.5.3 Identification and traceability (ISO 9001:2000-7.5.3)

1. HEC policy and objectives

HEC shall have procedures for identifying the status of a product with respect to required measurement and verification activities and, where traceability is a requirement, HEC shall identify the product throughout all processes. In particular, this shall apply to the component parts of the product where their interaction affects conformity with requirements.

2. Responsibilities

Top management, assisted by Section Managers, has overall responsibility for establishing, implementing and maintaining this activity.

3. Implementation

SP/5 - Documentation
SP/6 - Audits.

7.5.4 Customer property (ISO 9001:2000-7.5.4)

1. HEC policy and objectives

HEC shall ensure that all customer property while it is under HEC's supervision or being used by HEC is identified, verified, stored and maintained. Any customer property that is lost, damaged or otherwise found to be unsuitable for use shall be recorded and reported to the customer (see 7.2.3).

NOTE: Customer property may include intellectual property e.g. information provided in confidence.

2. Responsibilities

Top management, assisted by Section Managers, has overall responsibility for establishing, implementing and maintaining this activity.

3. Implementation

SP/5 - Documentation.

7.5.5 Preservation of product (ISO 9001:2000-7.5.5)

1. HEC policy and objectives

HEC shall ensure that during internal processing and final delivery of product to the intended destination that the identification, packaging, storage, preservation, and handling do not affect conformity with product requirements. This shall also apply to parts or components of a product and elements of a service.

Product release/delivery shall not proceed until all the specified activities have been satisfactorily completed and the related documentation is available and authorised.

2. Responsibilities

The Company Secretary, assisted by Section Managers, has overall responsibility for establishing, implementing and maintaining this activity.

3. Implementation

HEC QMS Part 3 - Quality Procedures
HEC QMS Part 4 - Work Instructions
SP5 - Documentation.

7.6 Control of measuring and monitoring devices (ISO 9001:2000-7.6)

1. HEC policy and objectives

As HEC's product is exclusively management system documents and reports this section is not applicable to HEC's business.

8 Measurement, Analysis and Improvement (ISO 9001:2000-8)

8.1 General (ISO 9001:2000-8.1)

1. HEC policy and objectives

HEC shall define, plan and implement measurement, monitoring, analysis and improvement processes to ensure that the QMS, processes and products conform to requirements and:

- the type, location, timing and frequency of measurements and the requirements for records shall be defined (see 5.5.7).
- the effectiveness of measures implemented shall be periodically evaluated.

HEC shall identify and use appropriate statistical tools and the results of data analysis and improvement activities shall be an input to the management review process (see 5.6).

2. Responsibilities

Top management, assisted by Section Managers, has overall responsibility for establishing, implementing and maintaining this activity.

3. Implementation

SP/5 - Documentation
SP/6 - Audits.

8.2 Monitoring and measurement (ISO 9001:2000-8.2)

8.2.1 Customer satisfaction (ISO 9001:2000-8.2.1)

1. HEC policy and objectives

HEC shall monitor information on customer satisfaction and/or dissatisfaction as one of the measurements of performance of the QMS. The methods and measures for obtaining and utilising such information and data shall be defined.

2. Responsibilities

Top management, assisted by Section Managers, has overall responsibility for establishing, implementing and maintaining this activity.

3. Implementation

SP/4 - Corrective and Preventive Action.

8.2.2 Internal audit (ISO 9001:2000-8.2.2)

1. HEC policy and objectives

HEC shall carry out objective audits in order to determine if the QMS has been effectively implemented and maintained and conforms to ISO 9001:2000. In addition, HEC may carry out audits to identify potential opportunities for improvement.

The audit process, including the schedule, shall be based on the status and importance of the activities and/or areas to be audited and the results of previous audits.

Note: see also ISO 10011-1, 10011-2 and 10011-3 for guidance.

2. Responsibilities

Top management has overall responsibility for establishing, implementing and maintaining this activity.

3. Implementation

SP/6 - Audits.

8.2.3 Monitoring and measurement of processes (ISO 9001:2000-8.2.3)

1. HEC policy and objectives

HEC shall monitor and measure processes to ensure they continue to satisfy their intended purpose.

2. Responsibilities

Top management, assisted by Section Managers, has overall responsibility for establishing, implementing and maintaining this activity.

3. Implementation

SP/6 - Audits.

8.2.4 Monitoring and measurement of product (ISO 9001:2000-8.2.4)

1. HEC policy and objectives

HEC shall monitor and measure the characteristics of the product to verify that the requirements for the product and/or service are met.

Evidence of conformance shall be documented and recorded. Records shall indicate the authority responsible for release of product (see 4.2.4).

2. Responsibilities

Top management, assisted by Section Managers, has overall responsibility for establishing, implementing and maintaining this activity.

3. Implementation

SP/6 - Audits.

8.3 Control of non-conforming product (ISO 9001:2000-8.3)

1. HEC policy and objectives

HEC shall ensure that products that do not conform to requirements are identified and controlled to prevent unintended use or delivery. These non-conformities shall be:

- corrected or adjusted to conform to requirements and re-validated; or
- accepted under concession, with or without correction or adjustment; or
- re-assigned for alternative valid application; or
- rejected as unsuitable.

2. Responsibilities

The Quality Manager, assisted by the Section Managers, has overall responsibility for establishing, implementing and maintaining this activity.

3. Implementation

SP/4 - Corrective and Preventive Action
SP/6 - Audits.

8.4 Analysis of data (ISO 9001:2000-8.4)

1. HEC policy and objectives

HEC shall analyse all applicable data to determine the suitability, adequacy and effectiveness of the QMS and use this to provide information relating to:

- customer satisfaction and/or dissatisfaction;
- conformance to product requirements;
- characteristics of trends and opportunities for preventive action;
- suppliers.

2. Responsibilities

Top management, assisted by the Section Managers, has overall responsibility for establishing, implementing and maintaining this activity.

3. Implementation

SP/4 - Corrective and Preventive Action
SP/6 - Audits.

8.5 Improvement (ISO 9001:2000-8.5)

8.5.1 Continual improvement (ISO 9001:2000-8.5.1)

1. HEC policy and objectives

HEC shall plan and manage the processes necessary for the continual improvement of the QMS through the use of a system level procedure that describes the use of quality policy, objectives, internal audit results, analysis of data, corrective and preventive action and management review to facilitate continual improvement.

2. Responsibilities

Top management has overall responsibility for establishing, implementing and maintaining this activity.

3. Implementation

SP/4 - Corrective and Preventive Action
SP/6 - Audits.

8.5.2 Corrective action (ISO 9001:2000-8.5.2)

1. HEC policy and objectives

HEC shall define the requirements for:

- identifying non-conformities (including customer complaints);
- determination of the causes of non-conformity;
- evaluating the need for actions to ensure that non-conformities do not recur;
- implementing corrective action;
- recording the results of actions taken;
- reviewing that corrective action taken is effective and recorded.

2. Responsibilities

Top management, assisted by the Section Managers, has overall responsibility for establishing, implementing and maintaining this activity.

3. Implementation

SP/4 - Corrective and Preventive Action
SP/6 - Audits.

8.5.3 Preventive action (ISO 9001:2000-8.5.3)

1. HEC policy and objectives

HEC shall define the requirements for:

- identification of potential non-conformities;
- determination of the causes of the identified potential non-conformities;
- determination of preventive action needed to eliminate causes of potential non-conformities;
- implementation of preventive action;
- recording the results of action taken;
- reviewing that preventive action taken is effective.

2. Responsibilities

Top management, assisted by Section Managers, has overall responsibility for establishing, implementing and maintaining this activity.

3. Implementation

SP/4 - Corrective and Preventive Action
SP/6 - Audits.

Annex A - HEC Organisation and Responsibilities

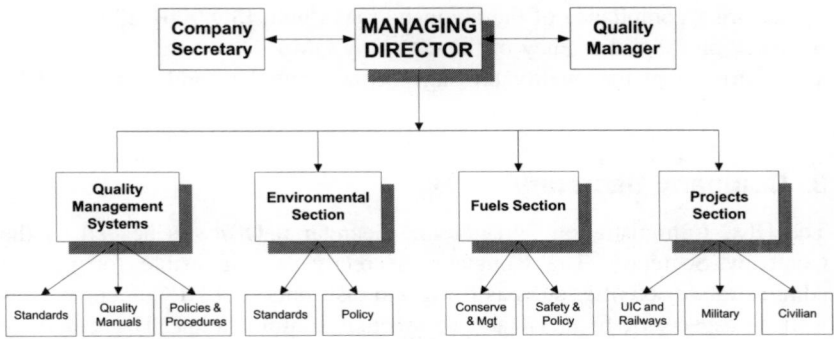

Figure 4 Herne European Consultancy Ltd – organisational chart

1. Managing Director

The Managing Director is responsible for the overall management of HEC. He is responsible for the overall and final success of all contracts undertaken, for providing guidance on all major issues and for ensuring that all HEC's products and services are produced and delivered to the highest possible level.

The Managing Director is responsible for:

- supervising the day-to-day running of HEC;
- the overall progress of the work with which he has been entrusted and the budget placed at his disposal;
- controlling budget, time schedules, Quality Plans, resources and quality within the company;
- approving changes to agreed time schedules, resources and budgets;
- ensuring that the organisation will, at all times, meet the business requirements and objectives (as stipulated in HEC Memorandum of Articles and Association) as well as keeping to the agreed time schedule;
- maintaining overall responsibility for all sections;
- preparing contracts for section members, in consultation with Section Managers.

2. Quality Manager

The Quality Manager is responsible for ensuring that the organisation's QMS is defined, implemented, audited and monitored in order to ensure that HEC's documents comply with the customers' quality standards as well as the ISO 9000 series of documents concerning 'Quality Management System'. The Quality Manager shall report directly to the Managing Director.

His tasks shall include:

- maintenance and effectiveness of the company QMS;
- ensuring compliance of the company QMS with ISO 9001:2000;
- ensuring the consistency of the company QMS;
- ensuring that the quality message is transmitted to and understood by everyone.

3. Company Secretary

The HEC Administration, Finance and Secretarial Office is headed by the Company Secretary. The Company Secretary is responsible for general administrative activities such as filing and distribution of HEC documents as well as aspects of financial and contractual administration. The Company Secretary shall report directly to the Managing Director.

His tasks shall include:

- the daily running of HEC Office;
- issuing financial reports;
- producing monthly financial statements to the Managing Director;
- the organisation of special meetings, workshops, seminars etc. when requested to do so by the Managing Director;
- arranging (and planning) publication of documents when required.

4. Section Managers

Section Managers are appointed by the Managing Director and are responsible for the general progress of their section, the budget placed at their disposal, for organising the work of their section and distributing this work between the sectional members according to the directives, procedures and instructions making up the HEC QMS whilst duly observing the requirements of HEC Memorandum of Articles and Association.

Section Managers shall report directly to the Managing Director and their tasks shall include:

- responsibility for the general progress of the work of their section and the management of their section's authorised budget;
- controlling the time schedules, work packages, resources and quality of the tasks allocated to their section;
- ensuring that the section will, at all times, meet the business needs and objectives of HEC;
- directing the studies of the section with the constant aim of achieving an accelerated and sustained tempo of the studies within the scope of their own particular Quality Plan and individual work packages;
- the progress and time management of all sub task(s).

5. Section Members

Section members shall carry out the accepted tasks assigned by their Section Manager, within the deadlines set.

6. Subcontractors and Consultants

When the work/studies of a section falls outside the scope of section members, the Managing Director may authorise the temporary co-operation of subcontractors and consultants.

A contract/agreement for the subcontractor's or consultant's participation will be concluded with his company or with his parent company by the Company Secretary.

The subcontractor or consultant shall be expected to make use of his personal knowledge and experience acquired both in and outside his company without, however, in any way committing the latter. The company who provides subcontractors or consultants shall, in return, grant them the greatest possible freedom of action and initiative and shall afford them the time and facilities required to carry out whatever work/studies they might be charged with in their capacity as a member of an HEC section.

Annex B - ISO 9001:2000 cross-check

Clause No	ISO 9001:2000 Title	Process	Quality Manual
4.2	Documentation requirements		
4.2.1	General		
4.2.2	Quality Manual	QP/5	
4.2.3	Control of documents	QP/1	
4.2.4	Control of quality records	SP/5, QP/5	
5	**Management responsibility**		
5.1	Management commitment		Sections 5-8
5.2	Customer focus		All
5.3	Quality policy		Section 1.5
5.4	Planning		
5.4.1	Quality objectives		Section 1.5
5.4.2	Quality management system planning		Sections 1.5, 2.1 & 2.2
5.5	Responsibility, authority and communication		
5.5.1	Responsibility and authority		Annex A
5.5.2	Management representative		Annex A
5.5.3	Internal communication	QP/10	
5.6	Management review		
5.6.1	General	QP/5	
5.6.2	Review input	QP/5	
5.6.3	Review output	QP/5	
6	**Resource management**		
6.1	Provision of resources	SP/1, SP/3	
6.2	Human resources		
6.2.1	General	SP/1	
6.2.2	Competence, awareness and training	QP/10	
6.3	Infrastructure	SP/3, SP/6, QP/5	

Clause No	ISO 9001:2000 Title	Process	Quality Manual
6.4	Work environment		HSE documents
7	**Product realisation**		
7.1	Planning of realisation processes	CP/1, SP/1, SP/2, SP/3, SP/4, SP/5, SP/6	
7.2	Customer-related processes		
7.2.1	Determination of requirements related to the product	CP/1, QP/6	
7.2.2	Review of requirements related to the product	SP/5	
7.2.3	Customer communications	SP/4	
7.3	Design and development		
7.3.1	Design and development planning	CP/1, SP/4, SP/5, SP/6	
7.3.2	Design and development inputs	CP/1, SP/4, SP/5, SP/6	
7.3.3	Design and development outputs	CP/1, SP/4, SP/5, SP/6	
7.3.4	Design and development review	CP/1, SP/4, SP/5, SP/6	
7.3.5	Design and development verification	CP/1, SP/4, SP/5, SP/6	
7.3.6	Design and development validation	CP/1, SP/4, SP/5, SP/6	
7.3.7	Control of design and development changes	CP/1, SP/4, SP/5, SP/6	
7.4	Purchasing		
7.4.1	Purchasing process	Subcontractor assessment procedures	
7.4.2	Purchasing information	Subcontractor assessment procedures	
7.4.3	Verification of purchased product	Subcontractor assessment procedures	

Clause No	ISO 9001:2000 Title	Process	Quality Manual
7.5	Production and service provision		
7.5.1	Control of production and service provision	SP/1	Part 3, Part 4
7.5.2	Validation of processes for production and service provision		
7.5.3	Identification and traceability	SP/5, SP/6	
7.5.4	Customer property	SP/5	
7.5.5	Preservation of product	SP/5	Part 3, Part 4
7.6	Control of monitoring and measurement devices		
8	Measurement, analysis and improvement		
8.1	General	SP/5, SP/6	
8.2	Monitoring and measurement		
8.2.1	Customer satisfaction	SP/4, QP/6	
8.2.2	Internal audit	SP/6	
8.2.3	Monitoring and measurement of processes	SP/6	
8.2.4	Monitoring and measurement of product	SP/6	
8.3	Control of non-conforming product	SP/4, SP/6	
8.4	Analysis of data	SP/4, SP/6	
8.5	Improvement		
8.5.1	Continual improvement	SP/4, SP/6	
8.5.2	Corrective action	SP/4, SP/6	
8.5.3	Preventative action	SP/4, SP/6	

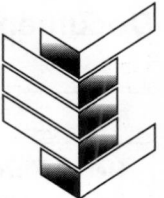

Herne European Consultancy Ltd

Quality Management System Part 2 - Quality Processes

This Quality Manual has been issued on the authority of the Managing Director of Herne European Consultancy Ltd for the use of all staff, subcontractors, clients or regulatory bodies to whom Herne European Consultancy Ltd may be required to provide such information to.

Managing Director
Herne European Consultancy Ltd

File No:	**H-QMS-030RLT00**
Version No:	**00.05**
Date:	**31.12.00**

Document Control Sheet

Title	This version	Date
Herne European Consultancy Ltd - Part 2 - Quality Processes	00.05	31.12.00
	File Number	No of Pages
	H-QMS-030RLT00	10

Abstract

The Herne European Consultancy Ltd Quality Management System is divided into four parts. This document is Part 2 and describes the Quality Processes adopted by Herne European Consultancy Ltd. It defines:

- the Quality Processes that have been developed to implement Herne European Consultancy Ltd's Quality Management System;
- the associated Quality Procedures that have been designed to enable Herne European Consultancy Ltd to carry out the policies of the Quality Management System.

The Quality Procedures designed to meet these processes are contained in Part 3 and the details of the Work Instructions are in Part 4.

Name	Function	Level
	Quality Manager	Prepare
	Managing Director	Agree
	Managing Director	Approve

Keywords

Core Business Process, ISO 9001:2000, Policy, Quality, Quality Management System, Quality Manager, Quality Manual, Quality Procedure, Supporting Process, Work Instruction.

Approved

_____ Date:_____

(Managing Director)

Amendments

Changes in the organisation of Herne European Consultancy Ltd or the environment in which it operates, may necessitate modifications, amendments, insertions and/or deletions to the overall quality management adopted by Herne European Consultancy Ltd and its associated documentation (e.g. Quality Procedures and Work Instructions). The contents of this Quality Manual may, therefore, be altered on an as required basis. All changes shall be subject to QP/8 - Change Control. Changes shall be deemed operational following approval by the authorised person/persons and published as updated sections of the Quality Manual.

No	Chapter	Amendment details	Date
01.00	All	First issue	28.06.93
02.00	All	Editorial revision	05.04.94
03.00	4	New flowchart	21.09.95
03.01	2	Revised and reworded	23.12.95
04.00	5	New flowchart	30.07.96
05.00	All	Revised to conform to ISO 9001:2000	31.12.00

Distribution List

1. Managing Director
2. Quality Manager
3. Company Secretary
4. Section Manager - Quality Management Systems
5. Section Manager - Environmental
6. Section Manager - Fuels
7. Section Manager - Projects
8. Spare

Contents

Abbreviations and acronyms

Abbreviation	Definition
CP	Core Business Process
HEC	Herne European Consultancy Ltd
ISO	International Standards Organisation
QM	Quality Manual
QMS	Quality Management System
QP	Quality Procedure
SP	Supporting Process
WI	Work Instruction

References

Ref.	Abbreviation	Title	Issue date
1.	ISO 9001	Quality Management Systems - Requirements	2000

1 Documentation

Herne European Consultancy Ltd (HEC) has four levels of documentation within their Quality Management System (QMS) which is structured as shown in the table below. This document is Part 2 and describes the Quality Processes adopted by HEC. It defines:

- the Processes that have been developed to implement HEC's QMS;
- the associated Quality Procedures that have been designed to enable HEC to carry out the QMS.

The Quality Procedures designed to meet these processes are contained in Part 3 and the details of the Work Instructions are in Part 4.

Table 1 Herne European Consultancy Ltd's Quality System - documentation

Part 1	Quality Manual	The main policy document that establishes the HEC's QMS and how it meets the requirements of ISO 9001:2000.
Part 2	**Quality Processes**	**The Core Business Process plus the primary and secondary supporting processes that describe the activities required to implement the QMS and to meet the policy requirements made in the Quality Manual.**
Part 3	Quality Procedures	A description of the method by which quality system activities are managed
Part 4	Work Instructions	A description of how a specific task is carried out

2 Processes

The HEC QMS is based on the requirements contained in ISO 9001:2000 with a common structure based on a Core Business Process model supplemented by a series of supporting process models.

The HEC QMS relies on the eight quality management principles contained in ISO 9001:2000 to enable a continual improvement of our business, our overall efficiency and to make us capable of responding to customer needs and expectations. These eight principles are:

- **Customer focused organisation** - HEC depends on our customers and is committed to understanding, anticipating and responding to every customer's requirements with product and service excellence.
- **Leadership** - Leaders establish unity of purpose and direction and create the environment in which people can become fully involved in achieving HEC's objectives.
- **Involvement of people** - HEC have created an environment which makes every employee a team member and encourages participation in achieving our goals.
- **Process approach** - The desired result is achieved by relating resources and activities to managed processes.
- **System approach to management** - Identifying, understanding and managing a system of interrelated processes for a given objective contributes to the effectiveness and efficiency of HEC.
- **Continual improvement** - Continual improvement is a permanent objective of HEC.
- **Factual approach to decision making** - Effective decisions are based on the logical and intuitive analysis of data and information.
- **Mutually beneficial supplier relationships** - Mutually beneficial relationships between HEC and its suppliers enhance the ability of both organisations to create value.

The organisational processes making up the HEC QMS comprise a Core Business Process (CP) (describing the end-to-end activities involved in HEC project management and the production of contract deliverables) supplemented by a number of supporting processes (SPs) which describe the infrastructure required to complete HEC projects on time and within budget.

To ensure achievement of process objectives, a process owner with full responsibility and authority for managing the process and achieving process objectives shall be nominated.

3 Quality Processes

Table 2 Quality Processes

Process no	Instruction title
CP/1	HEC Core Business Process
SP/1	Human Resources
SP/2	Quality
SP/3	Budget and Finance
SP/4	Corrective and Preventive Action
SP/5	Documentation
SP/6	Audits

4 Core Business process

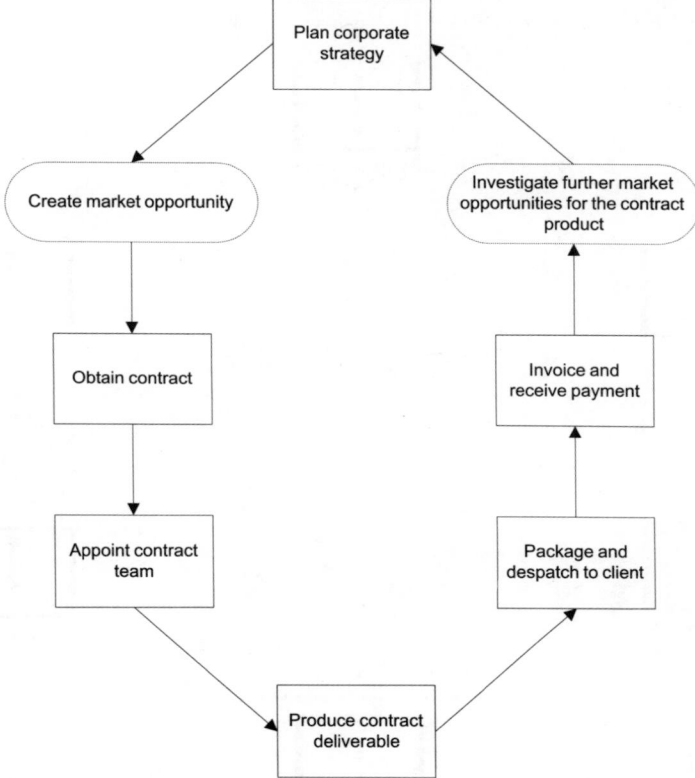

Figure 1 Core Business Process - overall

The HEC CP describes the end-to-end activities involved in the production of a contract deliverable. It is supported by a number of primary and secondary SPs, Quality Procedures (QPs) and Work Instructions (WIs).

5 Supporting Processes

The supporting processes are then made up of a number of QPs and WIs.

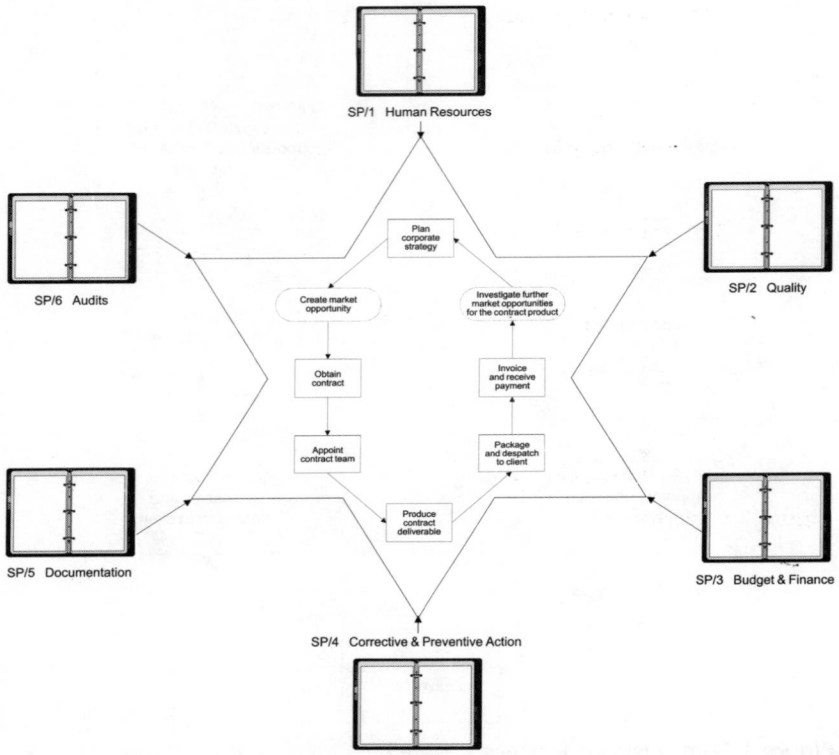

Figure 2 Supporting processes

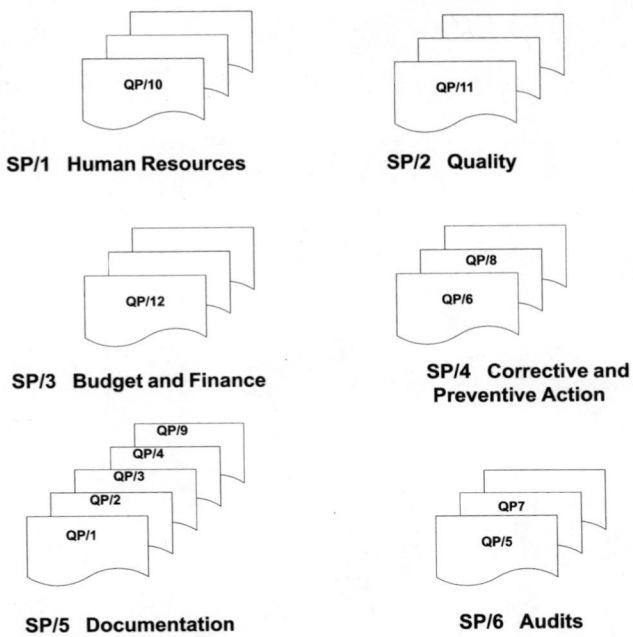

Figure 3 Quality Processes

Herne European Consultancy Ltd

Quality Management System
Part 3 - Quality Procedures

This Quality Manual has been issued on the authority of the Managing Director of Herne European Consultancy Ltd for the use of all staff, subcontractors, clients or regulatory bodies to whom Herne European Consultancy Ltd may be required to provide such information to.

Managing Director
Herne European Consultancy Ltd

File No:	**H-QMS-031RLT00**
Version No:	**00.05**
Date:	**31.12.00**

Document Control Sheet

Title	This version	Date
Herne European Consultancy Ltd - Part 3 - Quality Procedures	00.05	31.12.00
	File Number	No of Pages
	H-QMS-031RLT00	93

Abstract

Herne European Consultancy Ltd's Quality Management System is divided into four parts. This document is Part 3 and describes the Quality Procedures that have been designed to meet Herne European Consultancy Ltd's Quality Processes.

The Work Instructions associated with these Quality Procedures are detailed in Part 4.

Name	Function	Level
	Quality Manager	Prepare
	Managing Director	Agree
	Managing Director	Approve

Keywords

Approval, Audit, Budget, Change control, Customer feedback, Design control, Distribution, Document, Document control, File number, Filing, Finance, Investment, ISO 9001:2000, Meeting, Policy, Quality Procedure, Quality Management System, Report, Storage, Training.

Approved

_____ Date:_____
(Managing Director)

Amendments

Changes in the organisation of Herne European Consultancy Ltd or the environment in which it operates, may necessitate modifications, amendments, insertions and/or deletions to the overall quality management adopted by Herne European Consultancy Ltd and its associated documentation (e.g. Quality Procedures and Work Instructions). The contents of this Quality Manual may, therefore, be altered on an as required basis. All changes shall be subject to QP/8 - Change Control. Changes shall be deemed operational following approval by the authorised person/persons and published as updated sections of the Quality Manual.

No	Chapter	Amendment details	Date
01.00	All	First issue	28.06.93
02.00	All	Editorial review	05.04.94
03.00	12	New QP (QP/12)	21.09.95
03.01	4.3	Revised and reworded	23.12.95
04.00	All	Editorial revisions of all sections and annexes	30.07.96
05.00	All	Revised to conform to ISO 9001:2000	31.12.00

Distribution List

1. Managing Director
2. Quality Manager
3. Company Secretary
4. Section Manager - Quality Management Systems
5. Section Manager - Environmental
6. Section Manager - Fuels
7. Section Manager - Projects
8. Spare

Contents

Abbreviations and acronyms

Abbreviation	Definition
DCS	Document Control Sheet
HEC	Herne European Consultancy Ltd
ISO	International Standards Organisation
QM	Quality Manual
QMS	Quality Management System
QP	Quality Procedure
WI	Work Instruction

References

Ref.	Abbreviation	Title	Issue date
1.	ISO 9001	Quality Management Systems - Requirements	2000
2.	ISO 10011	Guidelines for auditing quality systems.	
		Part 1 - Auditing.	1990
		Part 2 - Qualification criteria for quality systems auditors.	1991
		Part 3 - Management of audit programmes.	1991

Documentation

Herne European Consultancy Ltd (HEC) has four levels of documentation within their Quality Management System (QMS) which is structured as shown in the table below. This document is Part 3 and describes the Quality Procedures that have been designed to meet HEC's Quality Processes.

The Work Instructions associated with these Quality Procedures are detailed in Part 4.

Table 1.1 Herne European Consultancy Ltd's Quality System - documentation

Part 1	Quality Manual	The main policy document that establishes the HEC's QMS and how it meets the requirements of ISO 9001:2000.
Part 2	Quality Processes	The Core Business Process plus the Primary and Secondary Supporting Processes that describe the activities required to implement the QMS and to meet the policy requirements made in the QM.
Part 3	**Quality Procedures**	**A description of the method by which quality system activities are managed**
Part 4	Work Instructions	A description of how a specific task is carried out

Quality Procedures

Quality Procedures (QPs) form the bulk of the QMS and describe how the policy objectives of the Quality Manual (QM) can be met in practice and how their processes are controlled. QPs contain the basic documentation used for planning and controlling all activities that impact on quality.

Each QP is unique and contains details of procedures directly applicable to HEC. By design, the QPs conform to the specific requirements contained in ISO 9001:2000, although in reality they often cover more as they are an efficient method of controlling every aspect of HEC business.

These documented procedures can be made available and used in either hard copy or electronic format and may be used as separate documents outside the QM in places of work.

Some procedures (e.g. QP/13) may contain data or information, the knowledge of which must remain restricted to HEC. These procedures are not included in the QM, beyond their title and reference number.

Current HEC QPs are listed in Table 1.2.

Table 1.2 Quality Procedures

Procedure no	Procedure title
QP/1	Document control
QP/2	Document Quality
QP/3	Design Control
QP/4	Document Approval
QP/5	Quality Management System Review
QP/6	Customer Feedback
QP/7	Internal Quality Audits
QP/8	Change Control
QP/9	Meetings and reports
QP/10	Training
QP/11	Production of a Quality Document
QP/12	Budget and Finance
QP/13	Investments

Procedure

The approval procedure for all QPs is as follows:

- The Quality Manager evaluates the requirement for a new QP, researches all available information (e.g. existing work procedures, work practices, standards etc.) and produces an 'Initial Background Draft'. This is then issued, for comment, to selected HEC staff who are directly involved in the procedure.
- The Quality Manager evaluates all comments received, co-ordinates all the necessary alterations, amendments, proposed modifications etc. and produces a Draft to the Managing Director for comment.
- Upon approval (or after modification) by the Managing Director, the QP is then issued as official HEC policy.

1 Quality Procedure 1 - Document Control

1.1 Scope

In conformance with the requirements of ISO 9000:2000, document control is essential for the overall efficiency and quality of HEC and its documents. QP/1 describes the document control procedures for HEC. It details the allocation of document codes and the procedures for distributing these documents. It describes the procedures for translating and filing (electronic and manual) these documents, how document changes are managed and the type of word-processing software and other software to be used. It does not, however, include the approval procedures for documents, which are described in QP/4 - Approval Procedures.

HEC document control procedures shall apply to all documents which are produced for the company, irrespective of from where they originate.

1.2 General

- The responsibility for all document control lies with the Company Secretary.
- A centralised filing system shall be retained in the main office.
- The term 'document' includes all HEC documents, letters, faxes, reports, minutes and contracts etc.

1.3 File numbering system

All HEC personnel shall make use of the company filing and numbering system when originating HEC documents, particularly where documents are to be distributed externally.

1.4 Document administration number

All documents which are received, despatched or processed by the main office shall receive a document administration number. A list of document administration numbers used by individual HEC consultants shall be maintained by them. Personnel based at the Head Office shall share one book, which shall be maintained by the Company Administrator. This is also the number by which the document is stored in the company computer. The number reverts to '001' at the beginning of each year.

All documents despatched by the Office shall be entered in the 'MAIL OUT' letterbook, while all documents received shall be entered in the 'MAIL IN' letterbook (for examples see Annexes A and B).

1.5 Documents produced by Herne European Consultancy Ltd

For all documents **produced** by HEC, the file reference number shall be in the footer, to the right, of every page, regardless whether the page is single or double sided. The format of this reference number shall be as follows:

H-XX-NNNAAAYY-VV.RR, where:

H	indicates that the document is related to HEC.
XX	is the file reference code (see Annex C).
NNNN	is the document administration number, which provides a unique reference for a particular document.
AAA	is the author's (or originator's) initials.
YY	is the last two digits of the year in which the document was written.
VV	indicates the version number of the document - also see paragraph 1.5.1.1 (Note: For preliminary or draft documents this number will always be '00'.).
RR	indicates the revision number of the document - also see paragraph 1.5.1.2.

Example: **H-16-1147RLT00-00.01**, where:

H	= an HEC document
16	= Financial (Insurance)
1147	= Document administration number 1147
RLT	= Author's initials (Ray Tricker)
00	= The year in which the document was written
00	= First draft
01	= Revision number 1.

1.5.1 Document changes

1.5.1.1 Version numbering

To indicate the version of the document two digits are included in the document reference number (see paragraph 1.5 above). For preliminary or draft document this number will always be '00'.

Example: H-16-1147RLT00-**01**, where:

01   = Version 1 of document 1147

Issued documents which have changed significantly from the previous version shall receive a new version number and the revision number (see paragraph 1.5.1.2 below) will revert to '00'.

1.5.1.2 Revision numbering

To indicate the revision number of the document, two digits are included in the document reference number as shown below.

Any documents or reports that have been changed shall receive a new (increased) revision number.

Example: H-16-1147RLT00-01.**02**, where:

02   = Revision 2 of version 1 of document 1147.

1.5.2 Identification of changes made to a document

Changes to consecutive revisions (of versions already having a revision number), should be identified by shaded and/or strikethrough typefonts (see Annex D to this section).

1.6 Letters produced by Herne European Consultancy Ltd

For all letters **produced** by HEC the reference number shall be in the relevant space on the first page. This number shall be repeated in the footer of every page, to the right, regardless of whether the page is single or double sided. The format of this reference number is similar to the example in 1.5, except that there is no requirement for a version or revision number. The format then shows as follows:

H-16-1147RLT00

All letters shall also have a reference indicating the person/persons, who dealt with the letter. This reference will consists of the initials of the involved persons separated by slashes (. . ./. . ./. . .) and shall be placed underneath the document reference number (on the front page only).

The first initials in the reference will be the person who initiated the letter. The middle initials are optional and are intended to indicate the person who actually wrote the letter. The last initials are the person who typed the letter.

Example: MD/QM/ANO, where:

MD   means that the Managing Director originated the document;
QM   means that the Quality Manager wrote the document;
ANO   means that the document was typed by A. N. Other.

1.7 Faxes and e-mails produced by Herne European Consultancy Ltd

For all faxes, **produced** by HEC, the reference number need only be included on the first page of the fax.

The format of this reference number is the same as the example in 1.5, except that there is no requirement for a version or revision number.

1.8 Contracts and minutes produced by Herne European Consultancy Ltd

For all contracts and minutes **produced** by HEC, the reference number shall be included in the footer of every page, to the right, in small characters regardless whether the page is single or double sided.

The format of this reference number is the same as the example in 1.5.

1.9 Documents received by Herne European Consultancy Ltd

All documents, **received** by HEC, shall have the file reference number clearly marked on the left hand side of the document, by hand, as follows:

H-XX-NNNN-DDMMYY, where:

H-XX-NNNN	is as shown in 1.5 above.
DD	is the day number of the date when the document was received.
MM	is the month number of date when the document was received.
YY	are the last two digits of the year number of the date when the document was received.

Example: **H-16-1147-260599**, where:

16	= is the document reference code (see Annex C).
1147	= document administration number 1147.
260599	= received on 26 May 1999.

1.10 Document Control Sheet

All documents shall include an HEC Document Control Sheet (DCS) as shown in Annex E to this Section. The form has seven separate parts as follows:

1.10.1 Document title

The title of the document should be kept as short as possible.

1.10.2 Version block

The version block indicates the status of the document in terms of issue and version number (also see 1.5.1.1 and 1.5.1.2).

1.10.3 Date

The date that this particular document was issued.

1.10.4 File number

The file number shall be in accordance with 1.5.

1.10.5 Number of pages

Here is shown the total number of pages making up this document, including incorporated annexes, if any.

1.10.6 Abstract

An executive overview of the document, which shall be kept as brief as possible.

1.10.7 Approval control block

The approval control block shows the responsible persons nominated to prepare, review, agree and approve the document (these responsibilities are tabled at Annex B to QP/8) and keywords.

1.11 Storing files on the server

In order to be able to retrieve stored files from the HEC server, each document shall be filed within a specific directory for that contract/section. Each contract/section shall have folder, with sub-folders for the various categories within each contract/section such as minutes, correspondence, reports, annexes, etc. The document numbering system shall be used. It is essential that the file reference number corresponds with the relevant part of the document number (see paragraph 1.5).

XX-NNNNAAYY, where:

XX　　is the file reference code (see Annex C) for the folder.
NNNN　is the document administration number (see paragraph 1.5 above).
AA　　is the author's (or originator's) initials.
YY　　is the last two digits of the year in which the document was written.

Example: **16-1147RLT00**, where:

16   = Financial (Insurance) folder
1147 = Document administration number 1147
RLT = Author's initials (Ray Tricker)
00   = The year in which the document was written.

1.12 Filing of documents (hard copies)

HEC file cabinets shall be located in the main office and are the responsibility of the Company Administrator.

1.12.1 File numbering and file cabinets

The document reference number, as described in paragraph 1.5, indicates where the document is to be filed.

Where possible, different files concerning one particular contract or section shall be grouped together.

If a received document concerns more than one contract or section, the document reference numbers of both shall be shown on that document.

1.13 Old and obsolete documents

Old and obsolete documents shall be removed from the file cabinet under the supervision of the Company Administrator. All removed documents shall be placed in file boxes, adopting the same method (used for filing documents), as described and clearly marked as 'CANCELLED'. File boxes shall be retained in the attic storeroom.

1.14 Headed Paper

All official HEC correspondence shall be printed on HEC paper using HEC logos.

1.15 Document distribution

Approved documents, working papers, reports and documents may be freely distributed to all HEC personnel as well as any personnel working for and on behalf of HEC. These papers shall all be clearly marked with the file reference number, status, originator, date and a distribution statement (e.g. **'not to be distributed outside HEC'**).

When a document is being sent to someone outside of HEC, the document or documents shall be approved by the Managing Director before dispatch and the cover letter shall include the Managing Director's signature block shown in Figure 1.1.

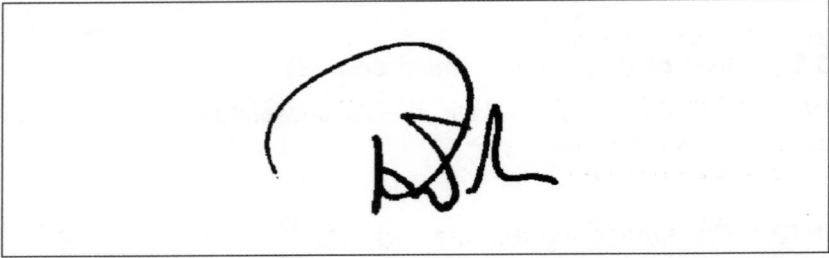

Figure 1.1 Managing Director's signature block

In exceptional cases the Managing Director may delegate approval of a specific document or documents to another officer (e.g. the Company Secretary). The actual signing (i.e. per pro) of the cover letter may also be delegated to a third party (e.g. the Company Secretary).

1.16 Draft documents

All draft versions of documents shall carry the following text on the front cover of the document:

'This is a draft version and may be used for information purposes only.'

Draft documents that do not pass approval shall be removed from circulation. If such documents have to be retained, they shall be kept in files marked **'NOT APPROVED'**.

1.17 Approved documents

All approved documents shall be uniquely numbered (see Section 1.5) and the main office will keep a register of all issued documents (see Annex F).

When a new version of an approved document is issued, copies of all previous versions shall be destroyed. This shall be covered by a statement in the covering letter to the effect that:

'On receipt of a new issue number the previous version is to be destroyed.'

1.18 Internal distribution

The Company Administrator is responsible for the distribution of all approved company documents, working papers, reports and documents within HEC.

1.19 External distribution

The Managing Director is responsible for (and shall decide on) the distribution of all approved documents, working papers, reports and documents outside of HEC (also see paragraph 1.15).

1.20 Press notices etc.

The Managing Director shall decide whether HEC approved documents, working papers, reports and documents shall be made available to the public. The Managing Director shall fix the right-of-use fee for these documents, with the Company Secretary deciding the copy price.

1.21 Software

1.21.1 Word processing

All HEC documents, working papers, and reports shall be made and stored using Microsoft® Word version 2000 format.

1.21.2 Spreadsheets and graphics

Spreadsheets and graphics for HEC documents, working papers, reports and documents shall be made using Microsoft® Office Professional 2000 and Visio Professional v5.

1.22 Copyright

The following shall be included on the front page of each deliverable:

QP/1 Annex A - Example of a mail in sheet

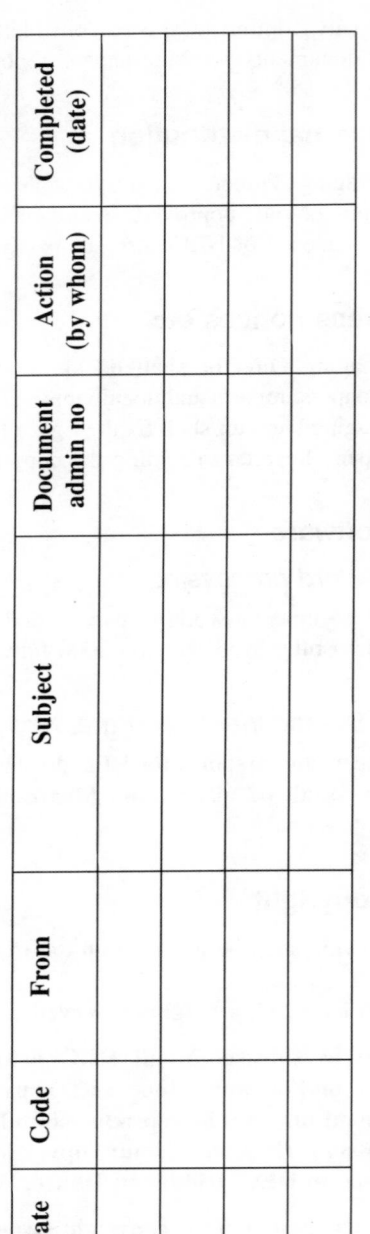

Mail in

Date	Code	From	Subject	Document admin no	Action (by whom)	Completed (date)

Code: a letter to describe the document, i.e. F = Fax, M = Minutes, L = Letter, etc.

QP/1 Annex B - Example of a mail out sheet

Mail out

Date	Code	To	From	Subject	Document admin no

Code: a letter to describe the document, i.e. F = Fax, M = Minutes, L = Letter, etc.

QP/1 Annex C - Examples of file reference codes

00-09 Administration
01   Accommodation - reservations, etc.
02   Internal quality audits
03   Meetings and reports
04   Office equipment
05   Stationery
06   Travel
07   Subcontractors

10-19 Finance
10   Audits
11   Annual accounts
12   Budgets
13   Contracts
14   Expenditure
15   Financial management
16   Insurance
17   Time and expense sheets

30-39 Public Relations
30   Articles
31   Brochures
32   General
33   Publications and presentations

40-49 Personnel Matters
40   Management
41   Social and welfare
42   Training
43   Health and safety

50-59 Quality Management System
50   Quality - General
51   Quality Manual
52   Quality Plans
53   Quality Policies and Procedures
54   Work Instructions
55   Quality Audits
56   ISO 9001:2000
57   Standards

60-69 Environmental
60   Policy
61   Standards
62   ISO 14001:1996

70-79 Fuels
70   Conservation
71   Management
72   Safety
73   Policy

80-89 Projects
80   UIC and railways
81   Military
82   Civilian

90-99 Technical
90   Manuals
91   Reference documents
92   National standards
93   International standards
94   Information Technology
95   Computer Network
96   Telephone Network

QP/1 Annex D - Identification of changes to a document

In addition to being ideal for controlling the quality of manufactured goods, Quality Plans are equally suited to the delivery ~~of~~ <u>processes and/or</u> services. The main requirement of a Quality Plan, however, is to provide the customer (and the workforce) with clear, concise instructions. These <u>instructions</u> must be ~~clearly~~ <u>adequately</u> recorded and be made available for examination by the customer. ~~It~~ <u>They</u> must leave no room for error but equally <u>they</u> should be flexible and written in such a way that it is possible to modify ~~its~~ <u>their</u> content to reflect changing circumstances.

QP/1 Annex E - Example of an HEC Document Control Sheet

Document Control Sheet

Title	This version	Date
Herne European Consultancy Ltd - Part 3 - Quality Procedures	00.05	31.12.00
	File Number	**No of Pages**
	H-QMS-031RLT00	84

Abstract

This Herne European Consultancy Ltd's Quality Management System is divided into four parts. This document is Part 3 and describes the Quality Procedures that have been designed to meet Herne European Consultancy Ltd's Quality Processes. The Work Instructions associated with these Quality Procedures are detailed in Part 4.

Name	Function	Level
	Quality Manager	Prepare
	Managing Director	Agree
	Managing Director	Approve

Keywords

Distribution, Document, Document control, File number, Filing, Quality Procedure, Storage

Approved

_____ Date:_____

(Managing Director)

QP/1 Annex F - Register of documents

HEC Document Administration Numbers

Date	Doc admin number	Type	To	Subject
01.03.99	1119	F	RLT	March activity report template
02.03.99	1120	M		Minutes of 5th Quality Meeting with TWB
03.03.99	1121	F	Hotel Europea	Hotel bookings for RLT
03.03.99	1122	L	Swift & Sure	Taxi bookings for RLT
04.03.99	1123	email	BH	Approval of Book 6
04.03.99	1124	L	Telemobile	Complaint re mobile phone repair
04.03.99	1125	R		QMS Report

2 Quality Procedure 2 - Document Quality

2.1 Scope

In addition to confirming that the technical and operational content of an HEC report, document or deliverable is acceptable, it is also important to ensure that these documents are complete, correctly formatted and do not contain any spelling mistakes etc. which could negate (to some extent) the considerable effort afforded in the production of these papers.

QP/2 describes the procedure to be adopted within HEC in order to ensure that all documents are of the correct format, content and quality.

This QP is to be read in conjunction with QP/1 - Document Control.

2.2 Document quality procedure

As the production of a document will normally require considerable time and effort, it is important that the documents themselves are of the required quality and reflect this.

Obviously the technical and operational content of a document is most important, but it is also important to ensure that these documents are of the correct format, content and quality. This can only be achieved by monitoring and confirming each stage of the document's production process, from acceptance of a task as a section work package to the actual distribution of the document. In effect, a cradle to grave approach.

The following flowchart and descriptive table shows the various points during the production of a document that require formal approval.

In producing and finalising HEC documents, the procedures contained in QP/1 - Document Control shall be observed especially those concerning the layout of documents.

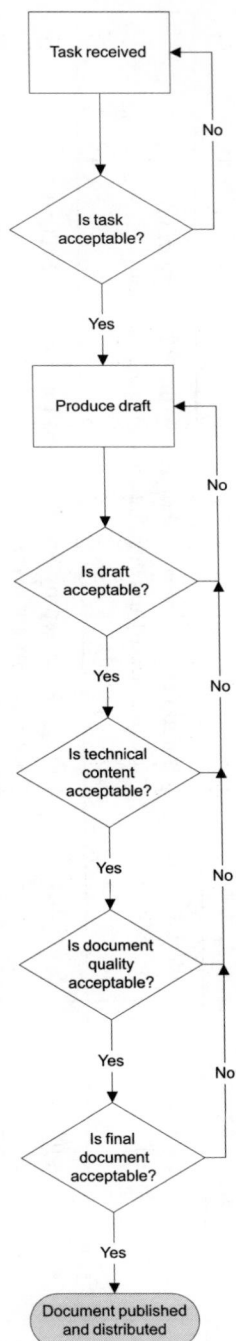

Figure 2.1 QP/2 - Document approval flowchart

Task	Description	Responsibility	Remarks	Signature and Date
(1)	• Task accepted and allocated to a section	Managing Director	Details of requirements, content, format and time frame received and approved by Managing Director.	
	• Task accepted by a section • Work package, time plan, etc. agreed	Section Manager	Task allocated to Division, Working Group or individual.	
(2)	• Draft document produced	Working Group or individual	Initial draft proposal elaborated by the Working Group (or individual) in consultation with other sections (if required).	
	• Draft approved	Specialist	Proposal agreed by Specialist and forwarded to Section Manager for approval.	
(3)	• Draft accepted	Section Manager	Draft proposals received by Section Manager and basic content agreed.	
	• Technical content approved	Section Manager	Section Manager evaluates and approves document for: • consistency with other technical documents; • overall technical content; • confirmation that all system and safety requirements have been met.	

(4)	Quality Manager	Editorial work completed on document to ensure correct cross-referencees, agreed layout, no obvious spelling mistakes and typographical errors, etc.	
	• Quality of the document approved		
(5)	Managing Director	Managing Director gives final approval to document, confirms that it meets the customer's full requirements and that it is ready for publication.	
	• Document approved by Managing Director		
(6)	Company Secretary	Company Secretary arranges for the document to be published and passed to Quality Manager for final approval prior to distribution.	
	• Document printed		
	Quality Manager	Quality Manager approves final document.	
	• Printing approved		
	Company Secretary	Company Secretary distributes copies of the document in accordance with the agreed distribution lists.	
	• Document distributed		

3 Quality Procedure 3 - Design Control

3.1 Scope

The primary function of HEC is to:

- provide advice and guidance on all quality matters;
- produce either complete Quality Management Systems, Quality Manuals, Quality Processes, Quality Procedures or Work Instructions (to suit individual customer requirements);
- provide qualified advice on environmental requirements (particularly for the electronics industry) and expert advice in fuel conservation, management and safety issues.

Although this is not a design activity in the true manufacturing sense, the principles described in ISO 9001:2000 for design are, in general, also valid for HEC. QP/3 details the requirements for Design Control within HEC.

3.2 Resourcing

The Managing Director shall assign system specification development responsibilities to Section Managers. Section Managers, in their turn, are responsible for ensuring completion of these tasks, for assigning the work to suitably trained and experienced specialists and for overseeing and supervising their output.

3.3 Planning

The Quality Manager is responsible for ensuring that the planning of all interfaces between the different activities is appropriate and that verification points are allocated and taken into account.

The Quality Manager shall approve the planning after each change and, where necessary, liaise with the Managing Director to ensure that more detailed plans are made in order that interfaces between the development activities are properly handled. The main objective is to see that the appropriate information concerning the requirements and specifications already developed and agreed on, is available to all parties - at any stage.

To facilitate this process, the Quality Manager shall use advance design planning and decision techniques (e.g. such as 'Teamwork') to control this requirement wherever appropriate.

To ensure overall task effectiveness, a time plan shall be maintained by the Company Secretary, throughout each individual contract's life and for all the main HEC activities.

3.4 Input

The input data for each stage of a contract shall (in consultation with the Quality Manager) be identified by the Section Manager, documented by the Company Secretary, and agreed with the Managing Director.

For each contract the same structure shall apply and the Quality Manager is responsible for ensuring that this actually happens.

3.5 Output

All documents shall be presented in the form as described in QP/1.

3.6 Verification

Verification of all HEC documents shall be in accordance with (when available) the relevant project or contract-specific Quality Plan and shall be documented.

Verification that documents are of the required format, content and quality shall be achieved via the procedures described in QP/1 and QP/2.

Approval shall be in accordance with QP/4.

The Quality Manager will advise the Managing Director on this subject on an as required basis.

3.7 Changes

All changes that could fundamentally influence the company scope, targets, organisation, budget, overall work breakdown structure, work packages and time plans shall be subject to the formal change control procedures described in QP/8.

4 Quality Procedure 4 - Document Approval

4.1 Scope

To achieve conformity and inter co-operation all official HEC documents[1], whether these be managerial, quality related, financial or technical, require some form of approval procedure. All official HEC documents shall be presented in the form of an official HEC document which will require the approval of the Managing Director. QP/4 details the requirements for Document Approval within HEC.

4.2 Approval procedure

4.3 General

4.3.1 Draft documents

For each type of document a number of different individuals and/or functions may be involved during the various stages of their production (i.e. from writing the initial document to final approval of the draft document). It is the responsibility of the Managing Director to assign suitably qualified persons (or sections) to complete this work. In doing so, the Managing Director shall ensure that all persons having qualifications related to the specific subject of a draft document shall participate in the preparation and approval stages (for example, the Quality Manager shall participate in all quality related matters).

When the draft document is finalised, it shall first be approved by the person assigned by the Managing Director and then by the Managing Director himself.

Draft documents are only approved when all persons assigned by the Managing Director agree unanimously. In cases where a decision cannot be taken unanimously, the Managing Director will be asked for a decision.

If an assigned individual cannot be present, he may identify a replacement who, following approval by the Managing Director, will have the authority to discuss and formally approve the document on his behalf.

The order of approval shall be:

- approve initial document (by the author(s) or their representative);
- agree contents of the draft document (Section Manager or suitably qualified person nominated by the Managing Director);
- approve the reviewed draft document (Section Manager or suitably qualified person nominated by the Managing Director).

[1] In this instance the term 'document' excludes letters, memos, faxes and e-mails.

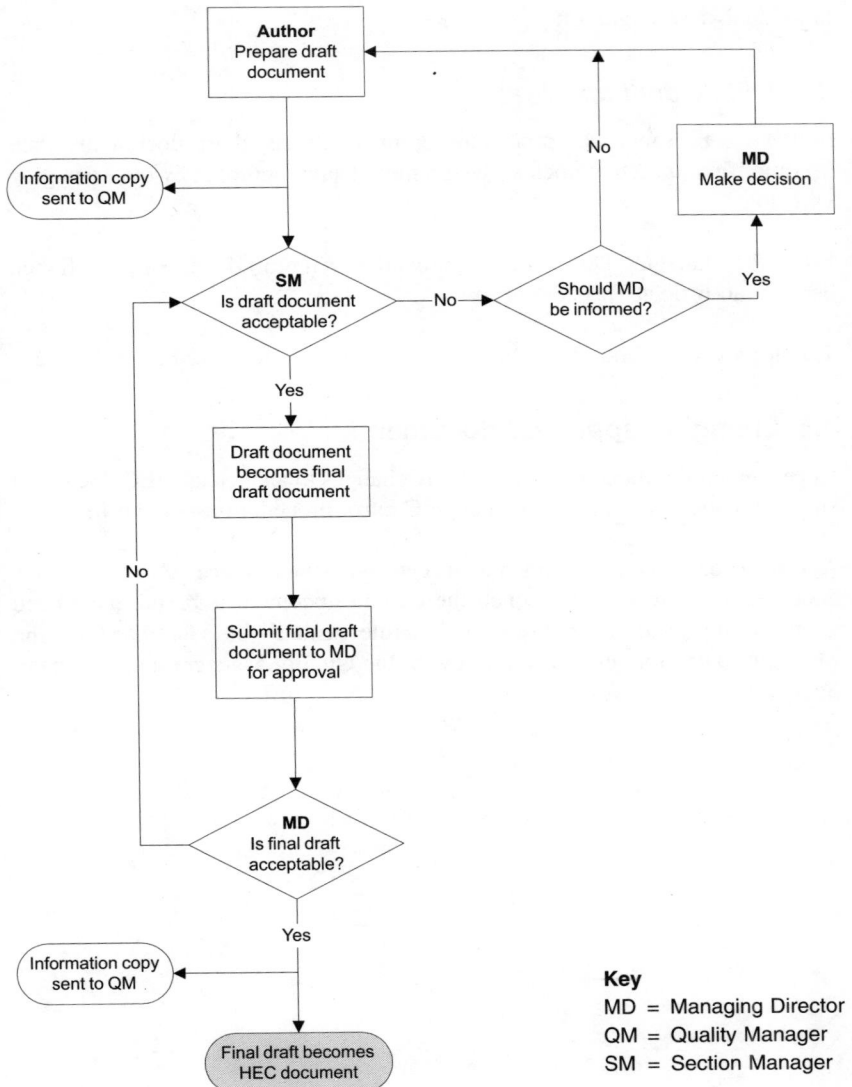

Figure 4.1 QP/4 - Document Approval flowchart

Approvals take place after the individuals representing a specific level have signed the Document Approval Form (see Annex A). A next higher hierarchical level cannot approve a document before all the assigned individuals have signed it.

4.3.2 Final draft approval

Following the approval procedure outlined above, draft documents then become 'final draft documents', which then require approval by the Managing Director.

When the Managing Director has approved a final draft document, it will then become an official HEC document.

The approval procedures for financial transactions are described in QP/12.

4.4 Changing approved documents

Once cleared by Managing Director any changes to an official HEC document shall be subject to the formal Change Control procedure as shown in QP/8.

Approval of a changed document can only take place if all previous documents and reports, on which the current document is based, have been formally approved. Exceptions to this rule need to be sanctioned by the Managing Director (in consultation with the Quality Manager and Company Secretary).

QP/4 Annex A - Document Approval Form

DOCUMENT APPROVAL FORM

Document title:	
File reference number:	

Task	Nominated authority	Approved (signature and date)
Prepare draft	Author	
Carry out quality check (QP/2)	Quality Manager	
Agree draft document	Section Manager	
Approve final draft	Managing Director	
Final quality check	Quality Manager	

5 Quality Procedure 5 - Quality Management System review

5.1 Scope

In accordance with the principles of ISO 9001:2000, bi-annual HEC QMS reviews are required in order to ensure that:

- HEC is effective in attaining its objectives as described in the QM;
- the QM remains effective and suitable for the requirements of HEC (in other words that it 'really works' in practice);
- the requirements and rules as described in the QM remain workable and are in accordance (as far as possible) with the way HEC personnel prefer to work - without losing the assurance that HEC delivers quality;
- HEC requirements are met and that the relevant rules are agreed on and are adhered to.

QP/5 details the requirements for Quality Management System reviews within HEC.

5.2 Quality Management System review

The initiative for the meetings of the Review Board shall be taken by the Quality Manager. He shall prepare an agenda and provide all relevant documents (e.g. reports of internal audits, results of product reviews, etc.). If necessary the Quality Manager shall draw attention to areas where HEC requirements are not being met or where rules are not followed. Whenever possible he will provide recommendations for improvements.

If the results of the review are such that corrective action is necessary, the Review Board shall agree on the corrective actions and suggest appropriate methods for their implementation. The Managing Director shall be responsible for ensuring the implementation of the agreed corrective actions.

The details of the review and the agreed corrective actions shall be recorded and the records shall be maintained in the company quality file.

The review shall cover all activities related to company and quality management as described in the QM, attached Quality Processes, QPs, WIs and Quality Plans.

5.3 Frequency of meetings

The Review Board shall meet every six months.

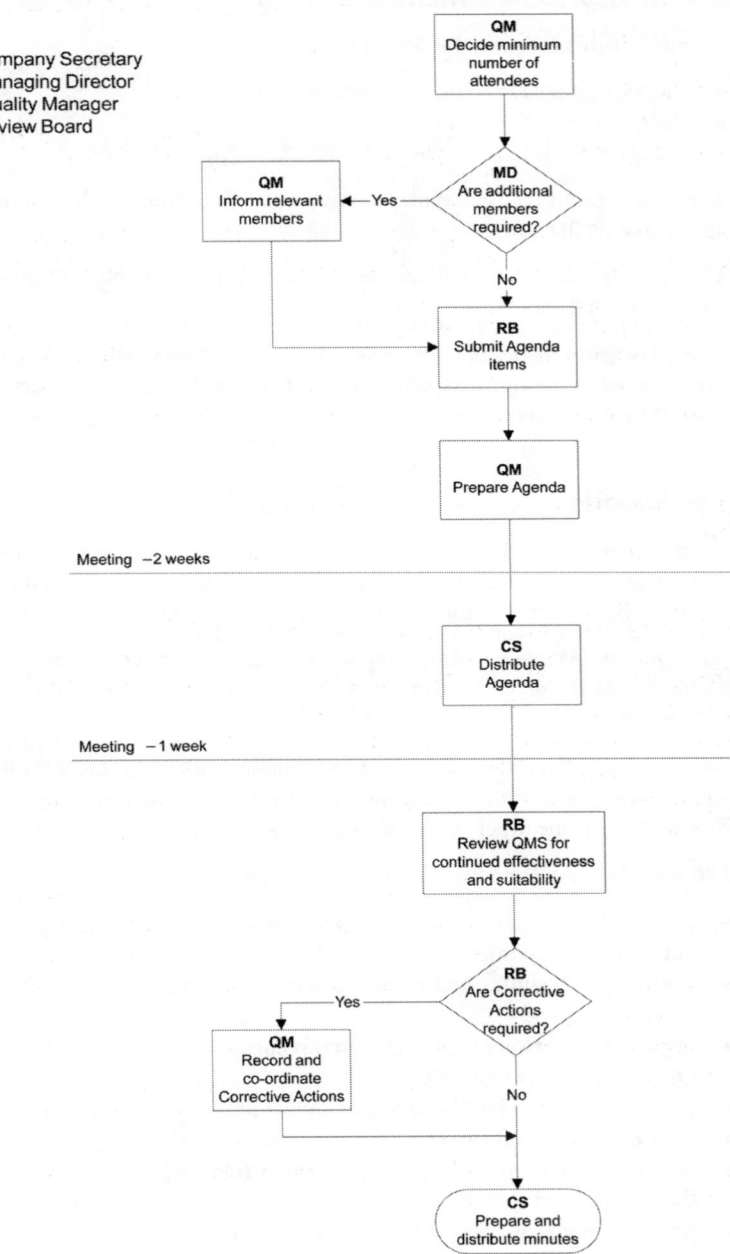

KEY
CS = Company Secretary
MD = Managing Director
QM = Quality Manager
RB = Review Board

Figure 5.1 QP/5 – QMS review flowchart

5.4 Review Board members

Permanent members of the Review Board are:

- the Managing Director (who acts as Chairman);
- the Company Secretary;
- the Quality Manager (who also acts as Deputy Chairman).

The exact number of attendees may vary according to the circumstances applicable at that time.

The Quality Manager shall decide on the minimum number of attendees for convening that meeting.

The Managing Director (in consultation with the Quality Manager) shall decide whether or not it is necessary to invite additional members and if so, who shall be involved.

5.5 Agenda

All members of the Review Board may contribute items for the agenda, but they must be submitted no later than two weeks prior to the actual date of the meeting. Such contributions shall be sent to the Quality Manager.

The Quality Manager shall prepare the agenda in consultation with the Managing Director and ensure that the relevant information documents are attached to it.

The Company Secretary shall distribute the agenda and attached information documents so that these are in the possession of all members of the Review Board at least one week prior to this meeting.

The agenda for a Review Board shall consist of:

- a review of all actions raised at the previous meetings and progressed at subsequent meetings;
- a review of minutes and actions arising from the minutes of the previous meeting;
- implementation and continued effectiveness of the QM, Quality Processes, QPs, WIs and Quality Plans;
- results of internal HEC audits and details of the corrective actions taken;
- previous HEC audit results;
- previous reports on all major deviations from HEC objectives related to time, costs and quality;
- previous consequences of changes (objectives, organisation, schedules, etc.);
- previous results of verifications on major HEC documents;
- previous results of actions agreed at previous meetings;
- customer complaints.

5.6 Meeting contents

The nature of the Review Board is such that all major issues affecting HEC shall be considered as appropriate.

In all cases the target shall be:

- to review if the QMS is still the most effective and suitable way to reach and achieve objectives and to ensure that HEC documents comply with the relevant quality and safety standards.
- to seek ways of improving HEC's QMS.

5.7 Actions

If the results of the review are such that corrective action is necessary, the Review Board shall:

- consider solutions and agree on the corrective action(s);
- agree on responsibility for the implementation of the corrective action chosen;
- agree on a timescale for the implementation and review of corrective action(s) taken.

The review and the agreed corrective actions shall be recorded in the company quality file by the Quality Manager.

The Quality Manager shall also be responsible for co-ordinating the completion of all corrective actions agreed by the Review Board.

All actions raised at previous meetings shall be reviewed and progressed at subsequent meetings.

5.8 Meeting records

The Company Secretary is responsible for ensuring that minutes of the meeting are prepared and distributed, promptly.

The minutes shall clearly state:

- actions agreed upon;
- the person responsible for implementing these actions (i.e. the Action List);
- the agreed completion date (i.e. the Time Plan).

The minutes of the meeting shall be retained kept in the company quality file.

6 Quality Procedure 6 - Customer Feedback

6.1 Scope

The successful completion of any report or specification relies on the customer commenting on the technical and operational contents of these reports and specifications.

QP/6 has been designed to ensure that any customer feedback and complaints raised against HEC reports, documents or specifications are adequately reviewed, appropriate action is taken and trends analysed.

6.2 Flowchart

See Figure 6.1 on page 283.

6.3 Initiation and assessment

All customer feedback including complaints received by the company office shall (following registration) be directed to the appropriate Section Manager for assessment.

Unless the issue raised by the customer is of a minor nature (e.g. a grammatical or typographic error) or a request for information that can be dealt with directly, the Section Manager shall initiate a Customer Feedback Form (see Annex A).

The Section Manager initiating a Customer Feedback Form shall ensure that:

- there is sufficient detail in Part A for the problem to be self-explanatory;
- customer details are included;
- any related documents are attached.

The form shall then be signed, dated and forwarded for review.

6.4 Initial review

The review shall be made either by the initiating Section Manager or referred to an internal section or QMS Review meeting for discussion. The review procedure shall ascertain if the problem can be resolved locally and if so, agree the appropriate action required.

6.5 Local action

If it is agreed that action shall be taken locally, then the Section Manager is responsible for ensuring that it is carried out and the results are detailed in Part B of the Customer Feedback Form. In taking action, full consideration shall be given to the root cause of the problem and how this may be resolved.

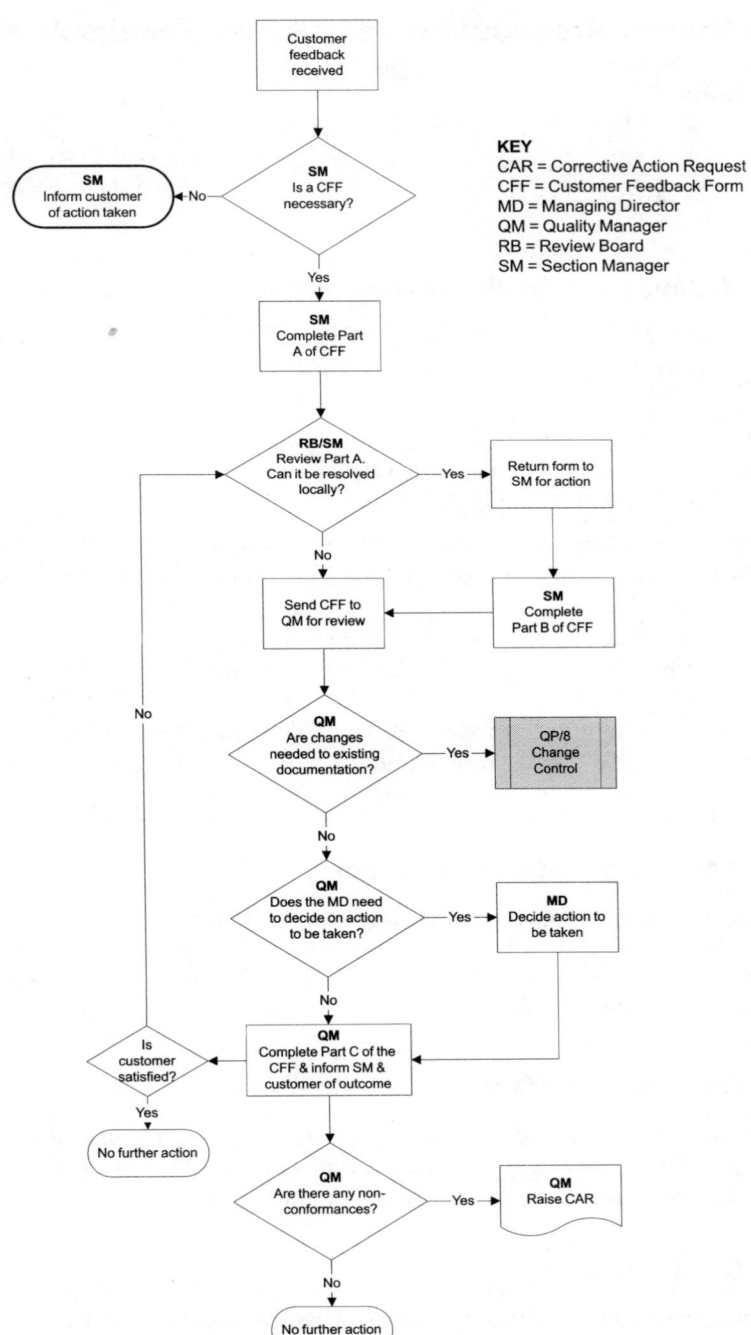

Figure 6.1 QP/6 - Customer feedback flowchart

This form shall then be signed and dated, with copies being forwarded to the Quality Manager.

If it is agreed that action shall **not** be taken locally, the original of the form shall be forwarded to the Quality Manager. Local recommendations may be made in Part B by the Section Manager if considered necessary and relevant.

6.6 Action taken by the Quality Manager

The Quality Manager shall review all forms received. Where action has been taken locally, the Quality Manager shall check that the action taken:

- is adequate;
- has no implications for other sections;
- has no implications on the HEC QMS.

Where action has not been taken locally, the Quality Manager shall review the problem and decide if it necessitates action through a Change Control Procedure (as described in QP/8) or consideration by the Managing Director.

The Quality Manager shall ensure that at all times the review considers the root cause of the problem and how this may be resolved.

Upon completion of the appropriate action, the Quality Manager shall ensure that Part B and Part C of the form are completed and that the original (or copy) is returned to the Section Manager who initiated the form.

6.7 Analysing non-conformances

The Quality Manager shall regularly review all Customer Feedback Forms to detect any trends that may have a detrimental effect on a project. When such a trend is found, the Quality Manager shall raise a Corrective Action Report (available from the Company Secretary) for review by the Managing Director.

6.8 Customer interface

The Quality Manager and/or Section Manager shall ensure that the customer, having made an enquiry, is kept informed of progress. They shall also seek comments from the customer on any action implemented.

6.9 Quality records

To ensure traceability and quality control, all records appertaining to customer feedback (and/or complaints) shall be retained by the Quality Manager in a separate quality file.

QP/6 Annex A - Customer Feedback Form

CUSTOMER FEEDBACK FORM

Ref no:		No of attached sheets:	
Customer:			
Related documents:			

Part A

Nature of feedback/complaint:	
Input:	face to face/letter/fax/phone/e-mail (delete as appropriate)

Signed:		Name:		Date:	

Part B

Action to be taken: (Section Manager/Review Board)	
Date action completed:	

Signed:		Name:		Date:	

Part C

Review by Quality Manager			
Refer to Managing Director?	Yes/No (delete as appropriate)	Raise CAR?	Yes/No (delete as appropriate)
		CAR No:	

Signed:		Name:		Date:	

7 Quality Procedure 7 - Internal Quality Audits

7.1 Scope

Although Quality Management System reviews are scheduled every six months (see QP/5), other internal quality audits shall be completed at key points throughout the company's life cycle.

These quality audits are completed so as to ensure that all activities within HEC are carried out according to the requirements, rules and procedures provided in the QM and its associated Quality Processes, QPs, WIs and Quality Plans.

QP/7 details the requirements for internal quality audits within HEC and describes the differences between a sectional quality audit and other internal quality audits.

7.2 Sectional quality audits

7.2.1 Frequency of audits

During each financial year, all sections shall be subject to at least three **complete** quality audits covering all relevant procedures. These audits shall be initiated by the Quality Manager and shall be scheduled at key points in relation to the status and importance of the various activities of a section.

It is the Quality Manager's responsibility to prepare (in consultation with the Section Managers) an audit schedule for the Managing Director's approval to cover the next 12 months (see Annex A).

7.2.2 Audit preparation and organisation

All audits shall be carried out by an audit team consisting of the Managing Director, Company Secretary and the Quality Manager (who will normally perform the function of lead auditor - but this need not always be the case).

The Quality Manager shall decide on the minimum number of attendees for convening that meeting and whether it is necessary to invite additional members and if so, who shall be involved. The exact number of attendees may vary according to circumstances applicable at that time.

In addition to agenda items, the audit team shall review, for adequacy, the Section Quality Plan together with its associated procedures. They shall resolve all concerns where the Section Quality Plan or the section's organisation is inadequate or inappropriate to meet HEC objectives as stated in the QM.

7.2.3 Agenda

The Quality Manager shall organise an agenda for each audit which shall include:

- scope and objectives of the audit;
- review of all actions raised at previous meetings and progresses at subsequent meetings;
- minutes of and actions arising from the last meeting.

7.2.4 Actions

If the results of the audit are such that corrective action or actions are necessary, the audit team shall:

- consider solutions and agree on the corrective action(s);
- agree on responsibility for the implementation;
- agree on a timescale for the implementation and review of corrective action(s) to be taken.

The review and the agreed corrective actions shall be recorded in the company quality file and a copy shall be retained by the section concerned.

7.2.5 Meeting records

The Quality Manager is responsible for ensuring that minutes of the meeting are prepared and distributed promptly.

The minutes shall clearly state the:

- actions agreed on;
- person responsible for implementing these actions (i.e. the Action List);
- agreed completion date (i.e. the time plan).

The minutes of the meeting shall be kept in the HEC quality file, by the Quality Manager, with a copy being circulated to all members of the audit team plus the section concerned.

7.3 Internal quality audits

Internal quality audits are initiated by the Quality Manager and shall be scheduled in relation to the status and importance of the various activities.

When deemed necessary, an internal quality audit may be completed by invited personnel (independent of the activity being audited), such as invited specialists from other ISO 9001:2000 certified companies.

The audits and all agreed corrective actions shall be recorded and these records shall be maintained in the company quality file by the Quality Manager.

7.3.1 Frequency of audit and audit schedule

Internal quality audits are either scheduled by the Quality Manager or completed at the request of a company officer (e.g. Managing Director, Company Secretary, Section Manager etc.).

The Quality Manager shall organise an agenda for each audit which shall include:

- scope and objectives of the audit;
- persons having direct responsibilities for the procedure(s) to be audited;
- reference documents;
- name of lead auditor and name(s) of assigned auditor(s);
- date when audit is to be concluded;
- audit report distribution.

7.3.2 Audit preparation and organisation

Depending on the complexity and the size of the audit, the Quality Manager may perform the audit himself, or he can assign a lead auditor and a team of auditors. (Note: This may be required when sections are too large, or when activities from other sections are integrated or are co-operating).

The lead auditor and the assigned auditor(s):

- shall examine all earlier audit reports on the same subject;
- shall prepare an audit check list (containing all of the topics/items to be covered and an audit programme.

The lead auditor shall report to the Quality Manager.

7.3.3 Audit execution

All audits shall be completed in accordance with the recommendations of ISO 10011.

An initial meeting between the auditor(s), the auditee(s) and the Quality Manager shall be held. During this meeting:

- a brief summary of the methods and procedures being used to conduct the audit shall be provided;

- the method of communication between auditor(s) and auditee(s) shall be agreed;
- the audit programme shall be confirmed.

The auditor(s) shall collect evidence via interviews, examination of documents and observation of activities. If possible information provided at interviews shall be checked for accuracy by acquiring the same information through independent sources.

If necessary (and required) changes to the audit programme may be made in order to achieve optimum audit objectives.

Auditors shall record all observations on the Audit Observation Sheet (see Annex B).

Auditors shall review the observations and determine which are to be reported as non-conformities.

Auditors shall discuss all observations with the Quality Manager and all observations of non-conformity shall be acknowledged by the manager (e.g. Section Manager) responsible for the activity being audited.

A closing meeting of auditor(s), auditee(s) and Quality Manager shall be held during which:

- audit observations shall be clarified;
- the critical significance of observations shall be presented;
- conclusions drawn about compliance shall be presented;
- system effectiveness in achieving the quality objectives shall be presented;
- corrective actions shall be agreed;
- the date for completion of the audit report shall be agreed.

Minutes of **all** relevant meetings, decisions and agreements shall be attached to the audit report.

7.3.4 Audit report

The lead auditor shall prepare an audit report using the Audit Report Form (see Annex C). The report must be signed by all members of the audit team, plus the Quality Manager, and copies sent to auditee(s) and company management as required.

Audit reports shall be retained in HEC quality files.

7.3.5 Corrective action

After the closing meeting the lead auditor shall prepare a Corrective Action Request (see Annex D) for each **agreed** corrective action. Corrective Action Requests shall state who is responsible for carrying out the corrective action and the timescale for its completion.

7.3.6 Follow up

The lead auditor is responsible for ensuring that corrective action has been carried out.

The lead auditor shall notify the Quality Manager of the status and/or completion of the corrective actions.

QP/7 Annex A - Audit Schedule

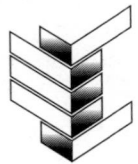

AUDIT SCHEDULE

1996-1997	Section			
Month	Quality	Environmental	Fuels	Projects
July	x			
August		x		
September			x	
October				x
November	x			
December		x		
January			x	
February				x
March	x			
April		x		
May			x	
June				x

QP/7 Annex B - Audit Observation Sheet

AUDIT OBSERVATION SHEET

Section/project to be audited:		
Reason for audit:		
Audit No:		**Date:**
Auditor:		**Sheet ... of ...**

Serial No	Observation/Supporting Evidence	Action required (Yes/No)

Circulation:	
Attached sheets:	

Signed:		Name:		Date:	

QP/7 Annex C - Audit Report Form

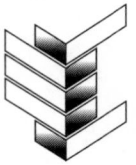

AUDIT REPORT FORM

Section/project audited:	
Audit No:	**Sheet ... of ...**
Person(s) contacted:	
Audit area(s):	
Reference documents:	
Summary:	

Audit Observation Sheet	Observation Number	Comments	Corrective Action Requirement

Prepared:		**Name:**		**Date:**	
Agreed:		**Name:**		**Date:**	
Circulation:		**Attached sheets:**			

QP/7 Annex D - Corrective Action Request

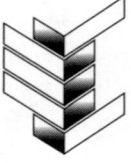

CORRECTIVE ACTION REQUEST

Section/project audited:				
Audit no:		**Audit date:**		
Auditor(s):		**Auditee(s):**		
Reference document(s):				
Non-conformance details:				
Signed: (Auditor)		**Name:**		**Date:**

Agreed corrective action:				
Signed: (Auditee)		**Name:**		**Date:**
Agreed time limit:				
Signed: (Actionee)		**Name:**		**Date:**

Progress	Signed	Date

* NB Use one sheet for each corrective action agreed

8 Quality Procedure 8 - Change Control

8.1 Scope

When a contract document reaches the stage where the information that it contains is being used (or relied on) by other sections, it is imperative that any proposed changes to the original document are not completed without the knowledge of all concerned.

In order to prevent this sort of situation occurring, a decision will be made (by the Managing Director, endorsed by the Section Managers) that at a particular stage **no** further changes, alterations, modifications, insertions or deletions will be made without the Change Control procedure described below being adopted.

QP/8 details the requirements for Change Control within HEC and is a requirement.

8.2 Procedure

All changes to HEC documents, procedures and specifications are, in principle, subject to a formal Change Control procedure.

Changes that could fundamentally influence the scope, targets, organisation, budget, overall work breakdown structure and time schedules (in addition to changes to approved HEC documents and other official documents), will have to be agreed by the Section Managers and approved by the Managing Director.

Proposals for changes shall be submitted to the Managing Director, in writing, using the Change Proposal Form shown at Annex A.

The Managing Director will ask the Company Secretary to distribute the proposals for changes to all Section Managers for discussion. The proposal for change will have to be distributed and received by all Section Managers at least four weeks prior to the next Section Managers' meeting.

Depending on the importance and impact of the proposed change(s) the Managing Director can decide to discuss the proposal in a scheduled Section Managers' meeting or call a special meeting.

A description of the types of impact and relevant approvals are listed in Table 8.1.

8.3 Impact Assessment

Depending on the classification of the proposed change, an 'impact assessment' may be required. The change classification (and, therefore, the

Table 8.1 Types of impact and relevant approvals

Change Classification	Impact Assessment	Final Approval by
A **Minor impact**: No other section or area affected. No change in man days, time schedule and costs.	No	Managing Director on advice from the Section Managers
B **Medium impact**: At least one other section or area affected. No (or little) change in man days, time schedule and costs.	To be decided by the Managing Director	Section Managers meeting
C **Major impact**: More than one other section or area affected. Significant change in man days, time schedule and costs.	Yes	Management Review Board Meeting

need for an impact assessment) will ultimately have to be sanctioned by the Managing Director. If the time, resources and budget required for an Impact Assessment are expected to be significant, formal approval by the Managing Director for carrying out this assessment is required. An example of an Impact Assessment Form is included at Annex B.

When the Section Managers have agreed to the proposed change it will be submitted to the Managing Director for final approval.

The Managing Director shall be responsible for implementing approved changes and shall make sure that all aspects which are affected by these changes are taken into consideration.

The Company Secretary shall be responsible for:

- incorporating the approved changes into existing technical documents;
- distributing these documents to the appropriate people;
- incorporating the approved changes into existing non-technical documents.

QP/8 Annex A - Change Proposal Form

CHANGE PROPOSAL FORM

Originator:			Section:		
File ref:		Date:		Serial No:	

Reason and description of change:	
Area(s) affected:	
Product(s) affected:	

Classification:	A/B/C	Impact assessment required?	Yes/No

Impact assessment summary (including man days, schedules, costs and risks)	

Full Impact assessment attached:	Yes/No

Authorisation/ Approval	Function	Name	Date	Signature
Change preparation				
Classification approval	Managing Director			
Recommendation (submit/reject)	Section Manager			
Approval	Managing Director			

Other points:	

QP/8 Annex B - Impact Assessment Form

IMPACT ASSESSMENT FORM

Originator:		Change Proposal Serial No:	

Description of proposed change:	
Impact upon (time, resources, cost, quality, etc.)	
Estimated cost of implementation of change	
Benefits:	
Recommendation	**Accept/Reject Change Proposal**
Comments:	

Signed:		Name:		Date:	

9 Quality Procedure 9 - Meetings and Reports

9.1 Scope

QP/9 describes how Management Review Board and Section Manager meetings are convened, the proposed agenda and how minutes should be produced. QP/9 also lays down the guidelines for the reporting procedure adopted by HEC.

9.2 Meetings

9.2.1 Management Review Board meetings

Management Review Board meetings shall normally take place twice a year in order to discuss important issues and to approve final documents. The Managing Director may convene additional meetings if required.

9.2.2 Section Managers' meetings

The Managing Director shall hold regular Section Manager meetings to discuss the methods and program to be adopted for the results, reports or other documents that have to be published. The preparation and detailed editing of reports and technical documents shall be carried out by section working groups or by small editing groups set up for that purpose.

Normally subcontractors and/or consultants shall only attend these meetings when their presence is deemed necessary by the Managing Director.

9.3 Discussion documents

The dates set for these meetings should allow sufficient time for the documents being discussed to be distributed far enough in advance of the meeting so as to enable members to consider them beforehand. In practice this means **at least** not later than two weeks before the meeting.

9.4 Agenda of meetings

In addition to those items covering technical aspects/problems, the agenda shall be established by the Company Secretary and the Section Managers (in agreement with the Managing Director) and shall contain the following points:

- approval of the minutes of the previous meeting;
- matters arising from the minutes of the last meeting;
- status report (verbal or written);
- budget and costs;
- date by which the work is to be completed;
- decision list and action list;
- place and date of the next meeting.

9.5 Guidelines for meetings

It is to be expected that a frank and objective atmosphere should prevail at HEC Management Review Board and Section Manager meetings, as well as with a mutual willingness to overcome problems so as to arrive, whenever possible, at a valid agreed solution.

The chair of the meeting shall direct the discussions towards a rapid solution of the problem raised without, however, sacrificing the liberty to exchange views, experience and ideas amongst the participants.

9.6 Minutes

The minutes of the Management Review Board and Section Managers' meetings shall be concise and only contain the essential points, the conclusions of the discussions and distribution of tasks between the members (i.e. the Action List).

The minutes shall, special cases excepted, normally only be sent to the Managing Director, the participants of the meeting and the Quality Manager. The minutes shall always be distributed within two weeks following the actual meeting.

9.7 Reporting

9.7.1 Company Status Report

Every six months a Company Status Report shall be written by the Quality Manager. This report will then be presented at the next Management Review Board meeting.

Following approval by the Managing Director, the Company Status Report will then be distributed to the members of the Management Review Board. These reports will contain an update of:

- overall progress;
- technical status;
- contractual status;
- financial status;
- liaison with the Railways;
- liaison with Industry;
- outstanding actions.

9.7.2 Financial reporting

See QP/12.

10 Quality Procedure 10 - Training

10.1 Scope

In conformance with ISO 9001:2000, one of the requirements of a QMS is to ensure that all HEC personnel are provided with training that will assist them in acquiring the skills and knowledge to perform effectively and to comply with HEC Quality and Safety Management Systems.

QP/10 details the requirements for training within HEC.

10.2 Responsibilities

Section Managers are responsible for ensuring that project tasks and activities are only assigned to staff qualified for that particular task or activity. This is on the basis of appropriate education, training and experience, in relation to staffing levels and HEC's current recruitment policy.

Top management identifies the need for staff training to handle the expected workload where special techniques or items of equipment are involved.

The Managing Director is responsible for ensuring that appropriate training is carried out so as to ensure that all staff involved are aware of the requirements, rules and procedures to which they are to conform and against which they will be audited.

The Managing Director is also responsible for ensuring that tasks and activities are only assigned to staff qualified for that particular task or activity and that this is on the basis of appropriate education, training and experience.

10.3 Identification of training needs

A training review may be carried out at any time, as necessitated by any of the following:

- appointment of new personnel;
- new equipment or working practices;
- change of duties or responsibilities;
- as a result of an audit or management review.

10.4 Training review

The Section Manager or manager undertaking the review shall, with the post holder:

- review training completed since the previous review;
- review and reschedule, where necessary, uncompleted training since the previous review;

- review the training needs of individual positions;
- review and identify current training requirements and ensure that the quality and safety requirements are fully covered;
- review and identify career development (where appropriate);
- ensure that the results of the review are recorded on the appropriate forms and forwarded to the Quality Manager.

10.5 Planning of training requirements

The Managing Director (with the assistance of the Company Secretary and the Quality Manager) shall budget and plan the training programme for all personnel under his responsibility. This shall also include any on-the-job training requirements.

10.6 Implementation of training requirements

The manager (e.g. Section Manager) responsible for planning training needs may either arrange training locally or subcontract formal external courses via the Company Secretary.

10.7 Training of new personnel

The Company Secretary shall ensure that all new personnel receive a local introduction briefing as detailed in the appropriate administration procedure (being prepared).

10.8 Training of Subcontractors and Consultants

The manager (e.g. Section Manager) employing subcontractors or consultants is responsible for either ensuring that they are already fully competent or that they can be trained to meet the contracted specification. The manager is also responsible for ensuring that all contracted personnel are made aware and understand the local arrangements for both quality and safety.

10.9 Quality Training

The Quality Manager is responsible for providing Induction and Refresher training courses in the HEC QMS.

10.9.1 Training courses and records

If external training is required then it shall only be obtained from established and recognised courses for which documented course content is available.

The appropriate Senior Manager shall retain records of all training. This shall include details of attendance, achievements, course content, scope, personnel who provided the training and those who received it.

All HEC personnel shall be issued with a copy of this QMS and the Quality Manager (as part of their introduction to HEC) shall brief its deliverables to them.

11 Quality Procedure 11 - Production of a Quality Document

11.1 Scope

To ensure conformity of all HEC documentation it is necessary to establish a process for the production, amendment and cancellation of all HEC Quality Processes, QPs and WIs (collectively known as 'quality documents') covering:

- initiation;
- review;
- authorisation;
- issue;
- amendment;
- cancellation.

QP/11 describes the production (and, if required, their eventual cancellation and destruction) of all new or revised HEC quality documents

11.2 Production of a quality document

11.2.1 Procedure

11.2.2 Initiation of a quality document

A written QP or WI is required for any HEC activity where consistency of quality output is likely to be impaired by its absence.

The need for a written quality document and its scope may be identified by:

- an individual;
- the results from an internal quality audit;
- the results from a company bi-annual QMS review.

Development of a quality document shall be agreed and co-ordinated by the Quality Manager who will issue and record a number, title and revision status for each document and maintain a master list.

A quality document shall be drafted by the Quality Manager or by an author nominated by the Quality Manager.

The Quality Manager shall record details of the initiator of the proposal and the author of the quality document.

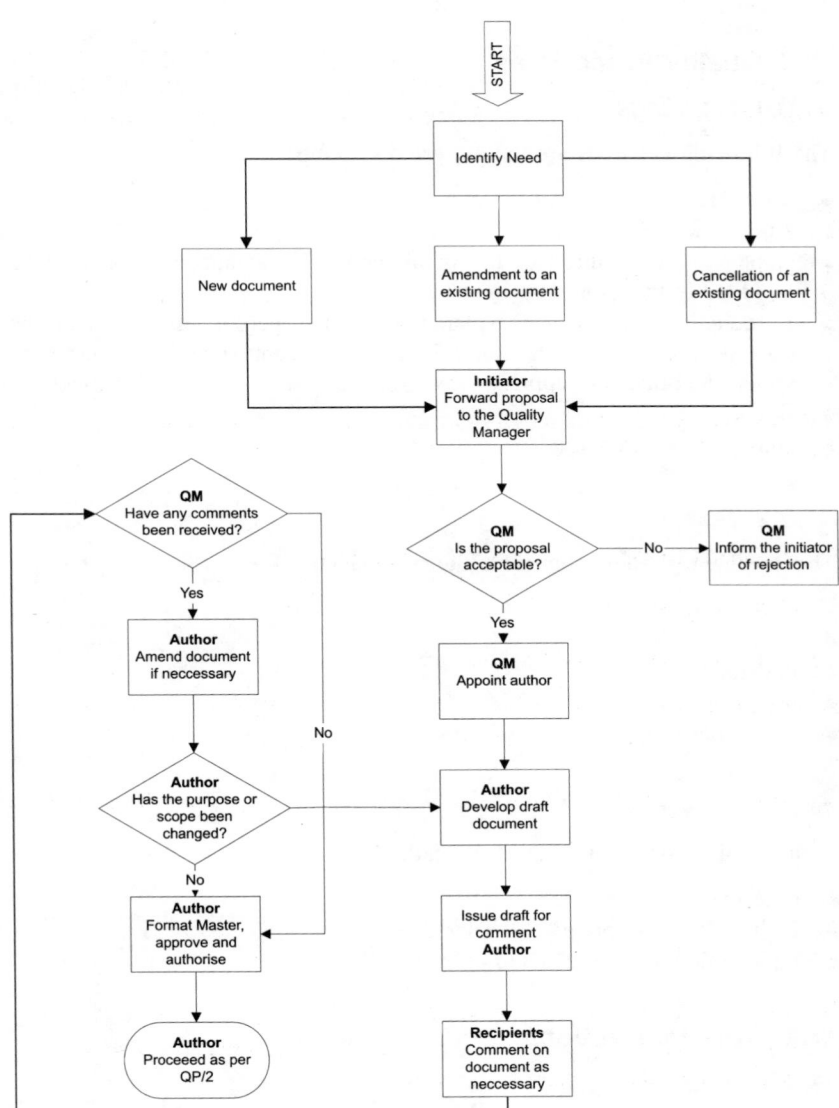

Figure 11.1 QP/11 Production of a quality document flowchart

11.2.3 Drafting

Drafts shall be prepared in accordance with QP/1 Document control and QP/2 Document Quality.

11.3 Quality Procedures

11.3.1 Headings

The following headings are the preferred contents:

- Title Page;
- Amendment Sheet;
- Contents - if required (a list of all annexes and attachments must be included in the Contents page);
- Introduction - a concise explanation of the specific objectives of the document together with a definition of the context and boundaries to which the document applies. Any exclusions shall also be identified;
- Detail;
- Annex(es) - if required.

11.3.2 Text

The document should comprise a logical sequence of text which must be easy to:

- read;
- understand;
- use;
- remember.

11.3.3 Flowchart

A flowchart is optional. If used, it shall:

- describe the main tasks;
- include decision points and related tasks;
- include details of associated QPs and WIs.

11.4 Work Instructions

11.4.1 Headings

The following headings are the preferred contents:

- Introduction - a concise explanation of the specific objectives of the document together with a definition of the context and boundaries to which the document applies. Any exclusions shall also be identified;
- Flowchart (if required);

- Detail, which must include:
  - the manner of production (and installation) where the absence of such controls would adversely affect quality;
  - measurable criteria for workmanship to ensure the required level of quality is being adhered to;
  - monitoring and quality control requirements;
  - the approval processes by which compliance can be identified;
  - who can carry out the procedure (including the minimum training requirements).
- Diagrams and tables (if required);
- Annex(es) - if required.

11.5 Review

In accordance with QP/1 Document Control, each title page of a draft for review shall be endorsed with the issue number and the current draft number (e.g. 00.04 - meaning the fourth amendment to the draft).

For control purposes, when a draft quality document is issued for comment, the date entry on the DCS page shall be the date of its production.

The Quality Manager shall circulate the draft quality document to the Managing Director, the Company Secretary and Section Managers for review. This shall be accompanied by a Request for Comments form (see Annex A) which will stipulate the closing date for responses.

On the Request for Comments form, recipients shall:

- enter appropriate comments (using additional sheets, if required);
- sign and date the form;
- return the form to the Quality Manager by the due date.

Note: If it assists the reviewer, the draft document may be 'marked up' and returned with the covering form.

Upon return of the completed Request for Comments form, the Quality Manager and/or author shall:

- evaluate and assimilate the reviewers' remarks;
- resolve conflictions, by convening meetings if necessary. (Note: final arbitration shall always rest with the Quality Manager and shall be documented accordingly);
- incorporate the comments into the revised document, dating affected page(s);
- repeat the review process if it has been necessary to make major changes to the document.

The Quality Manager shall then (with the assistance of the author - if appointed) complete the review and produce the final document.

11.6 Issue authority

A quality document shall not be issued formally until the review procedure described above has been satisfactorily completed.

Each quality document shall be issued in accordance with QP/4.

11.7 Amendments to approved documents

Amendments to an approved quality document may arise from:

- an individual applying formally to the Quality Manager (with sufficient information to support the case);
- the results from an internal quality audit;
- the results from a company bi-annual QMS review.

Each proposed amendment shall be considered in accordance with QP/8.

11.8 Cancellation

Cancellation of a quality document may be proposed by applying formally (with sufficient background to support the case) to the Quality Manager.

Each proposal for cancellation shall be processed in accordance with QP/8.

Cancellation of a quality document shall be approved and authorised in accordance with QP/8.

11.9 Local quality documents

Where the need arises for the provision of local quality documents (e.g. for a contract quality plan, specific location or section), the general principles of this procedure shall apply, although the management of its development shall be within the relative location or section. The authorisation of the documents shall be by the senior person at that location or within that section and its distribution shall be determined locally. Copies of **all** local quality documents and amendments to local quality documents shall be forwarded to the Quality Manager.

If the decision of the review (e.g. during an internal audit) is that the document should be cancelled, then the Quality Manager is responsible for ensuring that all copies of this document (issued and held in the library) are withdrawn and destroyed (also see QP/5 Quality Management System Review).

11.10 Quality records

To ensure traceability and quality control, the Quality Manager shall retain records of all quality documents (new, revised, amended or destroyed) in separate quality files.

QP/11 Annex A - Request for Comments form

REQUEST FOR COMMENTS

To: _____

Date: _____

Enclosures: _____

Subject: **Request for Comments**

Return by: _____

Please review the attached documents and return your comments by
the date specified above. You may continue your comments on a
separate sheet if desired, but please ensure you sign and date this
sheet and any additional pages you generate. When completed please
return to the above address.

COMMENTS

Quality Manager
Herne European Consultancy Ltd

12 Quality Procedure 12 - Budget and Finance

12.1 Scope

For all HEC contracts, the two main resources required are finance and manpower. QP/12 describes how both of these resources shall be managed within HEC.

Total cost management shall be computerised and controlled by the Company Secretary.

12.2 Procedure

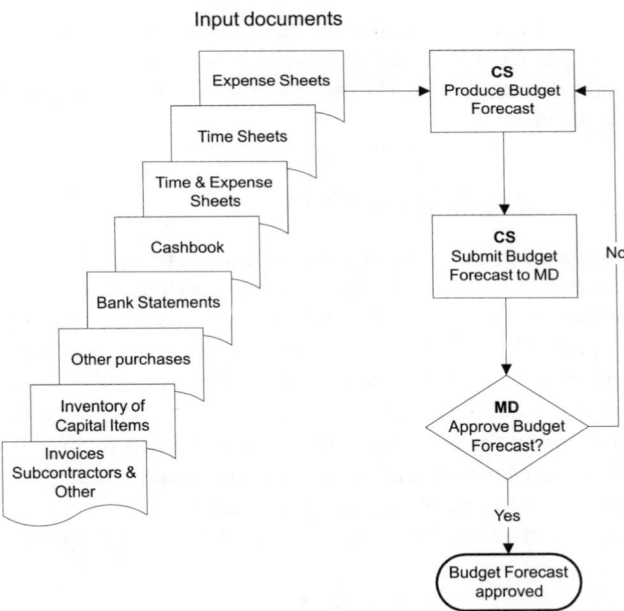

Figure 12.1 QP/12 - Budget and finance flowchart

12.3 Financial management

12.3.1 Delegation of financial authority

The Managing Director each year approves the HEC budget and delegates part of his authority to the Company Secretary.

The table at Annex A shows the delegation of authority for signing contracts and initiating orders, accepting deliveries (i.e. approving invoices), authorising payments and signing bank transfers. The amount each person is authorised to sign for is also indicated in this table.

Contracts, material orders or services may only be signed, or ordered, by the persons for whom an amount is listed in the columns 'Initiate orders and accept deliveries' or 'Sign contracts'. In cases where the Managing Director has to sign, the Section Manager is required to co-sign first.

Deliveries and invoices may only be accepted and approved by the persons for whom an amount is listed in the column 'Initiate orders and accept deliveries'. In cases where the Managing Director has to sign, the Section Manager is required to co-sign first.

In some circumstances a staff member's signature might be required prior to the Section Manager's signature.

Authorising payment and signing the bank transfers for invoices shall be limited to the persons for whom an amount is listed in the column 'Approve payment and sign bank transfer'. This action can only be completed after the delivery has been accepted.

12.3.2 HEC budget forecast

The HEC budget forecast shall consist of detailed financial budget planning for each contract and activity. The budget forecast shall include the following information:

- description;
- account;
- approved budget for each individual year and grand total;
- committed cost for each individual year and grand total;
- paid cost up to and including the cut-off date;
- result (i.e. difference between committed total and approved budget total);
- forecasted cost for succeeding years.

The budget forecast shall provide full details of **all** expenditures related to each contract and activity.

From the HEC budget forecast it shall be possible to extract the financial information for any particular year. The Company Secretary is responsible for this activity and shall provide details to the Managing Director.

12.3.3 Comparison of committed costs with approved budget

The Company Secretary shall carry out a continuous check on committed costs and the actual expenditures against the approved budget.

The Company Secretary shall inform the manager concerned if the total committed costs are higher than the approved budget for their particular activity or section.

The Company Secretary shall inform the Managing Director when it becomes likely that the total committed costs will exceed the total approved budget.

12.3.4 Administrating income and expenditure

All income to and expenditure from the HEC bank account shall be recorded by the Company Secretary in the HEC cashbook, which shall be kept in the main office.

The Company Secretary shall be responsible for the proper administration of the HEC bank account.

Copies of all transfer orders, bank statements and documents related to the HEC bank transfers shall be kept in one binder in the main office.

At the end of each month the Company Secretary shall present the cash book to the Managing Director for pre-audit.

12.3.5 Company financial audit

The Company Secretary shall, when requested, present all the required financial documents to the Company Auditor for verification.

12.4 Resource management

All manpower resources (e.g. permanent and part time staff, subcontractors and consultants) require a separate agreement/contract. These shall be initiated by the Company Secretary and signed by the Managing Director.

12.4.1 Contracts with subcontractors and consultants

All subcontractors and/or consultants working for (or on behalf of) HEC shall be required to agree to a contract which shall include the following elements:

- detailed task description (including documents);
- duration of the contract;
- fees;
- travel expenses and allowances;
- payment conditions;
- other terms and conditions.

The contract may be extended by mutual arrangement. Normally either party can terminate a contract by giving three months' notice.

12.4.2 Other purchases

Requests for the purchase of all other products or services (including major assets such as furniture and computers etc.) shall be submitted in writing (by the person requiring that product or service), to the Company Secretary. The Company Secretary shall, prior to requisition, obtain the Managing Director's approval.

The Company Secretary shall maintain an inventory of all capital items purchased for HEC.

12.5 Invoices

The Company Secretary shall stamp, date and sign all invoices received by HEC using the company stamp.

12.5.1 Subcontractors' invoices

Subcontractors and consultancies shall submit invoices for the manpower resourcing carried out and travel expenses incurred by their staff, directly to the Company Secretary for processing.

The Company Secretary shall check these invoices against the agreement/ contract previously decided. If inconsistencies are discovered, the Company Secretary shall contact the subcontractor/consultant concerned for further clarification.

Following verification by the Company Secretary, invoices shall then be sent to the Managing Director for endorsement.

Payment for invoices shall (following authorisation) be made from the HEC bank account by the Company Secretary.

12.5.2 Filing of invoices

After payment, all original invoices shall be filed, together with the following documents:

- a copy of the order form or letter (in case of a telephone order, a hand-written note from the initiating person will suffice);
- the original delivery note and a signed receipt by the initiator or the person authorised to sign on his behalf;
- a copy of the bank transfer note or cheque.

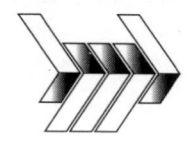

QP/12 Annex A - Delegation of Financial and Contractual Authority

DELEGATION OF FINANCIAL AND CONTRACTUAL AUTHORITY

Name	Initiate orders and accept deliveries	Maximum amounts		Example of signature
		Sign bank transfers and approve invoices	Sign contracts	
Herne European Consultancy Ltd Company stamp	Delivery as ordered	Payment authorised		
Managing Director	unlimited	unlimited	unlimited	
Section Managers	£6,000	£6,000	£6,000	
Company Secretary	£1,000	*	*	

* No authorisation

Herne European Consultancy Ltd

Quality Management System

Part 4 - Work Instructions

This Quality Manual has been issued on the authority of the Managing Director of Herne European Consultancy Ltd for the use of all staff, subcontractors, clients or regulatory bodies to whom Herne European Consultancy Ltd may be required to provide such information to.

Managing Director
Herne European Consultancy Ltd

File No:	**H-QMS-032RLT00**
Version No:	**00.05**
Date:	**31.12.00**

Document Control Sheet

Title	This version	Date
Herne European Consultancy Ltd - Part 4 - Work Instructions	00.05	31.12.00
	File Number	No of Pages
	H-QMS-032RLT00	23

Abstract
The Herne European Consultancy Ltd's Quality Management System is divided into four parts. This document is Part 4 and describes the Work Instructions that show how a specific task is carried out.

Name	Function	Level
	Quality Manager	Prepare
	General Manager	Agree
	Managing Director	Approve

Keywords
Document, ISO 9001:2000, Policy, Quality, Quality Management System, Quality Manager, Quality Manual, Quality Procedure, Work Instruction.

Approved
_____ Date: _____
(Managing Director)

Amendments

Changes in the organisation of Herne European Consultancy Ltd or the environment in which it operates, may necessitate modifications, amendments, insertions and/or deletions to the overall quality management adopted by Herne European Consultancy Ltd and its associated documentation (e.g. Quality Procedures and Work Instructions). The contents of this Quality Manual may, therefore, be altered on an as required basis. All changes shall be subject to QP/8 - Change Control. Changes shall be deemed operational following approval by the authorised person/persons and published as updated sections of the Quality Manual.

No	Chapter	Amendment details	Date
01.00	All	First issue	28.06.93
02.00	All	Editorial revision	05.04.94
03.00	4	Inclusion of WI/4	21.09.95
03.01	2.2	Revised and reworded	23.12.95
04.00	All	Editorial revisions of all sections and annexes	30.07.96
05.00	All	Revised to conform to ISO 9001:2000	31.12.00

Distribution List

1. General Manager
2. Quality Manager
3. Company Secretary
4. Section Manager - Quality Management Systems
5. Section Manager - Environmental
6. Section Manager - Fuels
7. Section Manager - Projects
8. Spare

Contents

Abbreviations and acronyms

Abbreviation	Definition
HEC	Herne European Consultancy Ltd
ISO	International Standards Organisation
QM	Quality Manual
QMS	Quality Management System
QP	Quality Procedure
WI	Work Instruction

References

Ref.	Abbreviation	Title	Issue date
1.	ISO 9001	Quality Management Systems - Requirements	2000
2.	ISO 10011	Guidelines for auditing quality systems. Part 1 - Auditing. Part 2 - Qualification criteria for quality systems auditors. Part 3 - Management of audit programmes.	1990 1991 1991

Documentation

HEC has four levels of documentation within their QMS which is structured as shown Table 1.1. This document is Part 4 and describes the WIs that have been adopted in order to carry out a specific task.

The QPs associated with these WIs are contained in Part 3.

Table 1.1 Herne European Consultancy Ltd's Quality Management System – documentation

Part 1	Quality Manual	The main policy document that establishes the HEC's QMS and how it meets the requirements of ISO 9001:2000.
Part 2	Quality Processes	The Core Business Process plus the primary and secondary supporting processes that describe the activities required to implement the QMS and to meet the policy requirements made in the QM.
Part 3	Quality Procedures	A description of the method by which quality system activities are managed.
Part 4	**Work Instructions**	**A description of how a specific task is carried out.**

Work Instructions

WIs describe how to perform specific operations and are produced for all of the relevant activities of HEC so as to ensure that the whole company can work to the same format.

WIs describe how individual tasks and activities are to be carried out. They describe, in detail, what is to be done, who should do it and when it has to be completed. They can, for example, cover simple issues such as making travel and hotel arrangements to more complex issues such as the structure of HEC reports.

They are produced for all of HEC's relevant activities so as to ensure that the whole company can work to the same format.

Current HEC Work Instructions are listed below:

Table 1.2 Work Instructions

WI No	Work Instruction Title
WI/1	Travel and Hotel Arrangements
WI/2	Timesheets and Expense Sheets
WI/3	Subcontractors' Invoices
WI/4	CD-ROM Distribution

Procedure

The approval procedure for all WIs is as follows:

- The Quality Manager evaluates the requirement for a new WI, researches all available information (e.g. existing work procedures, work practices, standards etc.) and produces an 'Initial Background Draft'. This is then issued, for comment, to selected HEC staff who are directly involved in the WI.
- The Quality Manager evaluates all comments received, co-ordinates all the necessary alterations, amendments, proposed modifications etc. and produces a Draft to the Managing Director for comment.
- Upon approval (or after modification) by the Managing Director, the WI is then issued as official HEC policy.

1 Work Instruction 1 - Travel and Hotel Arrangements

1.1 Scope

This procedure defines the actions to be taken for ensuring the timely and efficient handling of all travel requests.

1.2 Procedure

When HEC staff are required to travel away from their normal place of work for meetings etc. they shall complete a Travel Form (see Annex A), specifying the:

- name of the traveller;
- reason for the meeting(s);
- budget(s) to which the costs must be charged;

- start and end dates of the meeting(s);
- where the meeting is taking place;
- predicted departure and arrival times;
- hotel reservation and travel tickets, if required.

The Travel Form will be signed by the initiator and an information copy sent to the Company Secretary.

If hotel reservations and travel tickets are required, an information copy shall also be sent to the Company Administrator, who will make the appropriate arrangements.

After the staff member has returned from the journey he/she will add the actual data to the Travel Form, sign it and then submit it to the Company Secretary for reimbursement of expenses.

An allowance for travel expenses will be given on the basis of a lump sum per absence of (or fractions of) 24 hours, as determined by the departure and in conformance with the current, published, HEC rates.

WI/1 Annex A - Travel Form

TRAVEL FORM

Name	
Reason for travel:	

Reservations to be made by HEC?	Yes/No

Meeting Information

Start date	End date	Where	Client to be billed

Travel Information

		Predicted		Actual	
		Date	Time	Date	Time
From					
To					
From					
To					

Signed: (Initiator):		Name:		Date:	
Signed: (Company Secretary)		Name:		Date:	

2 Work Instruction 2 - Timesheets and Expense Sheets

2.1 Scope and objectives

To enable Section Managers to properly account for the hours spent by HEC staff (including management), it is necessary for this information to be freely available to them.

WI/2 describes the procedure for keeping track of all hours spent and shall be used by all HEC staff.

2.2 Time and expense sheets

The purpose of the time and expense sheets (see Annexes A and B) is to indicate the actual time spent on company and contract work as well as recording the actual travel cost (i.e. transport charges, meals, hotel and other authorised expenditure), incurred in connection with company and contract work.

During the agreement/contract period subcontractors and consultants shall (having first obtained the signature of the Section Manager concerned) send their time and expense sheets to the Company Secretary on the last day of each month.

The Company Secretary shall check the consistency of these reports **before** submitting them to the Managing Director for approval.

This WI should be read in conjunction with QP/12 - Budget and Finance.

2.2.1 Time sheets

The time sheet shall contain the following information:

- actual office hours (hours or days, depending on what is stated in the agreement or contract);
- travel time (for official HEC business);
- productive travel time (normally 50% of travel time).

The Company Secretary shall compare the time sheets with the budget and adjust the forecast when required.

2.2.2 Expense sheets

Travel costs (i.e. transport charges, meals, hotel, telephone charges and other authorised expenditure) may be charged to the company in accordance with the agreement/contract.

All costs shall be in the same currency as per the agreement/contract unless otherwise stipulated and/or agreed.

The Company Secretary shall compare the expense sheets with the budget and adjust the forecast when required.

The Company Secretary shall check and sign the expense sheets if he agrees with the contents. The expense sheets will then require approval by the Managing Director.

Personal expenditure incurred by a subcontractor/consultant is considered to be the responsibility of the subcontractor's/consultant's parent organisation. They are, therefore, responsible for reimbursing the subcontractor/consultant directly.

2.2.3 Time and Expense Reports

On a monthly basis, HEC staff shall consolidate the details contained in the Time and Expense sheets into a monthly Time and Expense Report (see Annex C).

WI/2 Annex A - Time Sheet

TIME SHEET

Name	
Month:		Year:	

Day	Actual office hours	Travel time	Productive travel time	Total productive hours
1				
2				
3				
4				
5				
6				
7				
8				
9				
10				
11				
12				
13				
14				
15				
16				
17				
18				
19				
20				
21				
22				
23				
24				
25				
26				
27				
28				
29				
30				
31				

Signed:		Name:		Date:	

WI/1 Annex B - expense sheets

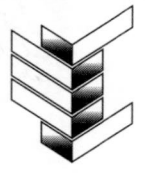

EXPENSE SHEET

Name	
Month:	**Year:**

							TOTALS
Week No	(1)						
Week ending	(2)						
Air fares	(3)						(10)
Tube & train fares	(3)						(10)
Coach fares	(3)						(10)
Taxi fares	(3)						(10)
Hotel	(4)						(10)
Meals	(5)						(10)
Entertainment	(6)						(10)
Telephone	(7)						(10)
Other expenses	(8)						(10)
TOTALS	(9)						(11)

Signed:		Name:		Date:	
Signed:		Name:		Date:	

Here follows a brief description how to use the Expense Sheet.
1) Week number.
2) Date of the Sunday of the week reported in this line.
3) Travel costs by air, train, taxi, etc.
4) Hotel costs.
5) Meal costs, if you were not at your principal location.
6) Entertainment costs for company guests.
7) Costs for official telephone calls.
8) Other costs, like material, books, software etc. (**to be approved by the Company Secretary**).
9) The total of all costs for the week concerned.
10) Total costs of your travel, hotel, meals, etc.
11) Total of all costs for the month concerned, again **except** your personal fees.

WI/1 Annex C - Time and Expense Report

TIME AND EXPENSE REPORT

Name	
Month:	Year:

Time Card

Week ending	Subject	Days spent	Location	Expenses						
				Travel expenses Train/Air fares	Hotel	Taxi	Meals	Other expenses	Totals	
				Allowance:						
Totals:				Totals:					End total:	

3 Work Instruction 3 - Subcontractors' invoices

3.1 Scope

WI/3 covers the approval procedure and payment for invoices from subcontractors.

3.2 Approval of invoices

Invoices from subcontractors shall be sent directly to the Company Secretary who shall:

- stamp the invoice and fill in the date and data as appropriate;
- keep a copy of the invoice;
- send the stamped original to the Section Manager for agreement against the planned work achievement/payment schedule as indicated in the contract.

3.3 Payment of invoices

All invoices submitted for approval must be accompanied by a copy of the approved Subcontract Approval Form.

Invoices shall be paid within one month of receipt of the invoice or of the work being completed, whichever is the latest.

3.4 Invoice records

The Company Secretary shall keep records of the invoices received and their subsequent payment.

4 Work Instruction 4 - CD-ROM Distribution

4.1 Scope

HEC are frequently requested to provide copies of contract deliverables to clients, section team members and third parties. The simplest and most cost effective way of distributing this information is via CD-ROM. WI/4 describes this process.

4.2 Procedure

Section Managers and specified individuals are responsible for (and shall decide on) the external distribution of all approved deliverables, working papers, reports and documents outside the project. (Also see QP/4 - Document Approval).

Section Managers (and specified individuals) shall determine:

- the requirement (need) to distribute copies (or parts of) HEC deliverables;
- the manner in which HEC deliverables may be distributed to clients, project team members and third parties;
- their availability and distribution.

4.2.1 Distribution list

The distribution of all HEC CDs shall be completed by the Company Secretary who shall maintain a distribution list, which will be updated every time a new delivery is made. The list shall include details of the person to whom the CD was distributed, its contents, the date of distribution and the selling price.

4.2.2 Updating previous distributions

Section Managers shall advise the Company Secretary every time a new version of a CD is issued and the Company Secretary shall inform all persons having received a previous version of that CD that a new version is available and (on request) provide replacement (i.e. updated) copies of that CD.

4.2.3 Price guidelines

The price charged by HEC for a CD shall depend on:

- the type of contract;
- the method of transmitting (i.e. sending) this information to the company;
- the type and amount of information contained on the CD;
- the time spent preparing the CD.

4.2.4 CD type

All HEC deliverables shall be distributed using electronic files formatted onto a CD-ROM which is readable by any standard CD-ROM reader.

4.2.5 CD labelling

All CD-ROMS provided by HEC shall be labelled. These labels shall be identified by a circular label (see example below) containing the HEC logo and details of the contract deliverable.

Figure 4.1 Example of a CD-ROM label

4.2.6 Plastic case - front

The front of the CD-ROM's plastic case shall be similar to the CD-ROM label and shall contain the HEC logo together with details of the contract deliverable and a copyright statement as shown in Figure 4.2.

Figure 4.2 Example of the front cover of the plastic case

4.2.7 Plastic case - back

The back of the CD-ROM's plastic case shall contain the text shown in Figure 4.3.

Installation and User Instructions

This CD-ROM contains data files only. It does not contain any application software.

A PC operating in a Windows environment with a CD-ROM drive and loaded with the Acrobat reader software is required to read the data contained on this CD.

The Adobe Acrobat Reader is free software produced by Adobe and can be obtained from Adobe Systems Incorporated. Details can be found on the Internet (*www.adobe.com/acrobat/*).

The data files can be opened using the File Manager menu command.

1. Insert the CD in to CD-ROM drive and select File Manager/ Explorer (depending on version of Windows being used).
2. Select the drive containing the CD. (This will usually be the 'D' drive).
3. From the directory structure displayed, select the **Readme.txt** file.
4. From the directory structure displayed select the **index.pdf** file and open it.

Figure 4.3 Example of the back cover of the plastic case

4.2.8 Plastic case - spine

The spine of the CD-ROM's plastic case shall contain details of the contract deliverable.

4.2.9 Internal matter

An optional sheet (the same size as the CD case) may be included at the discretion of the Section Manager so as to include details of the deliverable, its potential use, any limitations etc.

4.2.10 Draft deliverables

All draft versions of HEC deliverables shall carry the following text inside the front cover of CD case:

> **This is a preliminary version distributed for information purposes only. It should not, therefore, be used to extract definitive information from. Neither HEC nor its participating members are liable for any damage (including, but not limited to, claims from third parties) caused by information extracted from this preliminary version.**

4.2.11 Approved deliverables

When a new version of an approved deliverable is issued, copies of all previous versions shall be destroyed. This shall be covered by a statement in the covering letter to the effect that:

> **On receipt of this CD, all previous versions are to be destroyed.**

Part Seven _____

Self-assessment

So by now you should have your own organisation-specific Quality Management System, but how do you monitor its effectiveness?

Part Seven covers the often-overlooked topic of self-assessment. Methods for completing management reviews and quality audits (internal or via third party assessment) are discussed.

Also included are:

- self-assessment checklists against the requirements of ISO 9001:2000;
- examples of audit stage checklists;
- annexes listing:
  - the headings of ISO 9001:2000;
  - the likely documentation that an organisation would need to meet the requirements of ISO 9001:2000;
  - a complete index to the ISO 9001:2000 standard.

7
Self-assessment

7.1 How ISO 9000 can be used to check an organisation's Quality Management System

Having set up your own Quality Management System (QMS), how can you prove to a potential customer that it fully meets the recommendations, requirements and specifications of ISO 9001:2000? Indeed, how can you check a subcontractor's or a supplier's QMS?

If management obey the requirements of the QMS standards that have been described so far, then they will be well on their way to running a quality organisation. The requirements of QMS do not rest there, however. The organisation must continually review their QMS as to its continuing suitability and success, reveal defects, danger spots or irregularities, suggest possible improvements, eliminate wastage or loss, check the effectiveness of

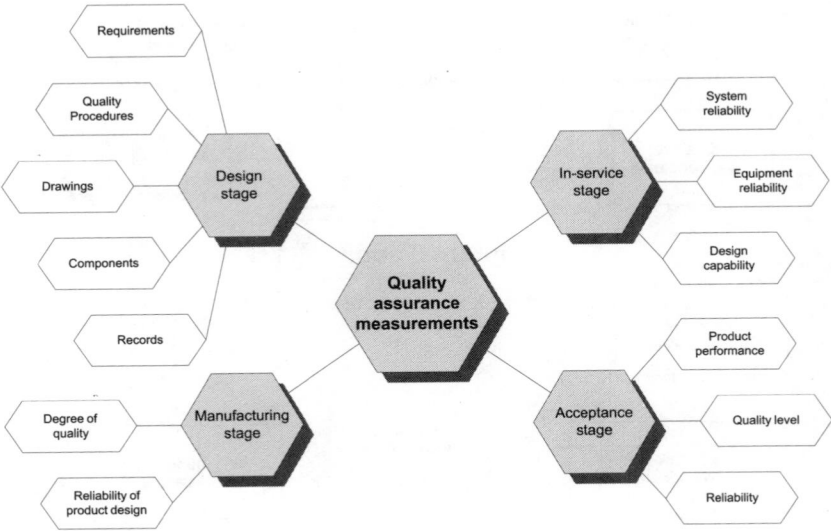

Figure 7.1 Quality assurance measurements

management at all levels and be sure that managerial objectives and methods are effective and achieving the desired result. Above all an organisation must be prepared to face up to an audit of their quality procedures from potential customers.

7.2 Internal audit

The purpose of an internal quality audit is to identify potential danger spots, eliminate wastage and verify that corrective action has been successfully achieved. The procedures with which to carry out these audits should always be documented and available.

An audit plan determines whether the QMS is effectively achieving its stated quality objectives and should be established as soon as possible. Indeed, it is a requirement of ISO 9001:2000 that an assessment is regularly completed by the organisation of all the production and manufacturing techniques that they use together with the elements, aspects and components belonging to that organisation's QMS.

The type and content of an internal audit varies with the size of the organisation. In some circumstances it can even mean going as far as having to review the statistical control methods that are used to indicate or predict the need for corrective action being carried out.

Another very important reason for carrying out an internal audit is obviously that it provides a comparison between what the QMS or Quality Plan stipulates should be done and what is actually being done.

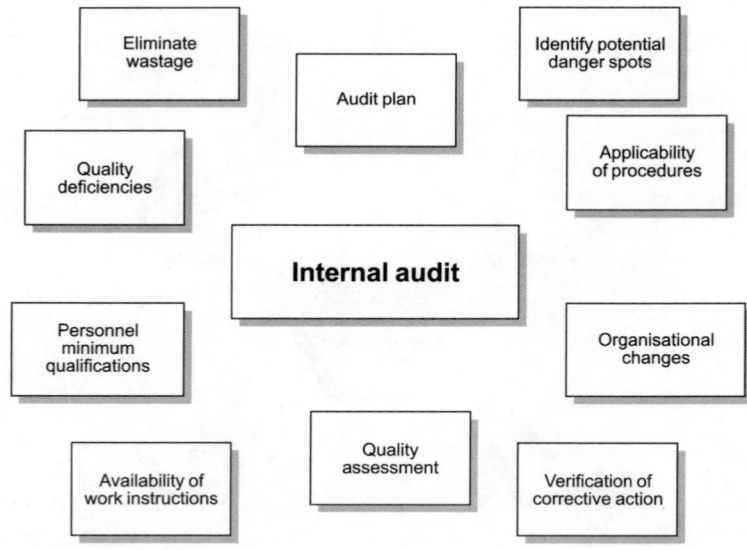

Figure 7.2 Internal audit

The main aim, however, of an internal audit is to confirm that everything is OK.

This verification activity will, depending on the size and activities of the organisation, include testing and monitoring the design, production, installation and servicing processes, the design reviews and the method of auditing the QMS.

The audit should be capable of identifying such things as non-compliance with previously issued instructions and deficiencies within the QMS. The audit should recommend any corrective actions that can be achieved to improve the system.

It is essential that management shall take timely corrective action on all deficiencies found during the audit. Follow-up actions should include the verification of the implementation of corrective action, and the reporting of verification results.

7.2.1 Audit plan

To be effective, an 'internal audit' must be completed by trained personnel and where possible by members of the quality control staff – provided, that is, that they are **not** responsible for the quality of that particular product.

This does not, of course, stop the management from using an outside agency (i.e. a third-party certification) if they wish to, thereby gaining a completely unbiased view of the general success of their QMS.

The selection of the department to be audited should always be on a random basis and normally these internal audits will be completed every three months or so. Ideally the audit should be pre-planned so that it covers all aspects of quality control within one calendar year.

There are many reasons why an internal audit should be carried out, and provided they are completed by qualified personnel, they are usually successful.

The audit plan should cover:

- all the specific areas and activities that are to be audited;
- the reasons why an internal audit is being completed (e.g. organisational changes, reported deficiencies, survey or routine check);
- stipulate the minimum qualifications of the personnel who are to carry out the audit;
- describe how the audit report should be finalised and submitted.

7.3 External audit

Although the supplier may have been able to convince the purchaser that their QMS is effective, it is in the interests of the purchaser to conduct their own evaluation (audit) of the supplier. This is usually done on an irregular basis.

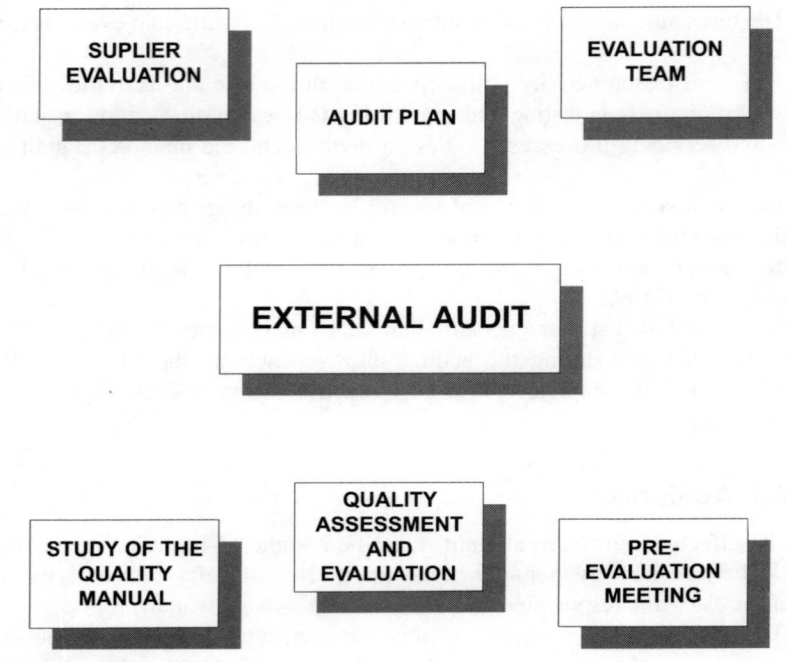

Figure 7.3 External audit

The supplier must, of course, agree to the principle of purchaser evaluations being carried out and it is usual to find this as a separate clause in the contract.

Normally these audits are pretty simple, but – particularly when the material, product or service being purchased is complex – the purchaser will need to have a reasonably objective method of evaluating and measuring the efficiency of the quality control at the supplier's factory and be certain that the system established by the supplier complies with the laid down standards and is, above all, effective. This method is known as the 'supplier evaluation'.

7.3.1 Supplier evaluation

Part of the initial contract will stipulate that the supplier provides access to the purchaser's inspectors and sometimes even accommodation and facilities to enable the purchaser's representatives to conduct their activities and evaluations. These facilities depend upon the level of surveillance, but could require the supplier to provide:

- suitable office and administrative facilities;
- adequate work space for product verification;

- access to those areas where work is in progress or to those which affect the work;
- help in documenting, inspecting and releasing material and services;
- the use of inspection and test devices and availability of personnel to operate them are necessary.

7.3.1.1 Evaluation team

Two or more inspectors from the purchaser's organisation will form the evaluation team. These inspectors must be thoroughly skilled in the requirements of quality assurance and are normally drawn from the purchaser's own quality control section.

7.3.1.2 Pre-evaluation meeting

Before the evaluation team visits the supplier's premises they must first be given the chance to:

- meet the supplier's staff to discuss the procedures being used;
- identify the supplier's divisions that will be tested;
- decide which representatives of the organisation will be required to accompany the evaluation team during their inspection;
- agree dates and outline timetables, etc.

7.3.1.3 Study of the quality manual

The purchaser must then be given a copy of the supplier's Quality Manual. The Quality Manual will be scrutinised not only for its accuracy and clarity but also its position compared to national and international standards and to see that it conforms to the relevant sections of ISO 9001:2000.

When the manual has been thoroughly examined, the purchaser will then send a team of inspectors to the supplier's premises to fully scrutinise every aspect of the supplier's design office, purchasing, storekeeping, manufacturing, assembly and test facilities to see that the work carried out complies with the procedures (promises!) made in their Quality Manual.

7.3.1.4 The evaluation

Having completed the pre-evaluation, the purchaser is now able to visit the supplier's premises for a complete inspection.

During the actual evaluation, the department heads will first be required to describe to the team exactly how their quality control system works. They will have to provide examples of their quality control documentation and possibly even be required to prove that certain divisions have the correct documentation and that it is up to date. The department heads will then have to show how stock is received, accounted for and withdrawn from stores, how the appropriate drawings are issued, updated and eventually disposed of. The evaluation team will want to see the route cards and/or 'travellers' that accompany partially completed work.

The purchaser will, as part of their QMS audit, possibly carry out an evaluation of the sampling procedures used by the supplier – to ascertain whether they conform to those laid down in the Quality Plan for that particular product.

During their evaluation it is also possible for the purchaser's team to ask for a previously inspected batch to be rechecked so they can see if a similar or comparable result is obtained.

Other aspects of the manufacturer's facilities that the inspectors might well want to look at (particularly if the supplier is an organisation actually manufacturing a product) could include:

- evidence that their test equipment and other instruments have been regularly maintained and calibrated against a known source;
- that rejected or unacceptable components and assemblies are clearly marked and segregated to avoid any chance of their accidental inclusion with other items that have already been accepted.

At the end of this evaluation, a meeting will be arranged between the evaluation team and the factory management to discuss their findings and to be sure that there are not any misunderstandings, etc.

The eventual evaluation report will then be formally presented at a meeting with the management. The result of this meeting could be one of the following:

7.3.1.4.1 Acceptable system control

This means that the evaluation has shown that the supplier has a satisfactory QMS, there are no deficiencies and the supplier has been able to give an assurance of quality. When this happens, there should be no reason why the purchaser should feel it necessary to demand any radical changes to the supplier's system.

But even though the supplier may have proved that they are up to a satisfactory standard, the purchaser will still have the right to (and often does) insist on making further inspections throughout the duration of the contract.

7.3.1.4.2 Weak system control

This covers the situation where the evaluation team find several significant weaknesses in the supplier's system.

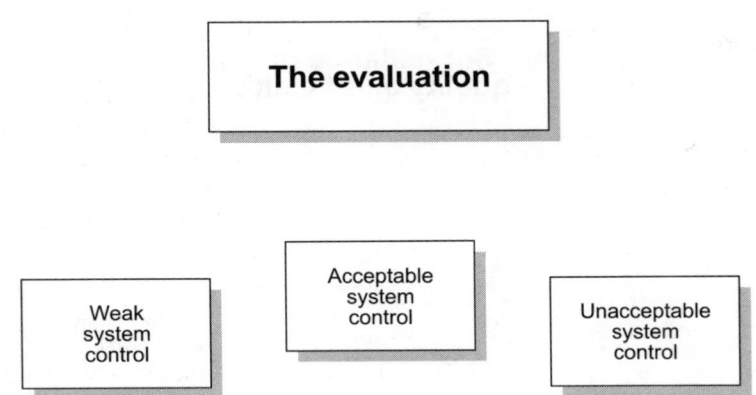

Figure 7.4 The evaluation

If this happens, the supplier will have to take steps to overcome these failures and improve their QMS. Having done this, the supplier can then ask for another evaluation to be carried out to confirm that their quality now meets the required standards.

7.3.1.4.3 Unacceptable system control

This is the result of an evaluation team finding that the number of deficiencies – or the lack of quality discipline at the supplier's premises – mean that the supplier will have to make radical changes to improve their overall QMS before they are anything like acceptable to the potential purchaser.

When the supplier has completed the necessary changes, they will then require a second evaluation to see that their improvements are satisfactory. Unfortunately this could be as much as a year later, by which time the purchaser may well have found an alternative source or decided that the initial organisation's quality is definitely not up to standard – and virtually blacklisted that particular supplier!

Having been inspected, it is important that the records of this inspection are safely filed away in case they may be required to reinforce some point at a later stage or to provide statistical data for the analysis of a supplier's performance. This is sometimes referred to as vendor rating.

In Britain, the Department of Trade and Industry (DTI) publish comprehensive lists of manufacturers who have proved that their QMS fully satisfies the requirements of ISO 9001:2000.

7.4 The surveillance or quality audit visit

Although an organisation may well have successfully passed an initial evaluation of their facilities and the purchaser may well be satisfied that the supplier is capable of providing an assurance of quality, it cannot be assumed

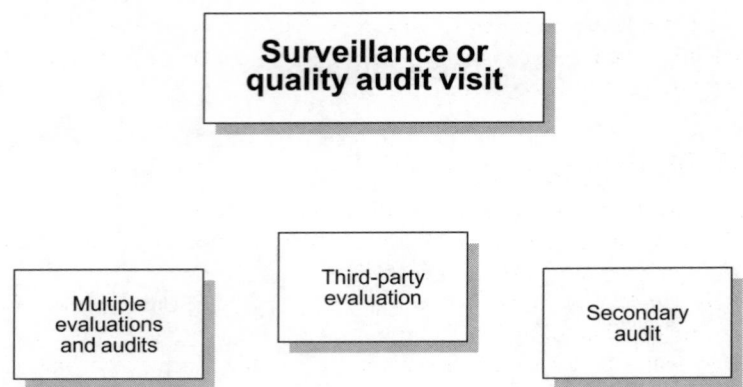

Figure 7.5 The surveillance

that the supplier will be able, or even capable of, retaining this status forever. Many things can happen to change this situation such as staff moving through promotion or natural wastage, changes in the product design that may or have been necessary, or perhaps even a new man-management philosophy.

The purchaser needs, therefore, to be informed of any changes in the organisation and personnel that might affect the overall quality of the product.

It is quite possible that the purchaser might want to make irregular surveillance visits of the supplier's premises to examine a particular aspect of their QMS. These surveillance or audit visits by the purchaser will be run on exactly the same lines as the supplier evaluation and are aimed at providing the purchaser with a confidence in the supplier and an assurance that they are capable of in fact still providing the purchaser with the quality of goods that they require. The aim of these audit visits should be that all the important aspects of the quality control system are checked, in rotation.

7.4.1 Multiple evaluations and audits

It is possible that some suppliers might well be providing the same product to several different customers and it could just happen that all of these customers ask to have an audit – at the same time! This obviously cannot be allowed to happen as the manufacturer would forever have people visiting the factory and disturbing, not only the labour force, but also the production line! Thankfully there are quite a number of ways around this problem such as secondary audit or third-party evaluation.

7.4.2 Secondary audit

If a purchaser indicates that they want to carry out an audit, the supplier can offer to provide the details of another customer's audit that has recently been carried out at their premises. If this does not quite cover the problem area sufficiently, then the supplier could offer to check in more detail the appropriate points raised by the purchaser.

7.4.3 Third-party evaluation

As an alternative to the secondary audit, a third-party evaluation team (i.e. one that is not directly involved in either the supply or purchase of the article) could be employed to carry out an audit.

There are several firms that have been specifically set up to do this and these are capable of determining if a supplier's product, premises and management are capable of meeting (and still meet) the laid down standards.

Probably the most famous of these (especially for British firms) is the British Standards Institution. BSI regularly produce a certified list of all suppliers whose products meet the requirements of ISO 9000. This list is also published by the Department of Trade and Industry.

7.5 ISO 9001:2000 checklist

Self-assessment can be a very useful tool to evaluate improvement and ISO 9004:2000 helps organisations by providing an annex containing 'guidelines for self-assessment'. I have included a number of annexes to this chapter specifically aimed at helping small businesses complete a self-assessment of their QMS and cost-effectively work in conformance with the requirements of ISO 9001:2000. These consist of:

7.5.1 ISO 9001:2000 headings

A complete list of the sections and sub-sections making up ISO 9001:2000 requirements (Annex A).

7.5.2 ISO 9001:2000 explanations and likely documentation

A brief explanation of the specific requirements (i.e. the 'shalls') of each element of ISO 9001:2000 together with a description of the likely documentation that an organisation would need to have in place to meet the requirements, as well as an outline of this content (Annex B).

7.5.3 Example audit checklist

A list of the most important questions an external Quality Auditor (e.g. BSI, TÜV, Yardely, etc.) would be likely to ask. If an organisation can honestly answer 'yes' to all these questions then they would be quite entitled to say that they 'fully comply with the requirements of ISO 9001:2000' (Annex C).

7.5.4 Example stage audit checklist

Lists of the most important questions that an external Quality Auditor (e.g. purchaser) is likely to ask when evaluating an organisation for the:

- design stage;
- manufacturing stage;
- acceptance stage;
- in-service stage.

(Annex D).

7.5.5 Index for ISO 9001:2000

A unique and complete index to each section of ISO 9001:2000 enabling readers to quickly access the relevant passage or sentence in the standard (Annex E).

Annex 7A   ISO 9001:2000 headings

4   QMS Requirements
    4.1   General requirements
    4.2   Documentation requirements
          4.2.2   Quality Manual
          4.2.3   Control of documents
          4.2.4   Control of quality records

5   Management responsibility
    5.1   Management commitment
    5.2   Customer focus
    5.3   Quality policy
    5.4   Planning
          5.4.1   Quality objectives
          5.4.2   Quality management system planning
    5.5   Responsibility, authority and communication
          5.5.1   Responsibility and authority
          5.5.2   Management representative
          5.5.3   Internal communication
    5.6   Management review
          5.6.1   General
          5.6.2   Review input
          5.6.3   Review output

6   Resource Management
    6.1   Provision of resources
    6.2   Human resources
          6.2.1   General
          6.2.2   Competence, awareness and training
    6.3   Infrastructure
    6.4   Work environment

7 Product realisation
  7.1 Planning of product realisation
  7.2 Customer-related processes
      7.2.1 Determination of requirements related to the product
      7.2.2 Review of requirements related to the product
      7.2.3 Customer communication
  7.3 Design and development
      7.3.1 Design and development planning
      7.3.2 Design and development inputs
      7.3.3 Design and development outputs
      7.3.4 Design and development review
      7.3.5 Design and development verification
      7.3.6 Design and development validation
      7.3.7 Control of design and development changes
  7.4 Purchasing
      7.4.1 Purchasing process
      7.4.2 Purchasing information
      7.4.3 Verification of purchased product
  7.5 Production and service provision
      7.5.1 Control of production and service provision
      7.5.2 Validation of processes for production and service provision
      7.5.3 Identification and traceability
      7.5.4 Customer property
      7.5.5 Preservation of product
  7.6 Control of monitoring and measurement devices

8 Measurement, analysis and improvement
  8.1 General
  8.2 Monitoring and measurement
      8.2.1 Customer satisfaction
      8.2.2 Internal audit
      8.2.3 Monitoring and measurement of processes
      8.2.4 Monitoring and measurement of product
  8.3 Control of non-conforming product
  8.4 Analysis of data
  8.5 Improvement
      8.5.1 Continual improvement
      8.5.2 Corrective action
      8.5.3 Preventive action

Annex 7B ISO 9001:2000 – Explanations and likely documentation

Section no.	ISO 9001:2000 title	Explanation	Likely documentation
4	Quality Management System		
4.1	General requirements	A definition of the processes necessary to ensure that a product conforms to customer requirements that are capable of being implemented, maintained and improved.	Core Business Processes supplemented by: ● Supporting Processes; ● QPs; ● WIs.
4.2	Documentation requirements		
4.2.1	General	Documented proof of a QMS	Quality manual. High level policy statement on organisational objectives and quality policies. Procedures. Quality records.
4.2.2	Quality Manual	A document which describes an organisation's quality policies, procedures and practices that make up the QMS.	A Quality Manual containing everything related to quality controls within an organisation.
4.2.3	Control of documents	How an organisation's documents are approved, issued, numbered etc. How revisions are recorded and implemented and obsolete documents removed.	Document control procedures.
4.2.4	Control of quality records	What quality records need to be kept to demonstrate conformance with the requirements of an organisation's QMS and how they are identified, stored, protected etc.	Record keeping procedures.

Section no.	ISO 9001:2000 title	Explanation	Likely documentation
5	Management responsibility	Management responsibility and quality requirements.	Quality Manual.
5.1	Management commitment	A written demonstration of an organisation's commitment to: • sustaining and increasing customer satisfaction; • establishing quality policies, objectives and planning; • establishing a QMS; • performing management reviews; • ensuring availability of resources. • determining the legal and mandatory requirements its products and/or services have to meet; • continuous improvement.	High-level policy statement on organisational objectives and quality policies. A list of Government regulatory, legal and customer-specific requirements. • Procedures describing: – resource management; – contract review procedures; – management reviews; – financial business plan(s).
5.2	Customer focus	How an organisation ensures that customer needs, expectations and requirements are determined, fully understood and met.	Procedures describing: • resource management; • contract review procedures; • management reviews; • financial business plan(s).
5.3	Quality policy	How an organisation approaches quality and the requirements for meeting them, ensuring that: • They are appropriate for both customer and an organisation; • There is a commitment to continually meet customer requirements; • These commitments are communicated, understood and implemented throughout an organisation; • There is a commitment for continual improvement.	High-level managerial statement on an organisation's quality policy containing clear responsibilities, training and resources required for each organisational activity.
5.4	Planning	The planning of resources, etc. to meet an organisation's overall business objectives.	Quality Manual.

Section no.	ISO 9001:2000 title	Explanation	Likely documentation
5.4.1	Quality objectives	The quality objectives that an organisation expects to achieve within each function and level of the organisation.	Policy statements defining the objectives of the company and those responsible for achieving the objectives.
5.4.2	Quality management system planning	The identification and planning of activities and resources required to meet an organisation's quality objectives.	The processes and procedures used by senior management to define and plan the way that the organisation is run.
5.5	Responsibility, authority and communication	How the organisation has documented its QMS.	A Quality Manual containing everything related to quality controls within the organisation.
5.5.1	Responsibility and authority	A definition of the roles, responsibilities, lines of authority, reporting and communication relevant to quality.	Job descriptions and responsibilities. Organisation charts showing lines of communication.
5.5.2	Management representative	The identification and appointment of a 'Quality Manager' with responsibility for the QMS.	Job description and responsibilities. Organisation charts showing lines of communication.
5.5.3	Internal communication	How the requirements of an organisation's QMS are communicated throughout the company.	Team briefings, organisational meetings, notice boards, in-house journals/magazines, audio-visual and other forms of e-information.
5.6	Management review	How senior management reviews the QMS to ensure its continued suitability, adequacy and effectiveness, in the context of an organisation's strategic planning cycle.	Procedures concerning: • process, product and/or service audit procedures; • customer feedback; • process and product performance; • corrective and preventive action; • supplier performance; • record keeping.
5.6.1	General	The requirement for management to establish a process for the periodic review of the QMS.	Management review and QMS audit procedures.

Section no.	ISO 9001:2000 title	Explanation	Likely documentation
5.6.2	Review input	The documents and information required for management reviews.	Results of audits, customer feedback, analysis of process performance and product conformance, corrective and preventive action reports and supplier performance records.
5.6.3	Review output	Result of the review.	Minutes of the meetings where the overall running of the company is discussed.
6	Resource management	A description of resources with regard to training, induction, responsibilities, working environment, equipment requirements, maintenance, etc.	QPs, Quality Plans and WIs
6.1	Provision of resources	How resource needs (i.e. human, materials, equipment, infrastructure) are identified.	Quality Plans identifying the resources required to complete a particular project or activity.
6.2	Human resources	Identification and assignment of human resources to implement and improve the QMS and comply with contract conditions.	QPs, Quality Plans and WIs.
6.2.1	General	How an organisation assigns personnel on the basis of competency, qualification, training, skills and experience relevant to specific tasks.	Job descriptions and responsibilities. Training records. Staff evaluations. Project plans identifying the human resources required to complete the task.
6.2.2	Competence, awareness and training	Documents showing how an organisation selects, trains and assigns personnel to specific tasks.	System level procedures for: • training; • staff evaluations; • review of work assignments; • staff assessments; • records.

Section no.	ISO 9001:2000 title	Explanation	Likely documentation
6.3	Infrastructure	How an organisation defines, provides and maintains the infrastructure requirements to ensure product conformity (e.g. infrastructure, plant, hardware, software, tools and equipment, communication facilities, transport and supporting services, etc.).	Policies, procedures and regulatory documents stating the infrastructure requirements of an organisation and/or their customers. Financial documents. Maintenance plans. Project plans identifying the human resources required to complete the task.
6.4	Work environment	How an organisation defines and implements the human and physical factors of the work environment required to ensure product conformity (health and safety, work methods, ethics and ambient working conditions).	Environmental procedures. Project plans. Budgetary and legal processes and procedures.
7	Product realisation	The requirements for process control, purchasing, handling and storage, measuring devices, etc.	Quality Manual and associated Processes, QPs, Quality Plans and WIs.
7.1	Planning of product realisation	The availability of documented plans for all product processes required to realise a product, and the sequences in which they occur.	Process models (flow charts) showing the sequence of activities that an organisation goes through to produce a product. Documented QPs and WIs to ensure that staff work in accordance with requirements. Records that prove the results of process control. Quality Plans.
7.2	Customer-related processes	The identification, review and interaction with customer requirements and customers.	Quality Manual and Quality Plans.
7.2.1	Determination of requirements related to the product	How an organisation determines and implements customer requirements.	Contract review procedures. Regulatory and legal product requirements. Formal contracts.

Section no.	ISO 9001:2000 title	Explanation	Likely documentation
7.2.2	Review of requirements related to the product	How an organisation reviews product and customer requirements to check that they can actually do the job.	Contract review procedures. Regulatory and legal product requirements. Project plans showing lines of communication with the customer.
7.2.3	Customer communication	How an organisation communicates (i.e. liaises) with their customers, keeps them informed, handles their enquiries, complaints and feedback.	Project plans showing lines of communication with the customer.
7.3	Design and development	The control of design and development within an organisation.	Processes and procedures for design and development. Design plans.
7.3.1	Design and development planning	How an organisation goes about planning and controlling the design of a product (e.g. design stages, development processes, verification and validation, responsibilities and authorities).	Design and development plans. Procedures detailing the design process and how designs are verified and validated. Risk assessment. Job descriptions and responsibilities.
7.3.2	Design and development inputs	How an organisation identifies the requirements to be met by a product.	Project Plans (detailing policies, standards and specifications, skill requirements). Specifications and tolerances. Regulatory and legal requirements. Information derived from previous (similar) designs or developments. Environmental requirements. Health and safety aspects.
7.3.3	Design and development outputs	How an organisation ensures that the design output meets the design input requirements.	Drawings, schematics, schedules, system specifications, system descriptions, etc.

Section no.	ISO 9001:2000 title	Explanation	Likely documentation
7.3.4	Design and development review	How an organisation evaluates their ability to fulfil product requirements, identify problems and complete follow-up actions.	Procedures detailing how changes are made to designs and how they are approved, recorded and distributed. Design process review procedures. Management reviews and audit procedures. Records.
7.3.5	Design and development verification	How an organisation ensures that product specifications are fulfilled and that the design and development output meets the original input requirements.	Design process review procedures. Procedures for periodic reviews. Records.
7.3.6	Design and development validation	How an organisation ensures that the design is actually capable of doing it's intended job.	Procedures for in-process inspection and testing. Final inspection and test. Records.
7.3.7	Control of design and development changes	How changes to a design are approved, together with consideration of how these changes may influence other aspects of the business.	Procedures detailing how changes are made to designs and how they are approved, recorded and distributed. Design process review procedures. Management reviews and audit procedures. Records.
7.4	Purchasing	How an organisation controls the purchase of materials, products and services from suppliers and third parties.	Documented procedures for purchasing and the evaluation of suppliers.
7.4.1	Purchasing process	The controls that an organisation has in place to ensure purchased products and services are of an acceptable standard.	Approved list of suppliers. Supplier evaluations. Purchasing procedures. Purchase orders.

Section no.	ISO 9001:2000 title	Explanation	Likely documentation
7.4.2	Purchasing information	The details provided by an organisation when placing an order with a supplier and the approval process for purchasing documentation.	Approved list of suppliers. Supplier evaluations. Purchasing procedures. Purchase orders. Stock control procedures.
7.4.3	Verification of purchased product	The controls that an organisation has in place to ensure that products and services provided by suppliers meet their original requirements.	Approved list of suppliers. Supplier evaluations. Purchasing procedures. Purchase orders. Stock control procedures.
7.5	Production and service provision	The availability of a process to cover all production and service operations.	Documented Processes, QPs and WIs for production and service operations.
7.5.1	Control of production and service provision	The provision of anything required to control production and service operations.	Procedures for the provision of everything necessary for staff to carry out their work. Project plans and resources required to carry out a job.
7.5.2	Validation of processes for production and service provision	How an organisation identifies processes which cannot be verified by subsequent monitoring/testing/inspection (including the validation of these processes to demonstrate their effectiveness).	Procedures for tasks which cannot subsequently be proved to be acceptable.
7.5.3	Identification and traceability	The means by which the status of a product can be identified at all stages of its production/delivery.	Procedures for the provision of everything necessary for staff to carry out their work. Project plans and resources required to carry out a job.
7.5.4	Customer property	How an organisation looks after property provided by a customer, including identification, verification, storage and maintenance.	Procedure for the control of customer property.
7.5.5	Preservation of product	How an organisation looks after its own products (i.e. identification, handling, packaging, storing and protecting) including authorisation of release to a customer.	Product approval procedures. Procedures which ensure the safety and protection of products.

Section no.	ISO 9001:2000 title	Explanation	Likely documentation
7.6	Control of monitoring and measuring devices	The controls that an organisation has in place to ensure that equipment (including software) used for proving conformance to specified requirements is properly maintained, calibrated and verified.	Equipment records of maintenance and calibration. WIs.
8	Measurement, analysis and improvement	The measurement, monitoring, analysis and improvement processes an organisation has in place to ensure that the QMS processes and products conform to requirements.	Procedures for inspection and measurement.
8.1	General	The definitions of procedures to ensure product conformity and product improvement	Procedures for: ● product conformity; ● product improvement; ● statistical process review.
8.2	Monitoring and measurement	The analysis of customer satisfaction and the control of products and processes.	Procedures for inspection and measurement.
8.2.1	Customer satisfaction	The processes used to establish whether a customer is satisfied with a product.	Procedures for: ● customer feedback; ● change control; ● customer complaints.
8.2.2	Internal audit	The in-house checks made to determine if the QMS is functioning properly, that it continues to comply with the requirements of ISO 9001:2000 and to identify possibilities for improvement.	Audit procedure. Audit schedules. Audit plans, check sheets and records.
8.2.3	Measurement and monitoring of processes	The methods used to check if processes continue to meet their intended purpose.	Audit schedules. Audit plans, check sheets and records. Approval procedures for product acceptance. Processes for failure cost analysis, conformity, non-conformity, life cycle approach, self-assessment.

Section no.	ISO 9001:2000 title	Explanation	Likely documentation
8.2.3 cont.			Compliance with environmental and safety policies, laws, regulations and standards. Procedures for testing and monitoring processes. Performance and product measurement procedures.
8.2.4	Monitoring and measurement of product	How an organisation measures and monitors that product characteristics meet the customer's specified requirements.	Audit schedules. Audit plans, check sheets and records. Approval procedures for product acceptance. Processes for failure cost analysis, conformity, non-conformity, life cycle approach, self-assessment. Compliance with environmental and safety policies, laws, regulations and standards. Procedures for testing and monitoring processes. Performance and product measurement procedures. Supplier approval procedures.
8.3	Control of non-conforming product	The methods used to prevent the use or delivery of non-conforming products and to decide what to do with a non-conforming product.	Documented procedure to identify and control the use and delivery of non-conforming products. Approval procedures. Quarantine procedures. Change control procedure. Corrective and preventive action procedures. Audits.
8.4	Analysis of data	The methods used to review data that will determine the effectiveness of the QMS, especially with regard to customer satisfaction, conformance to customer requirements and the performance of processes and products.	Any data or statistics produced as a result of audits, customer satisfaction surveys, complaints, non-conformances, supplier evaluations, etc.

Section no.	ISO 9001:2000 title	Explanation	Likely documentation
8.5	Improvement	How an organisation controls corrective and preventive actions and plans for ongoing process and product improvement.	Documented procedures for: • corrective action; • preventive action; • product/process improvement; • customer complaints/ feedback; • non-conformity reports; • management reviews; • staff suggestions scheme;
8.5.1	Continual improvement	How an organisation goes about continually improving its QMS.	Procedures, minutes of meetings where improvement to the organisation's business is discussed. Management reviews.
8.5.2	Corrective action	What an organisation does to identify and put right non-conformities.	Process for eliminating causes of non-conformity. Documented complaints. Complaints procedure. Staff suggestions scheme.
8.5.3	Preventive action	The proactive methods an organisation employs to prevent non-conformities from happening in the first place.	Process for the prevention of non-conformity. Documented complaints. Complaints procedure. Staff suggestions scheme.

ANNEX 7C   Example ISO 9001:2000 checklists

4 Quality Management System

4.1 General requirements

Item	Requirement	Currently met? YES/NO	Document	Remarks
1.	Has a Quality Management System been established in accordance with the requirements of ISO 9001:2000?			
2.	Is the QMS:			
	● documented?			
	● implemented?			
	● maintained?			
	● continually improved?			
3.	Does the organisation have all the documents necessary to ensure the effective operation and control of its processes?			

Item	Requirement	Currently met? YES/NO	Document	Remarks
4.	Has the organisation:			
	• identified the processes needed for the QMS?			
	• determined the sequence and interaction of these processes?			
	• determined the criteria and methods required to ensure the effective operation and control of these processes?			
	• ensured that information necessary to support the monitoring and operation of these processes is available?			
5.	Does the organisation measure, monitor and analyse these processes?			
6.	Is the necessary action implemented to achieve planned results and continual improvement?			
7.	Does the organisation manage these processes in accordance with the requirements of ISO 9001:2000?			

4.2.1 General

Item	Requirement	Currently met? YES/NO	Document	Remarks
8.	Does the QMS documentation include:			
	• quality policy and quality objectives statements?			
	• documented procedures?			
	• a quality manual			

4.2.2 Quality Manual

Item	Requirement	Currently met? YES/NO	Document	Remarks
9.	Has the organisation established and maintained a Quality Manual?			
10.	Is it controlled?			
11.	Does it include details of:			
	• the scope of the QMS?			
	• justifications for any exclusions from the ISO 9001:2000 requirements?			
	• associated documented procedures (or reference to them)?			
	• the sequence and interaction of processes?			

4.2.3 Control of documents

Item	Requirement	Currently met? YES/NO	Document	Remarks
12.	Has the organisation established a documented procedure to control QMS documents?			
13.	Does this procedure include methods for:			
	● controlling distribution?			
	● approving of documents prior to issue?			
	● reviewing, updating and re-approving documents?			
	● identifying the current revision status of documents?			
	● ensuring that relevant versions of all applicable documents are available at points of use?			
	● ensuring that documents remain legible, readily identifiable and retrievable?			
	● identifying, distributing and controlling of documents from an external source?			
	● controlling obsolete documents?			
	● the identification and control of obsolete documents that have been retained for any purpose?			

4.2.4 Control of quality records

Item	Requirement	Currently met? YES/NO	Document	Remarks
14.	Does the organisation control quality records?			
15.	Do these records provide evidence of:			
	● the organisation's conformance to the ISO 9001:2000 requirements?			
	● the effective operation of the QMS?			
16.	Does the organisation have a documented procedure for quality records covering:			
	● identification?			
	● storage?			
	● retrieval?			
	● protection?			
	● retention time?			
	● disposition?			

5 Management responsibility

Item	Requirement	Currently met? YES/NO	Document	Remarks
17.	Does the organisation demonstrate its commitment to developing, establishing and improving the QMS through:			
	• management commitment?			
	• determining customer requirements and achieving customer satisfaction?			
	• a quality policy?			
	• quality objectives and quality planning?			
	• providing all the necessary resources to administer the QMS?			
	• regularly reviewing the QMS?			

5.1 Management commitment

Item	Requirement	Currently met? YES/NO	Document	Remarks
18.	Does the organisation demonstrate its commitment to developing, establishing and improving the QMS?			
19.	Does the organisation:			
	● ensure that all personnel are aware of the importance of meeting customer, regulatory and legal requirements?			
	● establish the quality policy and quality objectives?			
	● conduct management reviews?			
	● ensure the availability of necessary resources?			

5.2 Customer focus

Item	Requirement	Currently met? YES/NO	Document	Remarks
20.	Does the organisation ensure that customer needs and expectations are determined?			
21.	Are these customer needs and expectations converted into requirements?			
22.	Does the organisation ensure that customer requirements are fulfilled?			

5.3 Quality policy

Item	Requirement	Currently met? YES/NO	Document	Remarks
23.	Is the organisation's quality policy:			
	• controlled?			
	• appropriate?			
	• committed to meeting requirements?			
	• communicated and understood throughout the company?			
	• capable of continual improvement?			
	• a framework for establishing and reviewing quality objectives?			
	• regularly reviewed for continued suitability?			

5.4 Planning

Item	Requirement	Currently met? YES/NO	Document	Remarks
24.	Is the organisation's quality planning documented?			
25.	Does it include:			
	• quality objectives?			
	• resources?			

5.4.1 Quality objectives

Item	Requirement	Currently met? YES/NO	Document	Remarks
26.	Has the organisation established quality objectives for each relevant function and level within the company?			
27.	Are the organisation's quality objectives measurable and consistent with quality policy?			
28.	Do they include:			
	• a commitment for continual improvement?			
	• product requirements?			

5.4.2 Quality management system planning

Item	Requirement	Currently met? YES/NO	Document	Remarks
29.	Does the organisation's quality planning cover:			
	• the processes required in the QMS (as mentioned in section 4)?			
	• any permissible exclusions (to the requirements of ISO 9001:2000)?			
	• the requirements for continual improvement?			
	• the requirements for change control?			
30.	Does the organisation's quality planning ensure that the QMS is maintained during this change?			

5.5 Responsibility, authority and communication

Item	Requirement	Currently met? YES/NO	Document	Remarks
31.	Is the administration of the organisation's QMS documented?			
32.	Does it cover:			
	• responsibilities and authorities?			
	• management representative's duties?			
	• internal communication?			
	• the Quality Manual?			
	• control of documents?			
	• control of quality records?			

5.5.1 Responsibility and authority

Item	Requirement	Currently met? YES/NO	Document	Remarks
33.	Are the functions and inter-relationships of all the organisation staff defined?			
34.	Are the responsibilities and authorities of all the organisation staff defined?			

5.5.2 Management representative

Item	Requirement	Currently met? YES/NO	Document	Remarks
35.	Has the organisation management member(s) been appointed as management representative(s)?			
36.	Does the management representative(s):			
	● ensure that the QMS processes are established, implemented and maintained?			
	● report (to top management) on the performance (and methods for improving) the QMS?			
	● promote awareness of customer requirements throughout the organisation?			
	● liaise with external parties on all matters relating to the QMS?			

5.5.3 Internal communication

Item	Requirement	Currently met? YES/NO	Document	Remarks
37.	Does the organisation ensure that there are lines of communication between all members of staff to ensure the effectiveness of the QMS processes?			

5.6 *Management review*

Item	Requirement	Currently met? YES/NO	Document	Remarks
38.	Does the organisation top management regularly review the QMS at planned intervals?			

5.6.1 General

Item	Requirement	Currently met? YES/NO	Document	Remarks
39.	Does the QMS review cover the continuing suitability, adequacy and effectiveness of the QMS?			
40.	Does the review evaluate the:			
	● need for changes?			
	● quality policy?			
	● quality objectives?			

5.6.2 Review input

Item	Requirement	Currently met? YES/NO	Document	Remarks
41.	Does the management review include:			
	● internal audit results?			
	● external and third party audit results?			
	● customer feedback?			
	● process performance?			
	● product conformance?			
	● preventive and corrective actions that have been implemented?			
	● outstanding preventive and corrective actions?			
	● results from previous management reviews?			
	● changes that could affect the QMS?			

5.6.3 Review output

Item	Requirement	Currently met? YES/NO	Document	Remarks
42.	Do the outputs of management reviews include recommendations for:			
	● the improvement of the QMS and its processes?			
	● the improvement of product related to customer requirements?			
	● confirming and establishing resource needs?			
43.	Are the results of management reviews recorded?			

6 Resource management

Item	Requirement	Currently met? YES/NO	Document	Remarks
44.	Has the organisation documented procedures that adequately cover the requirements for:			
	● training?			
	● induction?			
	● responsibilities?			
	● working environment?			
	● equipment requirements?			
	● maintenance?			

6.1 Provision of resources

Item	Requirement	Currently met? YES/NO	Document	Remarks
45.	Does the organisation provide the resources required to:			
	● implement and improve the QMS processes?			
	● ensure customer satisfaction?			

6.2 Human resources

Item	Requirement	Currently met? YES/NO	Document	Remarks
46.	Has the organisation established procedures for:			
	● the assignment of personnel?			
	● training, awareness and competency?			

6.2.1 General

Item	Requirement	Currently met? YES/NO	Document	Remarks
47.	Are staff responsibilities defined in the QMS?			
48.	Are those members of staff assigned responsibilities based on their:			
	• competency?			
	• applicable education?			
	• training?			
	• skills?			
	• experience?			

6.2.2 Competency, awareness and training

Item	Requirement	Currently met? YES/NO	Document	Remarks
49.	Does the organisation:			
	• identify training requirements?			
	• provide appropriate training?			
	• evaluate the training provided?			
50.	Does the organisation ensure that all their staff appreciate the relevance and importance of their activities and how they contribute towards achieving quality objectives?			
51.	Does the organisation keep staff records covering education, experience, qualifications, training, etc.)?			

6.3 Infrastructure

Item	Requirement	Currently met? YES/NO	Document	Remarks
52.	Does the organisation identify, provide and maintain the necessary:			
	● workspace and associated facilities?			
	● equipment, hardware and software?			
	● supporting services?			

6.4 Work environment

Item	Requirement	Currently met? YES/NO	Document	Remarks
53.	Does the organisation identify and manage the work environment (including human and physical factors) to ensure conformity of product			

7 Product realisation

Item	Requirement	Currently met? YES/NO	Document	Remarks
54.	Has the organisation established the processes necessary to achieve the product?			

7.1 Planning of product realisation

Item	Requirement	Currently met? YES/NO	Document	Remarks
55.	Have the sequence of processes and sub-processes required to achieve the product been documented and planned?			
56.	Within this sequence of processes and sub-processes, has the following been determined:			
	● the quality objectives for the product, project or contract?			
	● product-specific processes, documentation, resources and facilities?			
	● verification and validation activities?			
	● criteria for acceptability?			
	● required records?			

7.2 Customer related processes

Item	Requirement	Currently met? YES/NO	Document	Remarks
57.	Has the organisation established procedures for the:			
	● identification of customer requirements?			
	● review of product requirements?			
	● customer communication?			

7.2.1 Determination of requirements related to the product

Item	Requirement	Currently met? YES/NO	Document	Remarks
58.	Has the organisation established a process for identifying customer requirements?			
59.	Does this process determine:			
	● customer-specified product requirements (e.g. availability, delivery and support)?			
	● non-specified customer requirements (e.g. those affecting the product)?			
	● mandatory requirements such as regulatory and legal obligations?			

7.2.2 Review of requirements related to the product

Item	Requirement	Currently met? YES/NO	Document	Remarks
60.	Has the organisation established a process for ensuring that product requirements have been fully established?			
61.	Does the process ensure that (prior to submission of tender or acceptance of contract):			
	● all customer requirements (plus any additional requirements determined by the organisation) have been defined and can be met?			
	● where no written requirements are available, that verbal customer requirements are confirmed before contract acceptance?			
	● any contract or order requirements differing from those previously express (e.g. in a tender or quotation) are resolved?			
	● the organisation has the ability to meet the defined requirements?			

7.2.3 Customer communication

Item	Requirement	Currently met? YES/NO	Document	Remarks
62.	Has the organisation established processes for:			
	• providing customers with product information?			
	• handling customer enquiries, contracts or orders (including amendments)?			
	• customer feedback and/or customer complaints?			

7.3 Design and development

Item	Requirement	Currently met? YES/NO	Document	Remarks
63.	Has the organisation a process and adequate procedures for their design and development activities?			

7.3.1 Design and development planning

Item	Requirement	Currently met? YES/NO	Document	Remarks
64.	Does the organisation plan and control design and development of the product by means of processes?			
65.	Do these processes include:			
	• stage review, verification and validation activities?			
	• identification of responsibilities and authorities?			
	• management of the interfaces between different groups that may be involved?			
	• provision of effective communication and clarity of responsibilities?			
	• product and planning reviews?			

7.3.2 Design and development inputs

Item	Requirement	Currently met? YES/NO	Document	Remarks
66.	Does the organisation define and document product requirement inputs?			
67.	Do these input requirements include:			
	● function and performance requirements?			
	● applicable regulatory and legal requirements?			
	● applicable requirements derived from previous similar designs?			
	● any other requirements essential for design and development?			
68.	Are inadequate, incomplete, ambiguous or conflicting input requirements resolved?			

7.3.3 Design and development outputs

Item	Requirement	Currently met? YES/NO	Document	Remarks
69.	Does the organisation define and document product outputs?			
70.	Are products approved prior to release?			
71.	Does the design and development output:			
	• meet the design and development input requirements?			
	• provide appropriate information for production and service operations?			
	• contain or make reference to product acceptance criteria?			
	• define the characteristics of the product that are essential to its safe and proper use?			

7.3.4 Design andr development review

Item	Requirement	Currently met? YES/NO	Document	Remarks
72.	Are systematic reviews of the design and development carried out at suitable stages?			
73.	Does the review:			
	● evaluate the ability of the product to fulfil the requirements?			
	● identify problems and propose solutions?			
	● include representatives from the functions concerned with the design and development stage being reviewed?			
74.	Are follow-up actions from the reviews recorded?			

7.3.5 Design and development verification

Item	Requirement	Currently met? YES/NO	Document	Remarks
75.	Does the organisation verify that the design output meets the design and development input?			
76.	Are these results and any necessary subsequent follow-up actions recorded?			

7.3.6 Design and development validation

Item	Requirement	Currently met? YES/NO	Document	Remarks
77.	Does the organisation validate that the product is capable of meeting the requirements of intended use?			
78.	Are these results and any necessary subsequent follow-up actions recorded?			
79.	Wherever applicable, is the validation completed prior to the delivery or implementation of the product?			
80.	If full validation is impractical prior to delivery or implementation of the product, is a partial validation performed to the maximum extent applicable?			

7.3.7 Control of design and development changes

Item	Requirement	Currently met? YES/NO	Document	Remarks
81.	Are all design and development changes identified, documented and controlled?			
82.	Does the organisation:			
	• evaluate the effect of the changes on constituent parts and delivered products?			
	• verify, validate and approve these changes before implementation?			
83.	Are these results and any necessary subsequent follow-up actions recorded?			

7.4 Purchasing

Item	Requirement	Currently met? YES/NO	Document	Remarks
84.	Does the organisation have processes for: • purchasing control? • purchasing information? • verification of purchased product?			

7.4.1 Purchasing process

Item	Requirement	Currently met? YES/NO	Document	Remarks
85.	Does the organisation have a process to ensure purchased products conform to requirements?			
86.	Does the organisation evaluate and select suppliers?			
87.	Are these evaluation and selection criteria defined?			
88.	Are these results and any necessary subsequent follow-up actions recorded?			
89.	Does the organisation complete periodic inspections and examinations of purchasing processes?			

7.4.2 Purchasing information

Item	Requirement	Currently met? YES/NO	Document	Remarks
90.	Does the organisation have documentation describing:			
	• the product to be purchased?			
	• requirements for approval or qualification (i.e. product, procedures, processes, equipment and personnel)?			
	• QMS requirements?			
91.	Does the organisation ensure the adequacy of the specified requirements contained in the purchasing documents prior to their release?			

7.4.3 Verification of purchased product

Item	Requirement	Currently met? YES/NO	Document	Remarks
92.	Does the organisation identify and implement the activities necessary for the verification of a purchased product?			
93.	Are these verification arrangements specified by the organisation or its customer if verification is to be carried out at the supplier's premises?			
94.	Is the method of product release specified in the purchasing documents if verification is to be carried out at the supplier's premises?			

7.5 Production and service provision

Item	Requirement	Currently met? YES/NO	Document	Remarks
95.	Does the organisation have procedures for the control of:			
	● production and service operations?			
	● identification and traceability?			
	● customer property?			
	● preservation of product?			
	● validation of processes?			

7.5.1 Control of production and service provision

Item	Requirement	Currently met? YES/NO	Document	Remarks
96.	Does the organisation control production and service operations?			
97.	Is this achieved through:			
	● information concerning the characteristics of the product?			
	● appropriate work instructions?			
	● the use and maintenance of suitable equipment for production and service operations?			
	● the availability and use of measuring and monitoring devices?			
	● the capability of implementing monitoring activities?			
	● processes to cover the release, delivery and post-delivery activities?			

7.5.2 Validation of processes for production and service provision

Item	Requirement	Currently met? YES/NO	Document	Remarks
98.	Does the organisation validate any production and service processes to demonstrate the ability of the processes to achieve planned results (where the resulting output cannot be verified by subsequent measurement or monitoring)?			
99.	Does this validation demonstrate the ability of the processes to achieve planned results?			
100.	Does the validation include:			
	● qualification of processes?			
	● qualification of equipment and personnel?			
	● use of defined methodologies and procedures?			
	● requirements for records?			
	● re-validation?			
101.	Does this validation include any processes where deficiencies may become apparent only after the product is in use or the service has been delivered?			

7.5.3 Identification and traceability

Item	Requirement	Currently met? YES/NO	Document	Remarks
102.	Does the organisation have procedures available to identify the product throughout production and service operations?			
103.	Is the product status identifiable with respect to measurement and monitoring requirements?			
104.	When traceability is a requirement, does the organisation control and record the unique identification of a product?			

7.5.4 Customer property

Item	Requirement	Currently met? YES/NO	Document	Remarks
105.	Does the organisation exercise care with customer property?			
106.	Does the organisation verify, protect and maintain customer property provided for use or incorporated into a product?			
107.	Are records maintained of any customer property that is lost, damaged or otherwise found to be unsuitable for use?			

7.5.5 Preservation of product

Item	Requirement	Currently met? YES/NO	Document	Remarks
108.	Does the organisation have set procedures for the identification, handling, packaging, storage and protection of products during internal processing and delivery to the intended destination?			

7.6 Control of monitoring and measuring devices

Item	Requirement	Currently met? YES/NO	Document	Remarks
109.	Where applicable, are measuring and monitoring devices:			
	• calibrated and adjusted periodically or prior to use, against devices traceable to international or national standards?			
	• safeguarded from adjustments that would invalidate the calibration?			
	• protected from damage and deterioration during handling, maintenance and storage?			
110.	Are the results of the calibration recorded?			
111.	Is the validity of previous results re-assessed if they are subsequently found to be out of calibration, and corrective action taken?			
112.	If software is used for measuring and monitoring, has it been validated prior to use?			

8 Measurement, analysis and improvement

Item	Requirement	Currently met? YES/NO	Document	Remarks
113.	Does the organisation define the activities needed to measure and monitor:			
	● product conformity?			
	● product improvement?			

8.1 General

Item	Requirement	Currently met? YES/NO	Document	Remarks
114.	Has the organisation defined, planned and implemented measures and monitoring activities needed to assure product continuity and achieve improvement?			
115.	Does this include the determination of the need for, and the use of, applicable methodologies including statistical techniques?			

8.2 Monitoring and measurement

Item	Requirement	Currently met? YES/NO	Document	Remarks
116.	Has the organisation procedures available to:			
	● ensure customer satisfaction?			
	● control internal audits?			
	● ensure effective measurement and monitoring of products and processes?			

8.2.1 Customer satisfaction

Item	Requirement	Currently met? YES/NO	Document	Remarks
117.	Does the organisation monitor information on customer satisfaction?			
118.	Does the organisation monitor information on customer dissatisfaction?			
119.	Are the methods and measures for obtaining such information defined?			
120.	Are these methods and measures utilised as part of the performance measurements of the QMS?			

8.2.2 Internal audit

Item	Requirement	Currently met? YES/NO	Document	Remarks
121.	Does the organisation conduct periodic internal audits?			
122.	Do these audits determine whether the QMS:			
	• conforms to the requirements of ISO 9001:2000?			
	• has been effectively implemented and maintained?			
123.	Are audits only carried out by personnel who are not associated with the activity or department being audited?			
124.	Are the audits planned to take into account:			
	• the status and importance of the activities and areas to be audited?			
	• the results of previous audits?			
125.	Are the audit scope, frequency and methodologies defined?			
126.	Does the organisation have a documented procedure for audits that includes:			
	• the responsibilities and requirements for conducting audits?			
	• the method for recording results?			
	• the method for reporting to management?			
127.	Does management take timely corrective action on deficiencies found during an audit?			
128.	Do these follow-up actions include the verification of the implementation of corrective action and the reporting of verification results?			

8.2.3 Monitoring and measurement of processes

Item	Requirement	Currently met? YES/NO	Document	Remarks
129.	Does the organisation apply suitable methods for the measurement and monitoring of processes:			
	• to meet customer requirements?			
	• to confirm the process's continuing ability to satisfy its intended purpose?			

8.2.4 Monitoring and measurement of product

Item	Requirement	Currently met? YES/NO	Document	Remarks
130.	Does the organisation apply suitable methods to measure and monitor the characteristics of the product at appropriate stages of the product realisation process?			
131.	Is there documented evidence of conformity with the acceptance criteria?			
132.	Are the responsibilities and authorities defined with regard to release of product?			
133.	Does the organisation ensure that the product is not released or the service delivered until all the specified activities have been satisfactorily completed (unless otherwise approved by the customer)?			

8.3 Control of non-conforming product

Item	Requirement	Currently met? YES/NO	Document	Remarks
134.	Has the organisation defined a procedure for the control of non-conformities?			
135.	Does this procedure ensure that:			
	• products which do not conform to requirements are prevented from unintended use or delivery?			
	• non-conforming products that have been corrected are subject to re-verification to demonstrate conformity?			
	• non-conforming products detected after delivery or use are either corrected or removed from service?			
136.	Is there provision for the notification of the customer, end user, regulatory or other body when required?			

8.4 Analysis of data

Item	Requirement	Currently met? YES/NO	Document	Remarks
137.	Does the organisation collect and analyse data to determine the suitability and effectiveness of the QMS and to identify improvements that can be made?			
138.	Does the organisation analyse the data to provide information on:			
	• customer satisfaction and/or dissatisfaction?			
	• conformance to customer requirements?			
	• the characteristics of processes, products and their trends?			
	• suppliers?			

8.5 Improvement

Item	Requirement	Currently met? YES/NO	Document	Remarks
139.	Does the organisation have procedures available for:			
	• planning continual improvement?			
	• corrective action?			
	• preventive action?			

8.5.1 Continual improvement

Item	Requirement	Currently met? YES/NO	Document	Remarks
140.	Does the organisation plan and manage the processes necessary for the continual improvement of the QMS?			
141.	Is the continual improvement of the QMS facilitated by the use of:			
	● the quality policy?			
	● quality objectives?			
	● audit results?			
	● analysis of data?			
	● corrective and preventive action?			
	● management reviews?			
	● concessions and approvals?			
	● concession scheme?			
	● defects and defect reports?			
	● bonded store?			

8.5.2 Corrective action

Item	Requirement	Currently met? YES/NO	Document	Remarks
142.	Has the organisation a documented procedure to enable corrective action to be taken to eliminate the cause of non-conformities and prevent recurrence?			
143.	Does this procedure define the requirements for:			
	• identification of non-conformities (including customer complaints)?			
	• determining the causes of non-conformities?			
	• evaluating the need for action to ensure that non-conformities do not recur?			
	• determining and implementing the corrective action needed?			
	• ensuring results of action taken are recorded?			
	• reviewing the corrective action taken?			

8.5.3 Preventive action

Item	Requirement	Currently met? YES/NO	Document	Remarks
144.	Has the organisation a documented procedure to enable preventive action to be taken to eliminate the causes of potential non-conformities and prevent occurrence?			
145.	Does this procedure define the requirements for:			
	● identification of potential non-conformities and their causes?			
	● determining and implementing the preventive action needed?			
	● ensuring results of action taken are recorded?			
	● reviewing the preventive action taken?			

Annex 7D Example stage audit checklists

Design stage

Item		Related item		Remark	Yes/no	Remarks
1	Requirements	1.1	Information	Has the customer fully described his requirement?		
				Has the customer any mandatory requirements?		
				Are the customer's requirements fully understood by all members of the design team?		
				Is there a need to have further discussions with the customer?		
				Are other suppliers or sub-contractors involved? If yes, who is the prime contractor?		
		1.2	Standards	What international standards need to be observed? Are they available?		
				What national standards need to be observed? Are they available?		
				What other information and procedures are required? Are they available?		

Item		Related item		Remark	Yes/no	Remarks
		1.3	Procedures	Are there any customer supplied drawings, sketches or plans?		
				Have they been registered?		
2	Quality Procedures	2.1	Procedures Manual	Is one available?		
				Does it contain detailed procedures and Instructions for the control of all drawings within the drawing office?		
		2.2	Planning Implementation and Production	Is the project split into a number of Work Packages?		
				If so:		
				Are the various Work Packages listed?		
				Have Work Package Leaders been nominated?		
				Is their task clear?		
				Is their task achievable?		
				Is a time plan available?		
				Is it up to date?		
				Regularly maintained?		
				Relevant to the task?		
3	Drawings	3.1	Identification	Are all drawings identified by a unique number?		
				Is the numbering system strictly controlled?		
		3.2	Cataloguing	Is a catalogue of drawings maintained?		
				Is this catalogue regularly reviewed and up to date?		

	Item	Related item	Remark	Yes/no	Remarks
		3.3 Amendments and Modifications	Is there a procedure for authorising the issue of amendments, changes to drawings?		
			Is there a method for withdrawing and disposing of obsolete drawings?		
4	Components	4.1 Availability	Are complete lists of all the relevant components available?		
		4.2 Adequacy	Are the selected components currently available and adequate for the task? If not, how long will they take to procure? Is this acceptable?		
		4.3 Acceptability	If alternative components have to be used are they acceptable to the task?		
5	Records	5.1 Failure reports	Has the Design Office access to all records, failure reports and other relevant data?		
		5.2 Reliability data	Is reliability data correctly stored, maintained and analysed?		
		5.3 Graphs, diagrams, plans	In addition to drawings, is there a system for the control of all graphs, tables, plans etc.? Are CAD facilities available? (If so, go to 6.1)		
6	Reviews and Audits	6.1 Computers	If a processor is being used: Are all the design office personnel trained in its use? Are regular back-ups taken? Is there an anti-virus system in place?		

Item		Related item	Remark	Yes/no	Remarks
	6.2	Manufacturing Division	Is a close relationship being maintained between the design office and the manufacturing division?		
	6.3		Is notice being taken of the manufacturing division's exact requirements, their problems and their choices of components etc.?		

Manufacturing stage

Item		Related item	Remark	Yes/no	Remarks
1	Degree of quality	1.1	Quality control procedures	Are quality control procedures available?		
				Are they relevant to the task?		
				Are they understood by all members of the manufacturing team?		
				Are they regularly reviewed and up to date?		
				Are they subject to control procedures?		
		1.2	Quality Control Checks	What quality checks are being observed?		
				Are they relevant?		
				Are there laid down procedures for carrying out these checks?		
				Are they available?		
				Are they regularly updated?		

Item	Related item		Remark	Yes/no	Remarks
2 Reliability of product design	2.1	Statistical data	Is there a system for predicting the reliability of the product's design?		
			Is sufficient statistical data available to be able to estimate the actual reliability of the design, before a product is manufactured?		
			Is the appropriate engineering data available?		
	2.2	Components and parts	Are the reliability ratings of recommended parts and components available?		
			Are probability methods used to examine the reliability of a proposed design?		
			If so, have these checks revealed design deficiencies such as:		
			● Assembly errors?		
			● Operator learning, motivational, or fatigue factors?		
			● Latent defects?		
			● Improper part selection?		
			(Note: If necessary, use additional sheets to list actions taken)		

Acceptance stage

	Item	Related item		Remark	Yes/no	Remarks
1	Product performance			Does the product perform to the required function?		
				If not what has been done about it?		
2	Quality level	2.1	Workmanship	Does the workmanship of the product fully meet the level of quality required or stipulated by the user?		
		2.2	Tests	Is the product subjected to environmental tests?		
				If so, which ones?		
				Is the product field tested as a complete system?		
				If so, what were the results?		
3	Reliability	3.1	Probability function	Are individual components and modules environmentally tested?		
				If so, how?		
		3.2	Failure rate	Is the product's reliability measured in terms of probability function?		
				If so, what were the results?		
				Is the product's reliability measured in terms of failure rate?		
				If so, what were the results?		
		3.3	Mean time between failures	Is the product's reliability measured in terms of mean time between failure?		
				If so, what were the results?		

In-service stage

	Item	Related item		Remark	Yes/no	Remarks
1	System reliability	1.1	Product basic design	Are statistical methods being used to prove the product's basic design?		
				If so, are they adequate?		
				Are the results recorded and available?		
				What other methods are used to prove the product's basic design?		
				Are these methods appropriate?		
2	Equipment reliability	2.1	Personnel	Are there sufficient trained personnel to carry out the task?		
				Are they sufficiently motivated?		
				If not, what is the problem?		
		2.1.1	Operators	Have individual job descriptions been developed?		
				Are they readily available?		
				Are all operators capable of completing their duties?		
		2.1.2	Training	Do all personnel receive appropriate training?		
				Is a continuous on-the-job training (OJT) programme available to all personnel?		
				If not, why not?		
		2.2	Product dependability	What proof is there that the product is dependable?		

Item	Related item		Remark	Yes/no	Remarks
			How is product dependability proved?		
			Is this sufficient for the customer?		
	2.3	Component reliability	Has the reliability of individual components been considered?		
			Does the reliability of individual components exceed the overall system reliability?		
	2.4	Faulty operating procedures	Are operating procedures available?		
			Are they appropriate to the task?		
			Are they regularly reviewed?		
	2.5	Operational abuses	Are there any obvious operational abuses?		
			If so, what are they?		
			How can they be overcome?		
	2.5.1	Extended duty cycle	Do the staff have to work shifts?		
			If so, are they allowed regular breaks from their work?		
			Is there a senior shift worker?		
			If so, are his duties and responsibilities clearly defined?		
			Are computers used?		
			If so, are screen filters available?		
			Do the operators have keyboard wrist rests?		

Item		Related item		Remark	Yes/no	Remarks
		2.5.2	Training	Do the operational staff receive regular on-the-job training?		
				Is there any need for additional in-house or external Training?		
3	Design capability	3.1	Faulty operating procedures	Are there any obvious faulty operating procedures?		
				Can the existing procedures be improved upon?		

Annex 7E Index for ISO 9001:2000

Subject title	ISO 9001 element
Identification and traceability	7.5.3
control (product)	7.5.3, 7.5.5
customer property	7.5.4
measuring and monitoring requirements	7.5.3, 7.6
status (product)	7.5.3
product	7.5.3
unique product identification	7.5.3
Improvement (also see continual improvement)	8.5
corrective action	8.5.2
planning for continual improvement	8.5.1
preventive action	8.5.3
Inspection and testing	7.1, 7.5.1, 8.1, 8.2.4
goods inwards	7.4.3
final inspection and testing	8.2.4
in-process inspection	7.5.1
Inspection and test status	7.5.1
authorised stamps, tags and labels	7.5.3
inspection records	7.5.3
product testing	7.5.1
production control	7.5.1
use of markings	7.5.3
Inspection, measuring and test equipment – control of	7.6
Internal audits, (of the Quality Management System)	8.2.2
corrective action	8.2.2
frequency	8.2.2
implementation and maintenance	8.2.2
methodologies	8.2.2
planning	8.2.2
procedure	8.2.2
records	8.2.2
reporting of results	8.2.2
requirements	8.2.2
scope	8.2.2
verification	8.2.2
Job descriptions	5.5.1
Maintenance of	
customer property	7.5.4
equipment	7.5.1c
quality management system	8.2.2b

References

Standards

Number	Date	Title
93/42/EEC	1993	European Community Council Directive concerning medical devices
94/408218 DC	2000	Draft for Comment on ISO 1005
A 137.1	1988	Ceramic tiles
ANSI 90 series		American quality standards
BS 0	1997	A standard for standards – guide to the context, aims and general principles
BS 0:–1	1991	A standard for standards – guide to general principles of standardisation
BS 0:–2	1991	A standard for standards – BSI and its committee procedures
BS 0:–3	1991	A standard for standards – guide to drafting and presentation of British standards
BS 3934	1965	Specification for the dimensions of semiconductor devices and integrated electronic circuits
BS 4778–1	1987	Quality vocabulary
BS 4778–2	1979	Quality vocabulary – international terms, national terms
BS 4778–3.1	1991	Quality vocabulary – availability, reliability and maintainability terms – guide to concepts and related definitions
BS 4778–3.2	1991	Quality vocabulary – availability, reliability and maintainability terms – glossary of international terms
BS 4891	1972	A guide to quality assurance
BS 5701	1980	Guide to number defective charts for quality control

Number	Date	Title
BS 5703	1980	Guide to data analysis quality control using cusum charting
BS 5750 series	1987	Quality systems – principal concepts and applications
BS 5750–1	1979	Quality systems – specification for design, development, production, installation and servicing
BS 5750–2	1979	Quality systems – specification for production and installation
BS 5750–3	1979	Quality systems – specification for final inspection and test
BS 6001	1999	Sampling procedures for inspection by attributes
BS 6002	1993	Sampling procedures for inspection by variables
BS 6143–1	1992	Guide to the economics of quality – process cost model
BS 6143–2	1990	Guide to the economics of quality – prevention, appraisal and failure mode
BS 7850–1	1991	Total quality management – guide to management principles
BS 7850–2	1992	Total quality management – guide to quality improvement methods
BS 7850–3	1994	Total quality management – guidelines for quality improvement
BS 8800	1996	Guide to occupational health and safety management systems
DEF STAN 13–131/2	1997	Ordnance Board safety guidelines for weapons and munitions
DIS ISO 9000	1999	Quality management systems – fundamentals and vocabulary
DIS ISO 9001	1999	Quality management systems – requirements
DIS ISO 9004	1999	Quality management systems – guidance for performance improvement
EN 29000	1987	Renumbered as ISO 9000/1
ISO 8402	1995	Quality management and quality assurance – vocabulary
ISO 9000		Quality management and quality assurance standards
ISO 9000	2000	Quality management systems – fundamentals and vocabulary

Number	Date	Title
ISO 9000–1	1994	Quality management and quality assurance standards – guidelines for selection and use
ISO 9000–2	1997	Quality management and quality assurance standards – generic guidelines for the application of ISO 9001, 9002 and 9003
ISO 9000–3	1997	Quality management and quality assurance standards – guidelines for the application of ISO 9001:1994 to the development, supply, installation and maintenance of computer software
ISO 9000–4	1993	Quality management and quality assurance standards – guide to dependability programme management
ISO 9001	1994	Quality systems – model for quality assurance in design/development, production, installation and servicing
ISO 9001	2000	Quality management systems – requirements
ISO 9002	1994	Quality systems – model for quality assurance in production and installation
ISO 9003	1994	Quality systems – model for quality assurance in final inspection and test
ISO 9004		Superseded by ISO 9004–1
ISO 9004	2000	Quality management systems – guidance for performance improvement
ISO 9004–1	1994	Quality management and quality system elements – guidelines
ISO 9004–2	1991	Quality management and quality system elements – guidelines for service
ISO 9004–3	1993	Quality management and quality system elements – guidelines for processed materials
ISO 9004–4	1994	Quality management and quality system elements – guidelines for quality improvement
ISO 10005	1995	Quality management – guidelines for quality plans
ISO 10011–1	1990	Guidelines for auditing quality systems – auditing
ISO 10011–2	1991	Guidelines for auditing quality systems – qualification criteria for quality systems auditors

Number	Date	Title
ISO 10011–3	1991	Guidelines for auditing quality systems – management of audit programmes
ISO 10012–1	1992	Quality assurance requirements for measuring equipment – metrological confirmation system for measuring equipment
ISO 10012–2	1997	Quality assurance for measuring equipment – guidelines for control of measurement processes
ISO 10013	1995	Guidelines for developing quality manuals
ISO 14001	1996	Environmental management systems – specifications with guidance for use
ISO 14010	1996	Guidelines for environmental auditing – general principles
ISO 14011	1996	Guidelines for environmental auditing – auditing procedures – Auditing of environmental management systems
ISO 14012	1996	Guidelines for environmental auditing – qualification criteria for environmental auditors
ISO TR 10017	1999	Guidance on statistical techniques for ISO 9001:1994
QS 9000	1995	Quality system requirements (for the automotive industry)
TR 9000		Quality system requirements (for the electronics industry)

Other references

Title	Author	Publisher
BS 5750/ISO 9000:1987 – a positive contribution to a better business		BSI pamphlet
Crusading for quality		*International Management*, July/August 1989
Letter for Oslo – voice of the other Europe	Fossli, Karen	*Management Today*, May 1989

Title	Author	Publisher
Operating degradations during the in-service stage	Tricker, R.L.	StingRay Management Consultants, 1999
Quality – its origin and progress in defence procurement	Drew, H.E.	Paper to the Institution of Production Engineers, 1971
Quality assurance	PSA	HMSO, 1987. ISBN 86177:143.53
Quality counts – developments in qualities and standards since 1982	White paper	HMSO
Quality Management Handbook (BSI)		BSI
Selling to the single market	DTI	June 1989
Setting the scene for European standards, testing and certification post 1992	Strawbridge, Geoff	BSI
Standards, quality and international competitiveness	DTI	October 1986
Standards, quality and international competitiveness	White paper	Cmnd 8621, July 1982
Statistical Process Control	Oakland, John	Butterworth–Heinemann, 1986
The History of Quality Assurance and EQD	Tennyson, Peter	
Working for Quality		BSI

Notes

Extracts from British Standards are reproduced with the permission of the British Standards Institute. Complete copies of all British Standards can be obtained, by post, from Customer Services, BSI Standards, 389 Chiswick High Road, London W4 4AL.

Books by the same author

Title	Details	Publisher
ISO 9001:2000 in Brief	A hands-on guide to the updated quality standard	Butterworth-Heinemann ISBN: 0 7506 4814 7
CE Conformity Marking	Essential information for any manufacturer or distributor wishing to trade in the EU.	Butterworth-Heinemann 2000
Environmental Requirements for Electromechanical and Electronic Equipment	Definitive reference containing all the background guidance, ranges, test specifications, case studies and regulations worldwide.	Butterworth-Heinemann ISBN: 0 7506 3902 4
MDD Compliance using Quality Management Techniques	Easy to follow guide to MDD, enabling purchaser to customise the Quality Management System to suit their own business.	Butterworth-Heinemann ISBN: 0 7506 4441 9
Quality and Standards in Electronics	Ensures that manufacturers are aware of all the UK, European and international necessities, know the current status of these regulations and standards, and where to obtain them.	Butterworth-Heinemann ISBN: 0 7506 2531 7

Abbreviations and acronyms

AFNOR	Association Francais de Normalisation
ANSI	American National Standards Institute
AQAP	Allied Quality Assurance Publications (NATO)
ASQ	American Society for Quality (was ASQC)
ASQC	American Society for Quality Control (now ASQ)
ASTM	American Society for Testing and Materials
BS	British Standard, issued by BSI
BSI	British Standards Institution
CCIR	International Radio Consultative Committee
CCITT	The International Telegraph and Telephony Consultative Committee
CECC	CENELEC Electronic Components Committee
CEN	Commission European de Normalisation
CENELEC	European Committee for Electrotechnical Standardisation
COS	Corporation of Open Systems
CP	Core Business Process
CSA	Canadian Standards Association
DCS	Document Control Sheet
DIN	Deutsches Institut für Normung (German Institute for Standardisation)
DIS	Draft International Standard
DTI	Department of Trade and Industry
DOD	(American) Division of Defence
EEC	European Economic Community
EMS	Environmental Management System
EN	European Number (for European standards)
EN HD	European Harmonised Directive
EU	European Union
FDIS	Final Draft International Standard
FIIE(elec)	Fellow of the Institution of Electronics and Electrical Incorporated Engineers
FinstM	Fellow of the Institute of Management
FR	Failure Rate

HEC	Herne European Consultancy Ltd
HSE	Health & Safety Executive (UK)
IAF	International Accreditation Forum
IEC	International Electrotechnical Commission
IEE	Institution of Electrical Engineers
IQA	Institute of Quality Assurance
ISO	International Organisation for Standardisation
ISO/CASCO	OSI Committee on Conformity Testing
ISO/TC176	The ISO Technical Committee responsible for the ISO 9000 series standards
IT	Information Technology
ITU	International Telecommunications Union
LAN	Local Area Network
MIQA	Member of the Institute of Quality Assurance
MIRSE	Member of the Institution of Railway Signal Engineers
MOD	Ministry of Defence
MSc	Master of Science
MTBF	Mean Time Between Failures
NATO	North Atlantic Treaty Organisation
NQIC	National Quality Information Centre
NSA	National Supervising Authority
NSO	National Standards Organisation
OSI	Open Systems Connection
PF	Probability Function
QA	Quality Assurance
QAI	Quality Assurance Inspector
QC	Quality Control
QM	Quality Manual
QMS	Quality Management System
QP	Quality Procedure
SP	Supporting Processes
SQP	Section Quality Plan
TQM	Total Quality Management (e.g. BS 7850)
UK	United Kingdom
VDE	Verband Deutsch Elektrotechniker
WI	Work Instruction

Glossary

As international trade increases, it is becoming more important than ever to know the exact meaning of some of the basic definitions when referred to the quality of a product or service – especially when used in the vernacular! To overcome this problem an international standard (ISO 8402:1994 – Quality management and quality assurance – vocabulary) was published in three languages (English, French and Russian).

ISO 9000:2000 was then developed within ISO/TC 176. It was developed by first screening existing quality standards (e.g. ISO 8402:1994) and publications that were available to determine the quality terms that could be included and then producing internationally acceptable definitions of them. Because of this 'international acceptability' many of these definitions and terms have specific meanings and applications as opposed to generic definitions that are normally to be found in dictionaries.

Acceptance – Agreement to take a product or service as offered.

Accreditation – Certification, by a duly recognised body, of facilities, capability, objectivity, competence and integrity of an agency, service or operational group or individual to provide the specific service/s or operation/s as needed.

Audit – Systematic, independent and documented process for obtaining evidence and evaluating it objectively to determine the extent to which audit criteria are fulfilled.

Audit client – Person or organisation requesting an audit.

Audit conclusions – Outcome of an audit decided by the audit team after consideration of all the audit findings.

Audit criteria – Set of policies, procedures or requirements against which collected audit evidence is compared.

Audit evidence – Records, verified statements of fact or other information relevant to the audit.

Audit findings – Results of the evaluation of the collected audit evidence against audit criteria.

Audit programme – Set of audits to be carried out during a planned time frame.

Audit scope – Extent and range of a given audit.

Audit team – One or more auditors conducting an audit, one of whom is appointed as leader.

Auditee – Organisation being audited.

Auditor – Person qualified and competent to conduct audits.

Bonded store – A secure place in which only supplies that have been accepted as satisfactory by the inspection staff are held.

Calibration – The operation that is required to determine the accuracy of measuring and test equipment.

Capability – Ability of an organisation, system or process to realise a product that fulfils the requirements for that product.

CEN (European Committee for Standardisation) – European equivalent of ISO.

CENELEC (European Committee for Electrotechnical Standardisation)
Certification body – An impartial body who have the necessary competence and reliability to operate a certification scheme.

Censored test – A test carried out on a number of items which is terminated before all the tested items have failed.

Certification – The procedure and action by a duly authorised body of determining, verifying and attesting in writing to the qualifications of personnel, processes, procedures, or items in accordance with applicable requirements.

Certification body – An impartial body, governmental or non-governmental, possessing the necessary competence and reliability to operate a certification system, and in which the interests of all parties concerned with the functioning of the system are represented.

Certification system – A system having its own rules of procedure and management for carrying out certification.

Chief inspector – An individual who is responsible for the manufacturer's Quality Management System (also referred to as the Quality Manager).

Company – Term used primarily to refer to a business first party, the purpose of which is to supply a product or service.

Compliance – The fulfilment of a Quality Management System or quality procedure of specified requirements.

Concession Authorisation to use or release a product that does not conform to specified requirements.

Concession/waiver – Written authorisation to use or release a quantity of material, components or stores already produced but which do not conform to the specified requirements.

Consignment – Products (or goods) that are issued or received as one delivery and covered by one set of documents.

Contract – Agreed requirements between a supplier and customer transmitted by any means.

Corrective action – Action taken to eliminate the cause of a detected nonconformity or other undesirable situation.

Customer – Ultimate consumer, user, client, beneficiary or second party.

Customer complaint – Any written, electronic, or oral communication that alleges deficiencies related to the identity, quality, durability, reliability, safety or performance of a device that has been placed on the market.

Customer dissatisfaction – Customer's opinion of the degree to which a transaction has failed to meet the customer's needs and expectations.

Customer organisation – Customer organisation or person that receives a product.

Customer satisfaction – Customer's opinion of the degree to which a transaction has met the customer's needs and expectations.

Defect – Non-fulfilment of a requirement related to an intended or specified use.

Design and development – Set of processes that transforms requirements into specified characteristics and into the specification of the product realisation process.

Design authority – The approved firm, establishment or branch representative responsible for the detailed design of material to approved specifications and authorised to sign a certificate of design, or to certify sealed drawings.

Design capability – The ability of a manufacturer to translate a customer requirement into a component that can be manufactured by their particular technology.

Design failure – A failure due to an inadequate design of an item.

Design review – A formal documented, comprehensive and systematic examination of a design to evaluate the design requirements and the capability of the design to meet these requirements and to identify problems and propose solutions.

Document – Information and its support medium.

Effectiveness – Measure of the extent to which planned activities are realised and planned results achieved.

Efficiency – Relationship between the result achieved and the resources used.

Environment – All of the external physical conditions that may influence the performance of a product or service.

Environmental condition – The characteristics (such as humidity, pressure, vibration etc.) of the environment in which the product is operating.

Equipment – Machines, apparatus, fixed or mobile devices, control components and instrumentation thereof and detection or prevention systems which, separately or jointly, are intended for the generation, transfer, storage, measurement, control and conversion of energy for the processing of material and which are capable of causing an explosion through their own potential sources of ignition.

Evaluation – The systematic evaluation of the effectiveness of a contractor's Quality Management System.

Failure – The termination of the ability of an item to perform a required function.

Failure mode, effect and criticality analysis (FMECA) – FMEA together with a consideration of the probability of occurrence and a ranking of the seriousness of the failure.

Failure mode/fault mode – One of the possible states of a failed (faulty) item, for a given required function.

Failure mode and effect analysis (FMEA) – A qualitative method of reliability analysis which involves the study of the failure modes which can exist in every subitem of the item and the determination of the effects of each failure mode on other subitems of the item and on the required function of the item.

Failure rate (instantaneous) – The limit, if this exists, of the conditional probability that the instant of time of a failure of an item falls within a given time interval to the length of this interval, when given that the item is in an up state at the beginning of the time interval.

Failure tree analysis (FTA) – The study, with the use of diagrammatic algorithms, of the possible sequence of events leading up to the failure of a product.

Fault – The state of an item characterised by inability to perform a required function, excluding the inability during preventive maintenance or due to lack of external resources or other planned action.

Fault tree – A logic diagram showing how a given fault mode of an item is related to possible fault modes of subitems or to external events, or combinations thereof.

Fault tree analysis – An analysis in the form of a fault tree in order to determine how a stated fault mode of the item may be the result of the fault modes of the subitems or of external events, or combinations thereof.

Final inspection – The last inspection by a manufacturer or supplier before delivery.

In-process inspection – Inspection carried out at various stages during processing.

In-progress-inspections – QA Inspectors perform these on a random basis or while assisting the technician. They may also be considered as 'Training' inspections and are meant to help the technician perform better maintenance whilst actually learning about the equipment.

Inspection – Activities such as measuring, examining, testing, gauging one or more characteristics of a product or service and comparing these with specified requirements to determine conformity.

Interested party – Person or group having an interest in the performance or success of an organisation.

Maintenance – The combination of technical and administrative actions that are taken to retain or restore an item to a state in which it can perform its stated function.

Management – Co-ordinated activities to direct and control an organisation.

Management system – To establish policy and objectives and to achieve those objectives.

Manufacturer The natural or legal person with responsibility for the design, manufacture, packaging and labelling of a device before it is placed on the market under his own name, regardless of whether these operations are carried out by that person himself or on his behalf by a third party.

May – This auxiliary verb indicates a course of action often followed by manufacturers and suppliers.

Measurement – Set of operations having the object of determining the value of a quantity.

Non-conformity – Non-fulfilment of a requirement.

Operational cycle – A repeatable sequence of functional stresses.

Operational requirements – All the function and performance requirements of a product.

Organisation – A company, corporation, firm or enterprise, whether incorporated or not, public or private.

Group of people and facilities with an orderly arrangement of responsibilities, authorities and relationships.

Organisational structure – Orderly arrangement of responsibilities, authorities and relationships between people.

Out-going inspections – These are performed after a job or task has been completed to verify that everything has been done correctly on a repaired equipment that is ready for return to the Customer. The Quality Assurance Inspector is normally required to check the item to see how it compares against the manufacturer's specification. Any item failing an out-going inspection has to be returned to the Technician or his Section Manager for corrective action. It will then be subject to a further out-going inspection by the QA Inspector.

Procedure – Describes the way to perform an activity or process.

Product – Result of a process.

> **Note**: There are four agreed generic product categories: hardware (e.g. engine mechanical part); software (e.g. computer program); services (e.g. transport); processed materials (e.g. lubricant).
>
> Hardware and processed materials are generally tangible products, while software or services are generally intangible.
>
> Most products comprise elements belonging to different generic product categories. Whether the product is then called hardware, processed material, software or service depends on the dominant element.

Project – Unique process, consisting of a set of co-ordinated and controlled activities with start and finish dates, undertaken to achieve an objective conforming to specific requirements, including the constraints of time, costs and resources.

Quality – Ability of a set of inherent characteristics of a product, system or process to fulfil requirements of customers and other interested parties.

Quality Assurance – Part of quality management, focused on providing confidence that quality requirements are fulfilled.

Quality Audit – A systematic and independent examination to determine whether quality activities and related results comply with planned arrangements and whether these arrangements are implemented effectively and are suitable to achieve objectives.

Quality Control – Part of quality management, focused on fulfilling quality requirements.

Quality costs – The expenditure incurred by the producer, by the user and by the community associated with product or service quality.

Quality level – A general indication of the extent of the product's departure from the ideal.

Quality loop – Conceptual model of interacting activities that influence the quality of a product or service in the various stages ranging from the identification of needs to the assessment of whether these needs have been satisfied.

Quality Manager – A person who is responsible for the manufacturer's Quality Management System (also sometimes referred to as the Chief Inspector).

Quality Management – That aspect of the overall management function that determines and implements the quality policy.

Note: The terms 'Quality Management' and 'Quality Control' are considered to be a manufacturer/supplier (or first party) responsibility. 'Quality Assurance' on the other hand has both internal and external aspects which in many instances can be shared between the manufacturer/supplier (first party), purchaser/customer (second party) and any regulatory/ certification body (third party) that may be involved.

Quality Management System – System to establish a quality policy and quality objectives and to achieve those objectives.

Quality Management System Review – A formal evaluation by top management of the status and adequacy of the Quality Management System in relation to quality policy and new objectives resulting from changing circumstances.

Quality Manual – Document specifying the quality management system of an organisation.

Quality Plan – Document specifying the quality management system elements and the resources to be applied in a specific case.

Quality Policy – The overall quality intentions and direction of an organisation as regards quality, as formally expressed by top management.

Quality Procedure – A description of the method by which quality system activities are managed.

Quality Records – Records should provide evidence of how well the Quality System has been implemented.

Quality System – The organisational structure, responsibilities, procedures, processes and resources for implementing quality management.